Does Tomorrow Exist?

This book takes up the question of whether past and future events exist. Two very different views are explored. According to one of these views (presentism), advanced by Nikk Effingham, the present is special. Effingham argues that only present things exist, but which things those are changes as time passes. Given presentism, although there once existed dinosaurs, they exist no more, and although you and I exist, at some time in the future we will come to exist no more. According to the alternative view (eternalism), advanced by Kristie Miller, our world is a giant four-dimensional block of spacetime in which all things, past, present, and future, exist. On this view, dinosaurs exist, it is just that they are not located at the current time.

The book considers arguments for and against presentism and eternalism, including arguments that appeal to our best science, to the way the world seems to us to be in our experiences of time, change, and freedom, and to how to make sense of ordinary claims about the past.

Key Features:
- Offers an accessible introduction to the philosophy of temporal ontology.
- Captures the process of philosophical debate, giving readers an insight into the craft of philosophy.
- Engages with and clearly explains state-of-the-art and cutting-edge research.

Nikk Effingham is Professor at the University of Birmingham where he works on metaphysics and the philosophy of religion. He is the author of *Time Travel: Probability and Impossibility* (2020) and *An Introduction to Ontology* (2013).

Kristie Miller is Professor of Philosophy at the University of Sydney, and Joint Director of the interdisciplinary Centre for Time. She works primarily in metaphysics, particularly on the nature of time, persistence, and personal identity. In addition to her articles, she has co-authored several books, including *Out of Time* (2022), *Everyday Metaphysical Explanation* (2022) and *An Introduction to the Philosophy of Time* (2018).

Little Debates About Big Questions
Tyron Goldschmidt
Fellow of the Rutgers Center for Philosophy of Religion, USA
Dustin Crummett
Ludwig Maximilian University of Munich, Germany

About the series:

Philosophy asks questions about the fundamental nature of reality, our place in the world, and what we should do. Some of these questions are perennial: for example, *Do we have free will? What is morality?* Some are much newer: for example, *How far should free speech on campus extend? Are race, sex and gender social constructs?* But all of these are among the big questions in philosophy and they remain controversial.

Each book in the *Little Debates About Big Questions* series features two professors on opposite sides of a big question. Each author presents their own side, and the authors then exchange objections and replies. Short, lively, and accessible, these debates showcase diverse and deep answers. Pedagogical features include standard form arguments, section summaries, bolded key terms and principles, glossaries, and annotated reading lists.

The debate format is an ideal way to learn about controversial topics. Whereas the usual essay or book risks overlooking objections against its own proposition or misrepresenting the opposite side, in a debate each side can make their case at equal length, and then present objections the other side must consider. Debates have a more conversational and fun style too, and we selected particularly talented philosophers—in substance and style—for these kinds of encounters.

Debates can be combative—sometimes even descending into anger and animosity. But debates can also be cooperative. While our authors disagree strongly, they work together to help each other and the reader get clearer on the ideas, arguments, and objections. This is intellectual progress, and a much-needed model for civil and constructive disagreement.

The substance and style of the debates will captivate interested readers new to the questions. But there's enough to interest experts too. The debates will be especially useful for courses in philosophy and related subjects—whether as primary or secondary readings—and a few debates can be combined to make up the reading for an entire course.

We thank the authors for their help in constructing this series. We are honored to showcase their work. They are all preeminent scholars or rising-stars in their fields, and through these debates they share what's been discovered with a wider audience. This is a paradigm for public philosophy, and will impress upon students, scholars, and other interested readers the enduring importance of debating the big questions.

Published Titles:

Does Tomorrow Exist?
A Debate
Nikk Effingham and Kristie Miller

Should Wealth Be Redistributed?
A Debate
Steven McMullen and James R. Otteson

Do We Have Free Will?
A Debate
Robert Kane and Carolina Sartorio

Is There a God?
A Debate
Kenneth L. Pearce and Graham Oppy

Is Political Authority an Illusion?
A Debate
Michael Huemer and Daniel Layman

Selected Forthcoming Titles:

Do Numbers Exist?
A Debate
William Lane Craig and Peter van Inwagen

What Do We Owe Other Animals?
A Debate
Bob Fischer and Anja Jauernig

Consequentialism or Virtue Ethics?
A Debate
Jorge L.A. Garcia and Alastair Norcross

Are We Made of Matter?
A Debate
Eric T. Olson and Aaron Segal

For more information about this series, please visit: www.routledge.com/Little-Debates-about-Big-Questions/book-series/LDABQ

Does Tomorrow Exist?

A Debate

Nikk Effingham and Kristie Miller

NEW YORK AND LONDON

Cover image credit: idizimage / Getty Images

First published 2023
by Routledge
605 Third Avenue, New York, NY 10158

and by Routledge
4 Park Square, Milton Park, Abingdon, Oxon, OX14 4RN

Routledge is an imprint of the Taylor & Francis Group, an informa business

© 2023 Taylor & Francis

The right of Nikk Effingham and Kristie Miller to be identified as authors of this work has been asserted in accordance with sections 77 and 78 of the Copyright, Designs and Patents Act 1988.

All rights reserved. No part of this book may be reprinted or reproduced or utilised in any form or by any electronic, mechanical, or other means, now known or hereafter invented, including photocopying and recording, or in any information storage or retrieval system, without permission in writing from the publishers.

Trademark notice: Product or corporate names may be trademarks or registered trademarks, and are used only for identification and explanation without intent to infringe.

ISBN: 978-0-367-61594-9 (hbk)
ISBN: 978-0-367-61596-3 (pbk)
ISBN: 978-1-003-10566-4 (ebk)

DOI: 10.4324/9781003105664

Typeset in Sabon
by Apex CoVantage, LLC

Contents

Foreword   x
JONATHAN TALLANT

PART I
Opening Statements   1

1   In Defence of the Block Universe View   3
KRISTIE MILLER

    1. Introduction 3
    2. Theories of Time: The Options 5
    3. The Argument From Special Relativity 17
    4. Arguments Against the Block: Change 25
    5. Arguments Against the Block: Temporal Phenomenology 27
    6. Arguments Against the Block: Free Will 33
    7. The Argument From Explanation for the Block 38

2   In Defence of Presentism   54
NIKK EFFINGHAM

    1. Introduction 54
    2. Making Sense of the Debate 56
    3. In Favour of Presentism 59
    4. Truthmaking 64
    5. Being Explains Truth 73
    6. Problems for Presentism 75
    7. A Proposed Solution 77
    8. Objections 78
    9. Comparison to Eternalism 81
    10. The Open Future 83

11. Presentism and Special Relativity 86
12. Conclusion 94

PART II
First Round of Replies 97

3   Past and Future Do Not Exist: Reply to Kristie Miller 99
    NIKK EFFINGHAM

    1. Introduction 99
    2. Change 100
    3. Direction, Asymmetry, and Explanation 109
    4. A Bad Presentist Explanation 114
    5. A Better Presentist Explanation 115
    6. Back to the Open Future 119
    7. Conclusion 122

4   The Past and Future Exist: Reply to Nikk Effingham 123
    KRISTIE MILLER

    1. Introduction 123
    2. The Argument From Ontological Parsimony 124
    3. Truthmaking and Parsimony 129
    4. The Objection From Relativity 140

PART III
Second Round of Replies 147

5   Back to the Block: Reply to Nikk Effingham's Reply 149
    KRISTIE MILLER

    1. Change 149
    2. Direction, Asymmetry, and Explanation 156

6   Presentism Returns: Reply to Kristie Miller's Reply 165
    NIKK EFFINGHAM

    1. Introduction 165
    2. Ontological Parsimony 166
    3. Truthmaking 170
    4. Ontological Parsimony Again: Qualitative Parsimony 172

5. Ontological Parsimony Again, Again:
   Quantitative Parsimony 174
6. Do Propositions Exist? 176
7. Permissivism 177
8. Conclusion 180

Suggested Readings	182
Glossary	187
References	191
Index	193

Foreword

St Augustine of Hippo summed up very nicely just how slippery time can seem when he wrote in his *Confessions* (Book XI, Chapter XIV), asking:

> What is time then? If nobody asks me, I know: but if I were desirous to explain it to one that should ask me, plainly I know not.

And when we move into the philosophy of time from that starting point, it can sometimes seem as if things remain just as confusing. Probably the most famous 20th century work on the philosophy of time is McTaggart's (1908) argument for the *unreality* of time. If we're interested in the philosophy *of* time, rather than its reality, this is an inauspicious start.

Happily, what we have in this current volume is a very clear and comprehensive introduction to some of the contemporary debates in the philosophy of time that have managed to move on at least a little from St Augustine and McTaggart.

A multitude of positions have been developed in the philosophy of time, but the two most often discussed in the literature are presentism and eternalism. In this volume, Kristie Miller takes to the stand to defend eternalism—the view that past, present, and future things all exist—whilst Nikk Effingham makes the case for presentism—the view that only present objects exist.

From that bare presentation of the two views, one might initially think that the difference between presentism and eternalism is *just* a disagreement about when in time things exist. The eternalist says that things exist in the past, present, and future; the presentist says that things only exist in the present. However, and as will become clear as you make your way through this volume, rather more can and needs to be said.

As Miller explains when she introduces the view, eternalism is best understood as the view that time is a lot like space. Just as objects exist, spread out through space, so too they exist spread out through time. The Big Bang is *out there* in time, just as Pluto is *out there* in space. Spatial distance and temporal distance are closely analogous. A natural consequence of this view is that events do not come into or go out of existence. The event of your birth exists.

The event of your death does, too. They're all out there in time. They're just separated from one another.

In some respects, that view seems highly intuitive. Time really *is* as it's represented by a timeline—the kind of thing that you might find pinned up around a school classroom. That crude timeline is a pretty good approximation of how reality really is.

However, in some other respects the view might seem somewhat lacking. After all, our experience of time seems to be of its *passing*. That is, things seem to *change*. What once was present, now is past. Things seem to flow; to be in a state of flux. And it can seem very hard to square that sense of flow and flux with the idea that reality is just as the timeline has it—in a sense, 'static', and like a block. If reality is static, then how can we understand and make sense of our *feeling* of time's passing—our *temporal phenomenology*? And, if reality is like a block, then in what sense do things *change*? Reality seems to be an unchanging and static thing. Finally, if the future is already 'out there' just as Pluto is 'out there', in what sense can we be said to have *free will*? I can't influence space such that Plato isn't out there, so how can it make sense to say that I can influence time to influence future states?

Historically, these have been some of the arguments that have motivated presentism; for presentism isn't just a thesis about when in time objects exist. Presentism is the view that various objects have existed and that others still will exist. Moreover, there's a kind of really robust temporal change and temporal passage. Objects come into existence in the present and go out of existence as they leave the present. Where eternalism seems static and to give us a block-like conception of reality, presentism eschews that entirely and denies that there is a close analogy between time and space.

Nonetheless, presentism does not face an easy time of it either. At this point, it's useful to see how Miller looks to illustrate the arguments against presentism and the arguments for eternalism. Her strategy is perhaps best understood as two parts offence, three parts defence. For the offence, Miller begins with an appeal to the special theory of relativity. As she notes, the special theory of relativity looks to have very particular consequences that make trouble for presentism. Very roughly—and both Miller and Effingham will do more justice to this later on—the idea is that two observers that are travelling at significant velocities with respect to one another will judge different sets of objects to be simultaneous. If you are on Earth and judge two explosions to occur at the same time, and I am in a rocketship travelling away from earth at high speed, I will *not* judge that the same two explosions occur at the same time.

Now, presentism is the view that only present objects exist. There will be a point at which you say that both explosions occur, and so you say that both are present, and both exist. I, however, will say that there is no such point where both are present, and both exist. We can't both be right about what exists. But since there doesn't seem any physical fact that we can appeal to in order to show that one of us is *correct*, it seems that the position that we should reach is that there is no fact of the matter as to whether the two explosions occur at the same time. That means that there is no fact of the matter as to whether or not the two explosions are present. The presentist, who says that *only present objects exist*, surely cannot allow that.

Phase two in Miller's offence focuses on temporal asymmetries. In the argument she surveys, Miller introduces epistemic asymmetries and asymmetries of influence. The idea here is that we can know about the past, not the future, and that we can influence the future and not the past. To develop her argument, Miller draws a distinction between the contents of time and the passing of time itself in a dynamic view. To get a handle on what the distinction comes to for the presentist, imagine watching a film backwards. When we watch the film backwards, we see the order of events reversed. If the film is of a goal being scored in soccer, then in the backwards film we might see a ball leap from the floor into the netting of the goal, then shooting out of the goal and onto the head of a striker, who then appears to be propelled backwards from mid-air onto their feet. Causation seems to go into reverse. Nonetheless, when we see the film, we don't seem to change the direction of *time*. Rather, in the backwards film, the events occur in a different orientation, but we continue to judge that time passes as per normal; it's the events that run backwards. Miller argues that our best physics suggests that reality leaves open a similar scenario: where the contents of time *run backwards* even though time's passing itself (given dynamism) continues to run forwards.

This is odd, Miller thinks. This possibility—of the contents of time running backwards—shows that it can't be that there's anything about the passing of time itself that explains why we have the asymmetries described; for, if the contents of time (and we are surely some of those contents) can run backwards, then our influence will flow in the other direction—even though time continues to flow forwards. And so, what we can influence, what we can know, would be fundamentally disconnected from time's passing if presentism is true; for the direction of time itself has not been changed. That seems to leave us with an asymmetry that we cannot explain: we cannot explain why we can influence the future and not the past, and know the past and not the future, because the passage of time, and the way that the contents of time change, can flow independently of one another.

To see why this will end up doubling as a motivational argument for eternalism, we need to understand just a little bit of Miller's defence. As you may recall, Miller considers three such arguments: *change*, *temporal phenomenology* and *free will*. In consideration of change, Miller goes back to the analogy between space and time. The argument against eternalism being able to accommodate change seems to turn on the idea that the whole—the block—does not change. There exists a static block; there is no scope for temporal passage or for the block as a whole to undergo change.

But, of course, that the block doesn't change doesn't prevent the contents of the block from changing. To get a feel for this idea, we can go back to the example of a timeline. If you imagine your own personal timeline, then you can probably imagine the time at which you weighed 10kg. You can probably also imagine the time at which you weighed 20kg. According to eternalism, both of those times exist, and you exist at those times, with those different weights. You've clearly changed—and changed by 10kg! And so there we have it; change. Change is just a matter of an object existing at (at least) two times and having different properties at those times. Now, to be sure, there's no *temporal passage* on such a model, where '*temporal passage*' in its italicised form is intended to evoke something over and above the timeline model of reality that the eternalist seems to commit to. But, says Miller, perhaps that's not so bad; for, she argues, one of the best alleged reasons to think that eternalism is false would be that we experience temporal passage as something over and above the timeline model of reality. Miller thinks, in fact, that we don't experience temporal passage as anything over and above something akin to a timeline. There is no phenomenology or 'feeling' of 'robust temporal passage'. So, there goes the argument from temporal passage and with it what would be the best argument against eternalism.

Putting all of that together enables us to return to Miller's argument from asymmetry *for* eternalism. The eternalist can agree that all objects (past, present, and future) exist, but does not have to agree that *time itself* has a direction over and above the 'direction' of change that the contents of time undergo. The eternalist is not committed to time's *passing* and so does not need to posit a direction to time. That being so, rather than saying that there is the direction of time *and* the direction of change (the 'direction' in which the film runs, forwards, backwards, etc.), there is just the direction of change and physical properties, such as entropy.

One might then think that this all serves to make a very strong case against presentism. We have a two-phase offence and a solid-looking defence. But as you make your way through the volume, Effingham will try to give you reasons to re-think that judgement. In his opening chapter, Effingham first looks to make really precise the difference between presentism and eternalism before turning his attention to reasons for believing presentism to be true.

The argument that Effingham initially advances in favour of presentism is an argument from *parsimony*. This argument begins with the idea that we should endorse the theory that posits the fewest objects in a way that we might find reminiscent of Ockham's razor. As Effingham notes, presentism posits only present objects. Eternalism posits objects that exist in the past and future, in addition to the existence of objects that are present. That looks to be a sizeable win for presentism, and so we should prefer presentism to eternalism.

From that starting argument, Effingham moves to defend presentism from arguments that have been put against presentism. At this point, his arguments are not in direct dialogue with Miller's, but he nonetheless considers and looks to try to block the argument from the special theory of relativity. I won't walk through this here since my goal in this section is just to give the reader a flavour of the sorts of consideration that are in play in the book, and we've already taken a look at the argument from relativity that Miller brings forward. Effingham then goes on to consider a further problem and further argument for presentism.

The problem facing presentism commences from a natural enough picture of truth. If we think about some familiar truths, there appears to be a connection between truth and the world. For instance, the proposition 'there is a glass on the table' is true only if there exists a glass, a table, and the glass is on the table. This is all very straightforward. But it points to a deeper insight, say some: truths are *made true* by what exists. What makes true 'there is a glass on the table' is what exists (namely, the state of there being a glass on the table).

However, if we try to extend that insight about the nature of truth into the temporal case, then the presentist will face a problem. After all, the presentist thinks that only present objects exist. But there are also truths about the past. It's true that Caesar crossed the Rubicon. And so, we face a problem: truths about the past need to be made true by what exists, but there are no past existents to make true truths about the past.

A significant part of Effingham's response to this argument is to point out that the alleged insight into the nature of truth might be based on a mis-step. We might have good grounds to deny that truths are made true by what exists. There are fairly obvious truths that seem to lack anything to make them true—that there could have been unicorns for instance. That's true, but nothing that actually exists seems to make true this truth about what is not but could have been. If there *are* some truths that don't need to be made true, then the presentist might say that truths about the past and future are like those truths and need nothing to make them true.

The final argument that Effingham brings in favour of presentism focuses on the open future. Where Miller focused on free will, Effingham's focus is slightly different and looks, not at what *we* can do, as putative free beings, but on the idea that the future itself is not fixed. Effingham's argument makes use of the notion of a fundamental fact—a fact for which there is no further explanation. As he notes, we typically try to minimise these in our best theories. It's a bad thing for a theory to posit an unexplained (/fundamental) fact.

Now, since the presentist believes that the future is 'open', so they also believe that there are no facts at all about how the future is. This, in turn, means that they're committed to the thesis that here are no fundamental facts about the future. In contrast, the eternalist posits a fixed future. That means that there are facts about the future and so there will be fundamental facts about the future. Presentism is thus to be preferred to eternalism.

With all of these arguments introduced—and with far greater nuance than I've managed here—the rest of the book brings Miller and Effingham into direct dialogue with one another. Each is given a chapter to respond to the arguments of the other, and so on until the end. The result is a refreshingly engaging work where the arguments aren't just left to rot on the page. If you want to know what one of the authors might say in response to a point, all that you have to do is keep turning the page. Whether you do so while time passes or simply across some region of a static block is something you will need to decide for yourself.

Jonathan Tallant

References

McTaggart, J. E. (1908). The Unreality of Time. *Mind* 68: 457–474.

Part I

Opening Statements

Chapter 1

In Defence of the Block Universe View

Kristie Miller

Contents

1. Introduction 3
2. Theories of Time: The Options 5
3. The Argument From Special Relativity 17
4. Arguments Against the Block: Change 25
5. Arguments Against the Block: Temporal Phenomenology 27
6. Arguments Against the Block: Free Will 33
7. The Argument From Explanation for the Block 38

1. Introduction

As you are sitting here reading this, close your eyes. Concentrate on what you can hear and smell and feel. Notice that this moment is changing: what you can hear and smell and feel is in flux. The strong scent of coffee from the next room wafts past and is then gone. The sharp call of a bird outside punctures your awareness and then is no more. This moment, so alive and colourful and noisy, is ever changing. We are located in the thrust and buzz and hub of the constantly changing now. New experiences come to be and old ones cease.

Are you feeling a little hungry? Are you thinking that soon, you will be eating a well-deserved lunch? Concentrate on that feeling. As you hear the ticking of the clock, perhaps it seems to you as though you are moving towards lunchtime and, in doing so, that you are moving ever further away from breakfast. Try to decide what to have for lunch. There are plenty of options; your pantry is well stocked. There are lots of different lunches you could have, and until you decide which, it seems to be unsettled what lunch will look like. Your lunch doesn't exist yet (though its ingredients do); it will come into existence when you decide what you want to eat and you make it.

The picture I just painted will probably seem intuitive. It's a picture that involves at least two aspects. First, it's a picture on which one moment is *really* present—the one you and I are in now—and which moment that is changes. At an earlier moment, you were eating breakfast, and lunch was quite some time away. But time has passed, and that moment is gone; now you are much closer to lunch. This phenomenon is known as *robust temporal passage* and I will have much more to say about what this is in section 1. Second, it's a picture on which some events are *temporary*. This view is known as *temporaryism*. This book mainly focuses on one way of combining robust temporal passage with temporaryism: *presentism*. Presentism is the view that only present things exist and that which things exist changes (temporaryism). It is this change in which things exist that constitutes there being robust temporal passage. So, on this view, your eating of breakfast is no more, and your eating of lunch has not yet come to be. Many philosophers have thought that both aspects of this picture are intuitive and have developed views on which our world is this way.

In this chapter, I argue that our world is not like this at all. Temporaryism is false, and *permanentism* is true. Whatever exists does so permanently. Nothing new comes into existence, and nothing ceases to exist. On this view, past, present, and future are equally real. All events that ever exist, exist *somewhere* and *somewhen in spacetime*. Your breakfast exists; your lunch exists; though, of course, neither of them exist right *here* or right *now*. In addition, there is no robust temporal passage. One moment is not marked out as being *really*, or *objectively*, present, with others marked out as either past or future.

Instead, whether an event is past, present, or future is an entirely relative matter. In this respect, past, present, and future are like north and south. Singapore is located to the north, relative to me (I am located in Sydney). But it is located to the south relative to someone in Vietnam. There is no sense in which Sydney can said to be simply objectively north (or south). The view I defend is known as the *block universe view*.

In section 2, I will begin by unpacking a few different accounts of the nature of time and explaining how each of these can be thought of as taking a stance on which of temporaryism or permanentism is correct and on whether or not there is robust temporal passage. This will allow us to better understand the block universe view and its competitors. Then, in section 3, I will present the first argument in favour of the block universe view. I call this the argument from special relativity. The aim of section 3 is to present the case in favour of the block universe in a way that avoids getting into the weeds of the maths and physics of special relativity (the interested reader can follow up on the details) but shows why, if we accept special relativity, we have strong reason to accept the block universe view.

The middle three sections of this chapter turn away from providing positive arguments in favour of the block and begin the task of defusing what might seem to be some powerful objections to the view.

In section 4, I outline and respond to the objection from change. According to this objection, very roughly, there is no change in a block universe; after all, everything is permanent. Since it is obvious that things change, the view must be false. I argue otherwise.

In section 5, I present the argument from temporal phenomenology. According to this argument, it powerfully seems to us that time robustly passes. Since, according to the block universe view, time does not robustly pass, defenders of this view must conclude that we are all subject to a massive and pervasive illusion. Since that is very implausible, we should conclude that the block universe view is false. I argue that the argument from temporal phenomenology is not a good one.

In section 6, I consider whether the block universe view is incompatible with there being free action. If the future exists, what we will do in the future exists. How can it be, though, that any of us can freely choose what to do if what we will do is already there in, as it were, black and white? In section 6, I outline the argument from free will and respond to it.

Finally, in section 7, I turn to providing one more positive argument in favour of the block universe view. There, I argue that there are various temporal asymmetries that we want to explain. We want to explain why we remember the past but not the future. Indeed, we want to explain why, in general, we have records of the past, but not the future. Further, we want to explain why we deliberate about the future, but not the past. On the face of it, it might seem as though views on which time robustly passes will do better in this regard; for they can say that these asymmetries in time are the product of time itself having a direction. In section 7, I argue that accounts of temporal asymmetries that appeal to robust temporal passage fail: temporal passage is explanatorily redundant. By contrast, the block universe theorist has an elegant explanation for these asymmetries.

2. Theories of Time: The Options

We can think of theories of time—theories of what time is like—as taking a stand on at least two sorts of questions. The first of these is the question of whether or not time robustly passes.[1] The second is the question of whether things in time exist permanently or temporarily. Different theories of time differently answer these two questions. Let's begin by considering this second question. There are answers to that question: *permanentism* and *temporaryism*.

---

1. Here and in what follows I talk about robust temporal passage rather than just temporal passage. That is to distinguish the notion I am interested in from a weaker notion of temporal passage that is consistent with the block universe view. On that latter conception, there is temporal passage just in case events occur in succession. This latter sense of temporal passage is sometimes known as *anodyne* passage.

Permanentism is usually defined as the view that always, everything always exists. This is a bit of a mouthful, but the idea is that, in some good sense of 'exists', there is no change in what exists. What is this sense of 'exists'? Sometimes philosophers distinguish between what they call a *tensed* reading of 'exists' and what they call a *tenseless* reading of 'exists'. Here's the idea. Consider the sentence 'Jemima is swimming'. That sentence is tensed: it's present-tensed. We might think of the sentence as saying something like: Jemima is swimming now, or Jemima is presently swimming. So, the sentence will be true just in case it is now the case that Jemima is swimming. If it is now time t, then the sentence will be true just in case, at t, Jemima is swimming. It doesn't matter what Jemima is doing at times other than t. As we will see later in the chapter, there is disagreement about what makes tensed sentences true. But for now, in order to get a handle on the relevant sense of existence that is at play here, let's suppose that a present-tensed claim such as 'Jemima is swimming' is true at a time, t, just in case, at t, Jemima is swimming. So far so good.

With this in mind, consider the sentence 'Dinosaurs exist'. On a tensed reading of 'exists', we should understand this sentence as saying something like 'Dinosaurs exist now'. So, imagine that Freddie utters that sentence some time in 2021. Then everyone, including permanentists, is going to agree that the sentence is false. That's because we don't find any dinosaurs located at any time in 2021.

This tensed reading of 'exists' is not what philosophers have in mind when they defend either permanentism or temporaryism. Instead, they have in mind what some call a tenseless reading of 'exists'. A tenseless reading of exists is a reading on which to say that dinosaurs exist is not to say that they exist *now*, or *presently*, it's just to say that they exist *somewhere* and *somewhen*. It's to say that, if we write down a list of absolutely everything that there is, dinosaurs will be on the list.

Another, and I think a better, way to get a handle on the distinction is not in terms of tensed and tenseless readings of 'exist' but in terms of whether we are using 'exists' in a *restricted* or an *unrestricted* way. Sometimes, when we talk of what exists, we mean to restrict our talk to a time or to a place. When I am standing on a beach in Sydney, I might say 'there are no crocodiles'. What I mean by that is that, unlike in Northern Australia, it's safe to swim in the water without threat from crocodiles. There are no crocodiles *here*, in Sydney. So, what I say is true when we read 'there are' in a restricted sense: to apply just to Sydney. But it's false if we read it in an unrestricted sense, since clearly there are indeed crocodiles. If I were to write down *all the things that exist, in the broadest possible sense* of this term, then I would write down 'crocodiles'.

We can think of one reading of 'exists' as restricting its scope to a particular time. On that reading, when we say, at t, 'dinosaurs exist' we mean that dinosaurs exist at t; that is, we mean that some dinosaurs are located at t.

We can think of the other reading of 'exists' as meaning 'exists' in the unrestricted sense: this is the sense in which we mean to pick out everything that exists anywhere at all in our universe, even if those things don't exist at the time at which we are located. In this sense, when we say, at *t*, 'dinosaurs exist' what we say might be true even if there are no dinosaurs located at *t*, so long as there are dinosaurs located somewhere in the universe. I will call this second sense of existence, existence simpliciter. By and large, it is this second sense of existence that will be at issue in this book.

Bearing this in mind, permanentists hold that there is no change in what exists, simpliciter. This does not mean that they think that there is no change in what exists in a restricted or tensed sense. They think there is; for there are certainly dinosaurs located at some times and not others; COVID 19 located at some times and not others. What permanentists hold is that, when we write down the list of absolutely everything that exists, simpliciter, it doesn't matter what time we make our list because that list always has the same things on it. That is because, according to permanentism, the *totality* of our universe never changes. The universe itself does not grow or shrink or otherwise change in any way.

> **Permanentism:** Always, everything always exists.

By contrast, *temporaryism* is the view that, sometimes, some things sometimes do not exist. Again, what is meant by 'exists' here is exists simpliciter. So, imagine, again we are asked to write the list of everything that exists in the broadest possible sense of that term. Temporaryism is the view that what is on our list will change depending on what time we write the list. For instance, it might be that sometimes dinosaurs will be on the list, and sometimes they won't. That is because temporaryists think that the *sum total of reality* itself changes.

> **Temporaryism:** Sometimes, some things sometimes do not exist.

Temporaryism and permanentism are views about whether what exists, simpliciter, changes or not. Permanentists say it does not, and temporaryists say it does. This means that there are different versions of permanentism and temporaryism, depending on which things the permanentist or temporaryist thinks exist simpliciter.

Let's start with permanentism. There are different views one can have about which events exist simpliciter. (In what follows, I will often jettison the 'simpliciter'. I will always mean existence simpliciter unless I specify otherwise.) For instance, one could think that only present events exist. On that view, it is always the case that only present events exist. It is not the case that any past events have ever existed nor that any future events will exist. If that were true, our world would literally contain a single moment: this one. But, of course, that is not how anyone supposes our world to be. Since we do think that things were some way in the past, and will be some way in the future, the most natural version of permanentism is one according to which *past, present, and future events permanently exist*. This view is often known as *eternalism*.

> Eternalism: Past, present, and future things exist.

According to eternalism, the Big Bang exists, the event of you eating your breakfast exists, the event of you eating your lunch exists, and so, too (let us suppose), does the event of the rise of robots.

To better understand eternalism, let's think about the case of space. You are located somewhere as you read this. Let's suppose you are in Birmingham in the UK. I am in Sydney in Australia. Although Birmingham exists, it doesn't exist *here*, where I am. That is to say, Birmingham exists, simpliciter, but it's not *located here*. Likewise, although Sydney exists, it does not exist *there*, where you are. That is to say, Sydney exists, simpliciter, but it's not located there.

Eternalists say the same thing about events in time. Eternalists hold that dinosaurs exist just the way that Birmingham does. But, just as Birmingham is not located right here, in Sydney, where I am, so too the dinosaurs are not located right here. Just as Birmingham is separated from me in space, the dinosaurs are separated from me in time.

So, when we use 'exists' in the unrestricted sense, eternalists say that 'dinosaurs exist' is true. By contrast, if we were using 'exists' in the restricted sense, to mean 'exists now', then eternalists will say that dinosaurs do not exist. By this, they just mean that dinosaurs are not to be found at this moment in time: they are not located here, in 2021. But, when we ask whether they exist simpliciter, the answer is that they do; for they are located 'out there' in spacetime. They are *somewhere* and *somewhen*; they are just not where we are, here and now.

What is *spacetime*? Spacetime is, very roughly, the product of fusing together the three spatial dimensions and the fourth temporal dimension into one four-dimensional thing. According to eternalists, our world is a giant, four-dimensional thing. It is extended along three spatial dimensions and one temporal dimension. So, according to eternalists, dinosaurs are located at other *times* in spacetime (times other than the one we are located at now) just as Birmingham is located at a different *place* (from the one I am located at here). But both exist simpliciter.

This is the only version of permanentism I will consider in this book.

Moving on, let's turn to temporaryism. One might hold that, at any particular time, only past and present things exist, but future ones do not. It is easy to see what is attractive about that view. You remember today's breakfast. There seem to be clear facts about it. Yet, it is clearly in the past. It cannot be changed or altered in any way. The present also clearly exists because we are in it and it is the time at which we act. But the future does not exist because, one might think, there are no facts about your future lunch. If one holds that view and one holds that certain future events *will* come into existence when they are present, then one is a temporaryist; for one thinks that the sum totality of reality changes. When we write the complete list of everything that exists, what we put on that list will depend on what time it is. For instance, perhaps the event of your eating breakfast on Tuesday will be on the list when it is Tuesday afternoon but not when it is Monday, since on Monday that event will not yet exist.

This kind of temporaryism is known as the *growing block view*. For it is the view that reality as a whole increases as new things comes into existence. On that view, things are constantly coming into existence. But once they come into existence, they stay in existence. Thus, our complete list of what exists will get longer as time passes.

> **Growing Block View:** Past and present things exist, but future ones do not. Reality grows as new things come into existence in the present.

Alternatively, one might hold that neither past nor present things exist. Then one thinks that the only things that exist are present things. Remember that this is not the trivially true claim that only present things exist *now*; for we are using 'exists' in the unrestricted sense. It's the claim that, when we make the complete list of everything that exists simpliciter, the only things on that list are the things that exist now.

If one combines this claim with the claim that the present changes as new things come into existence and previous things cease to exist, then one is a certain kind of temporaryist; for one thinks that sometimes a certain thing does not exist, then later it comes to exist, and later still, it ceases to exist. This view is known as *presentism*. On this view, only present things exist, but past things *did* exist, though they don't anymore, and future things *will* exist, though they don't exist yet.

> **Presentism**: Only present things exist, and which things exist changes.

According to eternalists, 'dinosaurs exist' is true when we read 'exists' in the unrestricted sense, while according to presentists, 'dinosaurs exist' is false when we read 'exists' in the unrestricted sense. Both views agree that it is false when read in the restricted sense.

So far, then, we have distinguished three views: eternalism, the growing block view, and presentism. Eternalism is a variety of permanentism, and the growing block view and presentism are varieties of temporaryism.

That brings us to the second way in which we can distinguish views about the nature of time: in terms of whether they are views that endorse *robust temporal passage* or views that deny robust temporal passage.

The first question we need to address is what it means to say that time robustly passes (or not). The reason I talk of *robust* temporal passage, rather than just temporal passage, is because there seems to be a trivial sense in which everyone agrees that time passes.

It is now 9.30AM. When I got up, it was 7.00AM. So, two and a half hours have elapsed between when I got up and this moment. The clock in this room measured that elapsed time. We can all agree that there is a certain temporal distance between the event of my getting up and the event of my writing this sentence, as measured by the clock in my living room. In *this* sense, we can certainly say that time has passed; indeed, two and a half hours have passed. This is uncontroversial, and is not what is typically meant by temporal passage when it is discussed in the philosophy of time. In what follows in this chapter, I will exclusively focus on robust temporal passage.

What is robust temporal passage? Time robustly passes if there is a change in the present moment.

> **Robust Temporal Passage**: There is a change in the present moment.

One way there can be a change in the present moment is if there are multiple moments, but *which* of them is present changes. Consider the growing block theory again. Recall that, on that view, the entire universe grows as new things come into being. The growing block theory is not merely a version of temporaryism. It is also a view on which there is robust temporal passage. That is because, according to such a view, the things that exist at the very end of the growing block are the things in the objectively present moment. They are the things that sit looking out into nothingness: the nothingness of the future. Which moment is present, however, changes as new things come into existence. The things that were present, by being at the very edge of being, cease to be present and become past when new things come into existence. So, which time is present changes. According to the growing block theory, then, we model temporal passage by the accretion of new things. What it is for time to pass is for new things to come into existence.

By contrast, it could be that the present changes not because there are multiple times and which is present changes, but instead because there is a single moment—the present—and what that moment is like changes. This is what presentists suppose is the case. So, presentists model temporal passage in terms of the change of a single present moment.

Views according to which time robustly passes are sometimes known as *A-theoretic* views, sometimes known as *temporally dynamical* views, and sometimes as *tensed* views. They are known as dynamical views because, on these views, time itself has a dynamical quality: time itself flows. They are known as tensed views because these are views on which the tenses we find in language—in particular, past, present, and future tenses—map onto objective features of time itself. I'll have more to say about this shortly.

By contrast, views that reject robust temporal passage are sometimes known as *static* views of time because time itself does not flow. Time itself is an unchanging dimension. The most common view of this kind combines eternalism—the claim that past, present, and future exist, simpliciter—with the claim that time does not robustly pass. This view is known as the *block universe view*.

> **Block Universe View:** (i) Past, present, and future exist. (ii) No moment is objectively present.

This view is sometimes also known as four-dimensionalism. That is because it is often spelled out as the view that time is a fourth dimension, which is a little like the three spatial dimensions. (This is not to say that the fourth temporal dimension is *just* like the spatial ones; that time is just like space. One could have such a view, but this is not the version of the block universe that most defenders of the view endorse. Instead, they hold that, although time is the fourth dimension, it is somewhat different from the three spatial dimensions.)

Four-dimensionalism is also often used to refer to a view about *persistence*. Persistence refers to the fact that objects exist through time. Four-dimensionalism is one view about the way in which objects persist through time. Henceforth, if we use 'four-dimensionalism' we will always use it to mean a view about persistence (which we will introduce later in the book).

According to the block universe view, our universe is bit like a giant Persian rug. All of the events that ever did happen, are happening, or will happen, are there, woven into the fabric of the rug. The rug has a complex pattern. It is multi-coloured. Some parts of it are gold and some, black. The rug tells the story of a great Persian prince, and it does so by having different parts of the rug tell different parts of the story. No two parts of the rug are the same. Still, the rug *itself* does not change. The rug itself does not shimmer or fade (even if it does have faded portions). This is why permanentism is true of the rug. So, too, for the block: the block *itself* does not change, even though different parts of the block are quite different from one another. For instance, one part of the block contains dinosaurs, and one part contains Facebook. But the block itself does not shrink or grow. It does not gain new parts or lose them. This is why the block universe view is a version of permanentism.

On this picture of reality, some events (things that happen in the block) are *earlier than* others, and some are *later than* others. So, for instance, the Big Bang occurs before the extinction of the dinosaurs: it is *earlier than* the extinction. These temporal relations of earlier-than and later-than are all part of the block and do not change. If the Big Bang is earlier than the extinction of the dinosaurs, it is always true that the Big Bang is earlier than the extinction of the dinosaurs. This is the sense in which the block universe is sometimes said to be 'static': the block itself does not change; instead, the block is full of events and things, located at different times, that bear unchanging relations of earlier-than and later-than to one another.

In turn, this means that the block universe view rejects robust temporal passage. No moment in the block is singled out as being the 'real' or 'genuine' present moment. It is not, for instance, the case that one moment in the block is 'lit up' with the light of presentness and that which time that is moves. There is no little *label* in the block which says 'present' and which attaches to a particular moment in the block, such that that label moves. Instead, according to the block universe theorist, every moment is 'the present' or 'now' for the people who are located at that time. Indeed, for block universe theorists, 'here' and 'now' function in a similar sort of way. 'Here' just picks out the place I happen to be at: Sydney, if I am in Sydney, and Birmingham, if I am in Birmingham. Likewise, 'now' just picks out the time I happen to be at (a moment in 2021 if that is when I am, or a moment in 1800 if that is when I am). And just as 'here' doesn't latch onto some special, mysterious metaphysical property of "hereness" that some locations have and others lack, so, too, 'now' doesn't latch onto a special, mysterious metaphysical property of 'nowness' that sometimes have and others lack.

To get a sense of how this is meant to go, we need to say a bit more about *indexicals* and about *tensed* and *tenseless truth conditions*.

Let's start by considering a tensed sentence:

S: I am swimming

This sentence is present-tensed. The word 'I' is an indexical. Indexicals are words or phrases whose meaning depends on the context in which they are uttered.

Or, as we might instead put it, they are words or phrases that express different propositions depending on the context in which they are uttered. So, the word 'I' is an indexical because, when I use it, I pick out myself (Kristie Miller) and, when you use it, you pick out yourself, and so on. So, when I say 'I am tall' I express the proposition <Kristie Miller is tall> and when Annie says it, she expresses the proposition <Annie is tall>. Likewise, 'next Tuesday' is an indexical because which proposition it expresses depends on when it is uttered.

Likewise, the word 'here' is an indexical. When I say 'I am here' and I am located in Sydney, I express the proposition <Kristie Miller is in Sydney>. That proposition, in turn, is true just in case I am, in fact, in Sydney. When Nikk utters 'I am here', he expresses the proposition <Nikk is in Birmingham>. Given that he is in fact in Birmingham, that proposition, too, is true. Quite generally, an utterance of 'I am here' by any speaker whatsoever will turn out to be true, regardless of where the speaker is, in fact, located, since 'here' simply picks out the speaker's location. When Nikk utters 'I am here' and he is in Birmingham, he utters the proposition <Nikk is in Birmingham>, and that proposition is true, since he is in fact in Birmingham. But Nikk's utterance would have been true if, instead, he had been located in Hobart, since, had he been in Hobart, he would have uttered the proposition <Nikk is in Hobart> when he said 'I am here'.

> **Indexical:** A term or phrase whose reference depends on the context in which it is uttered.

Let's suppose that Annie utters S. Then she utters the proposition <Annie is swimming>.[2] We can think of propositions as being what sentences *mean*. So, a sentence in English and a sentence in French can mean the same thing even though they are different sentences. In such cases, we say that the sentences *express the same proposition*.

What are the conditions under which the present-tensed sentence 'Annie is swimming' is true? Well, you might think that it will be true just in case there is some feature of reality itself that 'maps onto' or corresponds to the tense of the sentence. After all, the sentence will be true only if there is someone, Annie, and only if that someone is in water, moving about (i.e., swimming). Since the sentence is tensed, one might think we need to find something 'tensed' in the world which makes that sentence true.

We've just seen that temporaryists think that what exists (simpliciter) changes and that those who think that there is robust temporal passage think that this change in what exists is intimately connected to the passing of time. As time

---

2. I use angle brackets to pick out propositions.

passes, different things become objectively present, while those that were present become past. We've also seen that different views model this passage of time differently. The growing block models it in terms of the growth of the universe: as new things come into existence they become the present, and then they become past when still more things come into existence. Presentists model it in terms of the changing of the present moment: the present moment now contains a lot of COVID 19, but some time ago it did not contain any COVID 19.

Let's say that the fact that certain things are in the present (and perhaps that others are in the past, and still others are in the future), is *a tensed fact*. Then, according to temporaryists, the tensed facts change as time passes, since which things are present (and which past and future) changes.

So, one possibility is that tensed truths are true because of tensed facts. If that is right, we can say that tensed truths have *tensed truth conditions*. We will have much more to say about this in Chapter 2 of the book. But for now, all that really matters is that, on this view, tensed sentences (present-tensed, past-tensed, or future-tensed) are made true by reality itself containing something that corresponds to the tense of the sentences: they are made true by there being tensed facts, where these tensed facts consist in its being the case that some things are objectively present and that which things those are changes.

Notice that if tensed truths (i.e., true tensed sentences) have tensed truth conditions, then they are only true if there are tensed facts. So, there would be a very easy argument to the conclusion that time robustly passes. For surely many ordinary sentences such as 'yesterday I had breakfast' and 'I am swimming' and 'there were dinosaurs' and 'there will be killer robots' are true. If they are only true if there are tensed facts, then there must be tensed facts. And if there are tensed facts, then time must robustly pass. In turn, this would suggest that some version of temporaryism is true, since most accounts of robust passage are ones on which, which things exist, simpliciter, changes.[3]

Permanentists such as block universe theorists, however, reject the idea that tensed truths have tensed truth conditions. Instead, they hold that they have *tenseless truth conditions*. Very roughly, this means they think that such truths are made true not by there being tensed facts, but instead by various tenseless features of our world, coupled with various facts about where each of us is located relative to other things in our world. To see this, consider again the following sentence:

S: I am swimming.

Suppose Annie utters S at t. According to the block universe theorist, S is true just in case at t Annie is indeed swimming. The idea is that present-tensed

---

3. One possible exception is a version of the moving spotlight view, which we do not discuss in this book.

sentences are true at the time they are uttered just in case what they say—in this case, that Annie is swimming—is true at that time. In fact, many block universe theorists hold that, when Annie utters S at *t*, the proposition she expresses is <Annie is swimming at *t*>. That proposition is true just in case Annie is swimming at *t*. Moreover, *that* proposition is either true or false simpliciter. That is, consider its truth-value at, say, *t**. Is it true at *t** that <Annie is swimming at *t*>? Yes. So, if <Annie is swimming at *t*> is true at any time, it is true at *every* time. It never changes its truth-value. Of course, if Annie were to utter S at *t**, it would not express the proposition <Annie is swimming at *t*>, it would express the proposition <Annie is swimming at *t**> and *that* proposition might be false at *t** (if Annie is not swimming then). But the point is that the block universe theorist can say that propositions themselves do not change their truth-values. If it is ever true that Annie is swimming at *t*, then it is always true that she is. It is simply that *which* proposition is expressed by a tensed sentence, such as S, changes depending on when it is uttered, and so whether that sentence is true or not can also change depending on when it is uttered.

Importantly, though, none of this requires that any time is objectively present. What we laid out above are *tenseless truth conditions* for utterances of tensed sentences. They are tenseless because we had no need to appeal to facts about which time is really present. All we appealed to are facts about the time at which the sentence is uttered and facts about what is happening at that time (i.e., whether or not Annie is swimming at that time).

All it takes for a present-tensed sentence to be true at some times and false at others is that it expresses different propositions at different times and that sometimes what it expresses is true and sometimes false. S is true just when it is uttered at a time when Annie is swimming and false if it's uttered at a time when she is not. We don't need to try and find out *which* time is objectively present and then look to see if Annie is swimming *then* in order to work out if the sentence is true when it is uttered. Nor do we need to find a time that is objectively present in order to explain how that sentence can be true at some times, and false at others.

Now consider:

S*: I was swimming.

Suppose Annie utters S* at *t*. S* is past-tensed. The block universe theorist says that this sentence, too, has tenseless truth conditions. They say that S* is true when it is uttered at *t* by Annie just in case there is an earlier time at which Annie is swimming. The block universe theorist will say something similar about future-tensed sentences, but I leave it as an exercise for the reader to work out exactly what she will say.

The general point is that the block universe theorist will say that we can always provide a set of truth conditions for tensed sentences which appeal to nothing more than (a) the time at which the sentence is uttered and (b) things being some way or other either at the time of utterance (present-tensed sentences) or at an earlier time (past-tensed sentences) or at a later time (future-tensed sentences). There is no need to appeal to tensed facts.

With all this in mind, we can now see how the block universe theorist will make sense of claims that are directly about the past, present, and future. Consider the following sentence:

S1: I am present.

Suppose that Annie utters S1 at t. Then she utters the proposition <Annie is present>. According to the block universe theorist, the word 'present' is an indexical. It picks out whatever time one happens to be at. So, in this case, it picks out the time at which Annie says 'I am present', namely t. There's nothing more to that sentence being true, when uttered by Annie, than Annie being located at the time at which she utters the sentence (t). An utterance of that sentence would, in fact, be true if Annie were instead in 1800, since then it would express the proposition <Annie is in 1800> and that proposition would be true. So, to talk of being present is really just to talk about *when* one is located in the same way as to talk about being *here* is really just to talk about *where* one is located. In both cases, the relevant terms are indexicals that pick out the time/place of the speaker.

The block universe theorist, then, offers tenseless truth conditions for sentences like S1, too. She says that an utterance of that sentence is true just in case the speaker is located at the time of utterance (and it's super hard not to be located at the time you utter something!). These truth conditions are tenseless because they make no mention at all of tensed facts.

Something similar will be said about sentencing involving 'past' and 'future'. Suppose that Annie is located in Sydney in December 2020. Suppose that Annie says the following:

S2: The extinction of the dinosaurs is in the past.

Suppose Annie utters S2 at t. Then the block universe theorist will say that S2 is true at t, just in case there is an event of the extinction of the dinosaurs and that event is located earlier than t. And, again, these truth conditions are tenseless.

According to the block universe theorist, 'the past', in the block universe, just refers to that part of the block that is earlier-than where we happen to be located. Likewise, 'the future' just refers to that part of the block that is located later-than where we happen to be located. So, dinosaurs and their extinction are located in the past *related to Annie*, who is located at t. That's why, when Annie utters S2, she says something true. But of course, that very sentence would be false if it were uttered at certain other times. Consider the dinosaur, Maeve. If Maeve were to utter S2, what she says would be false; for the event of the extinction of the dinosaurs occurs later-than where Maeve is located and hence is *future* relative to her. So instead, if Maeve wants to utter a truth, she needs to utter the future-tensed statement 'the extinction of the dinosaurs is in the future'.

In this regard, the block universe theorist says that terms like 'past' and 'future' are a bit like terms like 'north' and 'south'. Suppose Annie is in Sydney. Then, for Annie, Singapore is to the north. Now consider Jeremy, located in Vietnam. For Jeremy, Singapore is to the south. Of course, Singapore has a perfectly objective location. It is just that whether Singapore is to the north or the south depends entirely on one's own location relative to Singapore. What is true of north and south is true of past and future on the block universe view.

In this book, I argue that our world is a block universe world, and my colleague Nikk argues that it's a presentist world.

I begin, in the next section, by presenting what I call the argument from special relativity. That argument is intended to show that we should endorse the block universe view.

Dynamical, or tensed, theories of time are ones that embrace both temporaryism and robust temporal passage. They hold that what exists changes and that it does so as time itself passes. On these views there is a fact of the matter as to which moment is truly present and which is past and which is future, and that fact changes as time passes. By contrast, static or tenseless theories of time, such as the block universe view, are ones that embrace permanentism and reject robust temporal passage. Such views hold that what exists does not change. Time does not pass. Instead, the sum total of reality is always the same. No moment is singled out as objectively present. Instead, we are all simply located whenever we happen to be located. Since being present is, on this view, just being located where one is, each of us is located in the present. Moreover, being past or being future is a relative matter. Something is past relative to a location just in case it is located earlier than that location, and it is future relative to a location just in case it is located later than that location.

3. The Argument From Special Relativity

Here is what I take to be a highly intuitive picture of our world. At the very first moment of time, a bunch of things came into existence. Let's call a thing that happens—such as something coming into existence or something moving or changing or being located at some place—an *event*. It is intuitive to think that a bunch of events occur at that very first moment of time in our universe. Those events occur at the very same time. They are *simultaneous* with one another. Then some different events occur. Those events are simultaneous with one another, and each of them is later than the first events that occurred. And so on.

On this picture, we can neatly divide up our universe into a sequence of times. Each time can then be ordered in terms of which time is earlier or later than which other time. At any time, there occur a bunch of events, and all of these events are simultaneous with one another. In turn, these events are all either earlier or later than events that occur at other times.

Dynamical theories of time—those according to which there is robust temporal passage—seem to presuppose something like this picture. Dynamists hold that there are objective facts about which events are present. But it seems very plausible to think that the present includes only those events that happen at the same time. In turn, it seems plausible to think that events happen at the same time just in case they are simultaneous with one another. So, two events are present only if those events are simultaneous. Let's call this the *presentness principle*.

> **Presentness Principle:** For any two events, E1 and E2, E1 and E2 are present only if E1 and E2 are simultaneous.

The Presentness Principle doesn't say that all that is required for two events to be present is for them to be simultaneous. After all, dynamists think that some pairs of events are simultaneous but are past. These are events that were both present at the same time—that is, were co-present—but are now both past. It just says that, if two events are present, then they must be simultaneous.

After all, dynamists hold that there is a fact of the matter regarding which events are present and which not. They deny, for instance, that there are pairs of events such that, if we ask the question, 'are both E1 and E2 present?', the answer is that there's no fact of the matter. Let's call this the Presentness Fact Principle.

> **Presentness Fact Principle:** For any two events, E1 and E2, there is a fact of the matter whether E1 and E2 are present.

If one accepts both the Presentness Principle and the Presentness Fact Principle, then one is committed to saying that there is always a fact of the matter as to whether any two events are simultaneous. For suppose there were some events, E1 and E2, and there were no fact of the matter regarding whether E1 and E2 are simultaneous. Then it will follow that there is no fact of the matter whether E1 and E2 are present, and hence it will follow that the presentness fact principle is false. So, dynamists who accept both principles are committed to the *Fact about Simultaneity Principle*.

> **Fact About Simultaneity Principle:** For any two events, E1 and E2, there is a fact of the matter whether E1 and E2 are simultaneous.

In what follows, I explain why the special theory of relativity shows us that the Fact about Simultaneity Principle is false. In turn, it shows us that dynamical theories of time are false. Since presentism is a dynamical theory of time, it follows that presentism is false. By contrast, I will argue, the block universe view can make good sense of the falsity of the Fact about Simultaneity Principle. So that gives us reason to endorse the block universe view.

Before I explain why the Fact about Simultaneity Principle is false, let's take a very quick detour. For you might be thinking that, unlike other dynamists, the presentist does not need to accept the Presentness Principle. After all, the presentist doesn't need to somehow distinguish all the events that are present from those that are either past or future; she doesn't think that there are any past or future things. So, the presentist could just say that the present things are just those things that exist and leave it at that, without mentioning simultaneity at all.

That, however, would be an implausible view. Suppose we just say that the present things are the things that exist, simpliciter. Then the block universe theory becomes a version of presentism. It just turns out that the present encompass both the dinosaurs and the sentient robots. Indeed, the present encompasses *everything*, and it just turns out that there is more of everything than presentists might otherwise have thought. Surely, though, this is not what the presentist wants to say. She wants to deny that dinosaurs exist, simpliciter. So, she needs to say more than that present things are just whichever things exist, simpliciter. The natural thing to say is that present things are those things that exist, simpliciter, where all of those things are simultaneous with one another. But then, the presentist is committed to the Presentness Principle.

So, what is the problem for dynamical theories that arises from special relativity? The problem is that dynamists are committed to the Fact about Simultaneity Principle, and science gives us good reason to think that that principle is false.

To see this, let's consider an example. George and Margaret are outside in their yard barbecuing. George gets out some eggs from the crate, cracks one on the side of the barbecue, and then upends the egg onto the hot surface and watches as it cooks. Then, he takes it off the barbecue and puts it onto Margaret's plate and she eats it. Let's call this sequence CRACK (for cracking the egg) then COOK (for cooking it) then EAT (for eating it). Let's also suppose that, while George is barbecuing the egg, his cat, Big Fur, is in the backyard. Big Fur is catching a rat, then eating the rat, then coughing up a part of the rat. Let's call this sequence of events CATCH, RAT, and COUGH. Margaret and George both observe the various events that take place in the yard. They both observe CRACK to occur before COOK, and COOK to occur before EAT. They also both observe CATCH to occur before RAT, and RAT to occur before COUGH. They also observe CRACK to be simultaneous with CATCH, and COOK to be simultaneous with RAT, and COUGH to be simultaneous with EAT (which is unfortunate, since no one really wants to be eating an egg at the same time as they are watching a cat cough up part of a dead rat).

So far, this is standard fare for a barbecue. But now suppose that George and Margaret have a friend, Jennifer. Jennifer did very well in the latest tech bubble, and she bought herself a single-woman star ship. A month ago, Jennifer boarded her ship and headed off at quite fast speed away from Earth. Tonight, Jennifer, still at high speed, travels past Margaret and George in their backyard and looks down to see what they are up to. What does Jennifer observe? Well, she observes that CRACK occurs before COOK, and that COOK occurs before EAT. She also observes that CATCH occurs before RAT, and that RAT occurs before COUGH. This should be a relief; observing COUGH to occur before RAT would be awful in a quite different way from observing RAT to occur before COUGH.

So far, this is what we would expect given the intuitive picture I painted at the beginning of this section. We all see eggs being cracked before being cooked and then eaten. But here is where things get weird. According to Margaret and George, who are sitting at rest in their yard, CRACK and CATCH are simultaneous. But according to Jennifer, who is moving at speed, they are not. Instead, Jennifer sees CRACK happen before CATCH. Likewise, while Margaret and George see COOK and RAT occur simultaneously, Jennifer sees COOK occur before RAT. And while Margaret and George observe EAT and COUGH to occur simultaneously, Jennifer observes EAT to occur before COUGH.

What's more, we know that, if there were someone else, also moving relative to Margaret and George, on the one hand, and Jennifer, on the other, they would agree with Jennifer that CRACK and CATCH, and COOK and RAT, and EAT and COUGH are not simultaneous, that person would see those events occur in the *opposite* order to the order Jennifer witnesses them.

What is going on? Consider, first, the events that Jennifer, Margaret, and George all agree about. These are events where light can travel from one to another. They are events that are potentially causally connected because one can send a signal from one event to the other. Indeed, these are events that, in this case, are causally connected. Big Fur eats the rat because her chasing it causes her to catch it. Margaret eats the cooked egg because the process of being on the hot barbecue causes it to be cooked. We know that events such as these will always be observed to occur in the same order regardless of who is doing the observing.

Below is figure 1.1 to help get a handle on this idea. What is depicted is known as a light cone, though it is really two cones. The cone on the bottom is known as the *backwards light cone*. The cone on the top is known as the *forwards light cone*. Everything on the surface of the backwards and forwards light cones are light-like separated from the point where the two cones meet (the point on which the light cone is centred). This means that, in order for something located on the surface of the backwards light cone to reach the point on which the cones are centred, it would need to travel at the speed of light. Likewise, something located at the point on which the cones meet would need to travel at the speed of light in order to reach any location on the surface of the forwards light cone. All of the locations *inside* the backwards and forwards light cone are said to be time-like separated from an event on the point of the cone. We can think of those events that are inside a point's backwards light cone as being in the past of that point, and we can think of those events that are inside the forwards light cone as being those in the future of a point. Everything outside of the light cones is in the *absolute elsewhere*. Events in the absolute elsewhere are said to be space-like, separated from the central point.

Events that are on or within the light cones will always be observed to be temporally separated, and their order will always be observed to be the same regardless of the relative motion of the observer. By contrast, events that are space-like separated, will be observed by some observers to be simultaneous

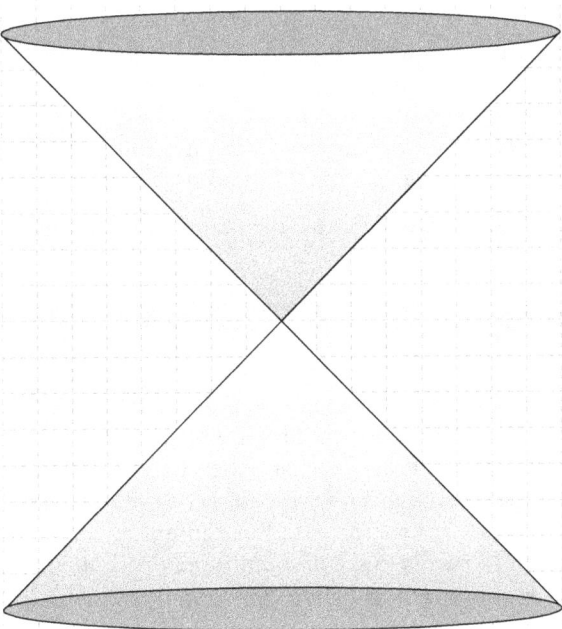

Figure 1.1 The Light Cone

and by other observers to be temporally separated, depending on the relative motion of those observers. When one observer is moving relative to the other, they will sometimes disagree about which events in the absolute elsewhere are simultaneous.

Now, so far that doesn't obviously give us as reason to suppose that there is no fact of the matter whether various events really are simultaneous. If I put Amy into a room with red lights and ask her what colour things are and I later put Jorge into the same room, but with white lights, and ask him what colours things are, they will disagree about the colours of the things in that room. But I might not conclude from this that there is no fact of the matter what the colours are of the things in that room. I might instead think that one observer is better placed to make colour judgments; namely, Jorge, because he is not looking at things under red light.

So, the fact that observers make different judgements about simultaneity does not show that there are no facts about simultaneity. It could be that some observers are getting things right and others are getting them wrong. Looking at the diagram above, it would be tempting to say that observers who are at rest get things right and those in motion are just experiencing an illusion. They are seeing things as simultaneous which really are not. The problem is that it is part of the very theories (general and special relativity), which predicted these observations and whose predictions have been confirmed, that motion is always relative. Earlier, I made it sound as though George and Margaret were at rest and Jennifer was moving. Now, of course, George and Margaret and Jennifer are moving with respect to one another. But it's not the case that *really*, Margaret and George are at rest in their backyard and Jennifer is moving. But if that is so, then we cannot say that really, George and Margaret get things right and Jennifer gets this wrong.

More generally, there is nothing in the theory of special relativity that gives us any reason to privilege one observer over another. This does not mean that we cannot *distinguish* some kinds of motion (or some kinds of trajectories) from others. For instance, we can distinguish inertial motion/trajectories from accelerating motion/trajectories. That is, while motion is relative, so that there is no fact of the matter as to whether one individual is at rest and another in motion, there is a fact of the matter about whether one individual is accelerating or not. Still, the point here is that, when we take individuals in inertial motion, there is no reason, given by the theory of relativity, to privilege one of their observations over the other's. But those individuals will sometimes disagree about which events in the *absolute elsewhere* —namely those outside of the backwards and forwards light cone—occur in which order.

Now, of course, we could simply posit, by fiat if you like, some special fact about who is right and who wrong. We could say that, even though it is not part of scientific theory that this is so, it is nevertheless the case. To do this, we would need to claim that there is some fact of the matter as to which observers are correct and that this fact makes no physical difference. It is not something that any empirical investigations could detect; for it is part of the scientific theories in question that, if there were privileged observers like this, we would not be able to determine which observers those are. So, if there are such observers, we could never to come to know that there are (and who they are) by scientific means. Then we would be positing what is known as *absolute simultaneity*; that is, we would be positing that there is some fact about which events *really are* simultaneous, even if we can never detect such a fact.

Making this posit strikes me as rather implausible. First, it's hard to know *which* observers we should think are the ones who are getting things right. Second, it is puzzling that, if there is a fact about simultaneity, it is not one that we can empirically detect. Surely, if anything is detectable, it would be this. Third, this seems methodologically dubious. Our best science says there are no privileged observers, or at least it says that we have no reason to suppose there are and no way to detect them if there were; but we decide to posit mysterious, undetectable, absolute simultaneity regardless. If that is the business we are in, why not start positing invisible, undetectable fairies dancing at the bottom of my garden?

So, I say, we should conclude the following:

> **No Absolute Simultaneity**: For any two events, E1 and E2, that are space-like separated, there is no fact of the matter whether E1 is simultaneous with E2.

The problem for the dynamist is that the truth of No Absolute Simultaneity entails the falsity of the Facts about Simultaneity Principle, and that is a principle the dynamist endorses.

So, the truth of one of our best-confirmed scientific theories, special relativity, gives us reason to think that dynamical theories are false. In turn, that gives us reason to think that the block universe view is true, at least on the assumption that the block universe theory is consistent with the theory of special relativity. We can frame the argument against dynamical views as follows:

> **Argument From Special Relativity**
>
> (1) Dynamical theories are inconsistent with the theory of special relativity
> (2) The theory of special relativity is true
> (3) Therefore, dynamical theories are false.

The argument from special relativity only tells us that we should reject dynamical theories. It does not yet tell us that we should endorse the block universe theory. But we can relatively straightforwardly make that case. We need to show that the block universe theory is, unlike dynamical theories, consistent with special relativity. So, that means that, unlike dynamical theories, it is not ruled out by best science.

We can show this to be so. According to the block universe view, there need be no one, correct way of 'slicing up' the block into slices, each of which contains absolutely simultaneous events. Instead, there are different ways of 'slicing' the block, corresponding to the different relative motions of observers. These represent the different sets of events that those observers will see as simultaneous.

To get a sense of this, imagine you have an unsliced loaf of bread in front of you and the bread is olive bread. The bread, in this analogy, is standing in for the block universe. The olives are standing in for events in the block. There is a fact of the matter as to the total distance between any two olives. This corresponds to there being a fact of the matter, in the block universe, as to which spatio-temporal distance obtains between any two events. Still, suppose you slice the bread into nice, straight slices. Then some olives will be on the same slice of bread, and some will be on different slices. This corresponds to the fact that, for some observers, the olives on the same slice of bread will appear to be simultaneous.

Now, imagine that we put the slices back together into a loaf, and this time we slice our bread on an angle. If we slice up the loaf like this, we will find that different olives are on the same slice. This corresponds to the fact that some observers will see olives on these slices of bread as simultaneous.

The lesson we should draw from this is that there is no *unique, correct* way of slicing up your olive bread into slices. So, it's not the case that some olives really are, objectively, on the same slice. Which olives are on which slice depends on how we slice the bread, and there is no one, correct way to do that. But that being so is consistent with there being some fact of the matter as what spatio-temporal distance there is between any two olives. It is just that, when observers move relative to one another, some see the distance between olives (as it were) as being made up of more spatial distance and less temporal distance, and some see it the other way around. So, some see a certain pair of olives as being on the same slice, and others see them as being on different slices. But that's just because they are 'slicing' up their bread in different ways.

This marks the end of the first argument in favour of the block universe view. Of course, it remains to be seen whether we should *accept* the block universe theory or not. Perhaps the block universe theory faces its own insurmountable problems, and so we have as much reason to reject it as we do to reject dynamical views like presentism. In the next section, I take up the task of considering several arguments against the block universe view, and I argue that these fail.

Perhaps the most powerful arguments against the block universe view are that it is incompatible with the truth of certain perfectly ordinary claims. Since those perfectly ordinary claims are clearly true, it must be that our world is not a block universe. There are lots of arguments we can mount to this conclusion, all of which have a common form:

---

(1) Our world contains_____.
(2) If our world is a block universe, our world does not contain_____.
(3) Therefore, our world is not a block universe.

We can then insert various different things into the missing slot, including *change, robust temporal passage,* and *an unsettled future*. I will consider each of these in turn throughout the next three sections, beginning with change.

> To sum up: our best theory is one on which simultaneity is not absolute. Since dynamical theories posit the existence of a privileged present moment, they posit the existence of a set of events that are absolutely simultaneous. Hence, dynamical theories posit something that is inconsistent with our best science, and this gives us good reason to reject those theories. The block view, by contrast, is compatible with there being no absolute simultaneity. Hence, we should prefer the block view to any of its dynamical cousins, presentism being one.

4. Arguments Against the Block: Change

Here is a datum we should take seriously: things change. But according to the block universe view, the universe as a whole does not change. For recall that the block universe view endorses permanentism, the thesis that nothing comes into, or passes from, existence. If permanentism is true then our world, considered as a whole, does not change. We can then offer the following argument:

---

(1) Our world contains change.
(2) If our world is a block universe, it does not contain change.
(3) Therefore, our world is not a block universe.

I will assume (1) is true. So, if (2) is true, the block universe view is in trouble. Is (2) true? It is easy to see why we might think (2) is true. We could argue as follows. If our world is a block universe, then the universe *as a whole* does not change. If the universe as a whole does not change, then there is no change in the universe and so our universe does not contain change. Therefore, if our world is a block universe, it does not contain change.

The question is whether, if our universe as a *whole* does not change, this means that our universe does not *contain* change. In what follows I will argue that this is false.

Let's take a step back and think about what change *is*. Every morning, my oats change from being raw oats to being porridge. What does this change consist in? Well, it consists in there existing raw oats at one time and cooked oats at another, with a sequence of times in between in which there exist oats of varying degrees of cookedness and rawness. Quite generally, if we were going to give an account of what it is for something to change, we would say that the thing must exist at multiple times (as the oats do) and that the thing must be different at some of those times. So, X changes just in case there are at least two times, t and t^* at which X exists, and X at t is different from X at t^*. That is, X's properties at t are different from X's properties at t^*. Since my oats exist at both t and t^* and have the property of being raw at one time and cooked at another, my oats change.

> **Change:** X changes iff X exists at (at least) two times, t and t^*, and X at t has different properties than X at t^*.

Can the block universe view accommodate there being change in this sense? Suppose we replace 'X' with 'the block'. Then it will certainly not be true that the block *itself* changes. After all, the block, *as a whole*, is the same regardless of what time it is. For nothing comes into or out of existence. Clearly, though, what is happening at one time in the block is often quite different from what is happening at some other time in the block. Consider Jemima. At one time in the block, Jemima is 10 years old and eating ice cream. At another time in the block, Jemima is 15 years old and knitting a pullover. At another time in the block, Jemima is 80 years old and stealing a car. So, if we replace 'X' with 'Jemima' we can certainly say that Jemima changes. In fact, for almost all the things we are familiar with, those things change. But surely the block contains change just in case it contains things that change. And, in that case, the block contains change. So, it does not follow from the fact that the block *itself* does not change that the block does not *contain* change. (2) is false; and we have no reason to reject the block universe view.

5. Arguments Against the Block: Temporal Phenomenology

Some philosophers have thought that it *seems* to us, or *feels* to us, as though time robustly passes. The idea is that it seems, or feels, to us as though there is a *whoosh* and *whizz* of time passing. It seems, or feels, as though the future is moving towards us, or we are moving towards it, and it seems, or feels, as though the past is moving away from us or we are moving away from it. We can very broadly call the way things seem, or feel, to us in this regard *our temporal phenomenology*.

There are two things we might be trying to get at when we say that our temporal phenomenology is this way. We might mean that our experiences have a certain *character*. The character of an experience is the way that experience feels to us. (Sometimes people use the term 'qualia' to mean something much like this.)

> **Character:** The felt quality of an experience.

So it might be that our experiences themselves have a sort of whooshy or whizzy feel. In that case, we could say that the character of our experiences is whooshy or whizzy.

Another possibility is that we might have perceptual experiences which represent that the world is some particular way: that it whooshes and whizzes. *Perceptual experiences* are the experiences we have via perception (or the experiences that are like these experiences). In having perceptual experiences, the world seems to us to be a certain way. When we have a perceptual experience of an elephant, by, say, seeing the elephant (or smelling it or feeling it), it seems to us as though there is an elephant. This is known as the *content* of the experience. One way to think about the contents of perceptual experiences is that they are the way things seem to us to be, on the basis of that experience.

> **Perceptual Content:** The contents of a perceptual experience; what that experience tells us the world is like.

So, it could be that some of our perceptual experiences are ones whose *content* is a sort of whoosh and whizz.

Importantly, experiences can have a certain content—they can say that the world is a certain way—even if the world is not that way. Suppose you are not in a zoo; you are sitting at home. You have the flu. You hallucinate an elephant standing in the corner of your dining room. You have a perceptual experience *as of* seeing an elephant. It perceptually seems to you as though there is an elephant. Indeed, things seem the same to you as they would if there really were an elephant present in your dining room. But there is no such elephant. To make this clear, we say that you have an experience *as of* there being an elephant. Your experience has a certain content: a content according to which there's an elephant. If there really is an elephant, then that experience is *veridical*. If there is no elephant (as in fact there is not) then your experience is either an *hallucination* or perhaps an *illusion*.

> **Veridical Experience:** A perceptual experience which says that the world is thus and so, and the world is thus and so.
>
> **Illusory Experience:** A perceptual experience which says that the world is thus and so, and the world is not thus and so.

The block universe theory faces what is known as the objection from temporal phenomenology. This objection is usually taken to centre around the idea that we have perceptual experiences whose content is this whoosh and whizz. That is, according to this objection, it seems to us, in perceptual experience, *as if* time robustly passes. Let's call this *our experience as of robust temporal passage*. When we talk about this experience, we are talking about having an experience in which it seems as though time robustly passes. If time does robustly pass, then the experience is *veridical*. If time does not pass, then the experience is *non-veridical*, or *illusory*.

What is often thought to be notable about our experience as of robust temporal passage is that it is pervasive. When I am in a forest, I have experiences of trees. When I am inside, I do not. When I am on the highway, I have experiences of cars. When I am inside, I do not. But our experiences as of robust temporal passage are not like this. Whether I am in the forest or on the highway or inside my living room or about to fall asleep, it seems to me as though time passes (or so the thought goes). This is what is meant by the claim that this experience is pervasive.

Given this, we can develop another argument against the block universe view.

> (1) Our world contains pervasive experiences as of robust temporal passage.
> (2) If our world is a block universe, then any experience as of robust temporal passage is illusory.
> (3) Therefore, if our world is a block universe, our world contains pervasive illusory experiences.
> (4) Our world does not contain pervasive illusory experiences.
> (5) Therefore, our world is not a block universe.

In Defence of the Block Universe View 29

The reason to accept (2) is that, if we have experiences as of robust temporal passage, then those experiences must be illusory if our world is a block universe. That is because there is no robust temporal passage in a block universe. So, if the block universe theorist wants to deny (5), she must either reject (1) or (4), given that she takes (2) to be true and (3) follows from (1) and (2).

A natural response to this argument might seem to be to deny (4). After all, why think we are not subject to a pervasive illusion? Well, consider the sorts of illusions we are familiar with from psychology, such as the Muller-Lyre illusion. In that illusion, it seems to us as though one line is longer than the other, even though they are the same length (see Figure 1.2).

The reason the two lines seem to be different lengths is that the angles act as depth cues that we associate with three-dimensional scenes. We incorrectly view the image as a three-dimensional drawing, and a size constancy mechanism—a mechanism that allows us to see some objects as being further away, rather than smaller—makes us think that one of the lines is longer. That is because, were the drawings three-dimensional, then that line would be further away and hence would, in fact, be longer than the other line. Although our perceptual system gets it wrong on this particular occasion, the error is the result of us having a perceptual system with certain features that, *in general*, allow it to correctly perceive depth and distance.

So, this illusion is the product of a mechanism that typically generates veridical experiences. We are not subject to a pervasive illusion in which we misjudge the length of *all* lines in *all* circumstances.

This is not just a feature of this illusion; in general, illusions tend to be like this. That can hardly be surprising. We evolved to be relatively skilful at perceiving our environment. If our ancestors were subject to pervasive illusions, then they would often have misjudged their environment. It is unlikely that those ancestors would have survived to reproduce. Being subject to pervasive illusions is not a great survival strategy.

What is more, it is not at all clear how anyone could come to have an experience of something that is *always* illusory. After all, think about the illusory experience of an elephant in your dining room, brought on by flu. Why is this

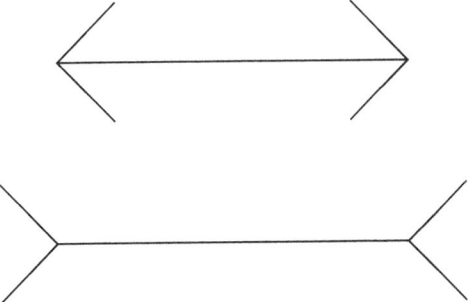

Figure 1.2 The Muller-Lyre Illusion

an experience as of an elephant rather than as of something else entirely? The obvious answer seems to be that this experience is just like the experience we have when we *in fact* see an elephant. So, we might say that what makes an experience an experience as of an elephant (rather than something else) is that it's the kind of experience that, usually, we have when we see elephants: they are experiences that, usually, are *caused* by there being elephants present. It is just that, on this occasion, it is *not* caused by there being an elephant present. But, if our world is a block universe, then there is no robust temporal passage anywhere in our world. So, none of our experiences are caused by robust temporal passage. In turn, it's not at all clear how we could come to have experiences as of time robustly passing, if all such experiences are illusory.[4]

Hence, we have two reasons to think that we are not subject to a pervasive illusion.

The block universe theorist could still try to show that we are subject to such an illusion. She might argue that this illusion is the product of the functioning of certain of our cognitive mechanisms and that, since the illusion is harmless, it has not been subject to elimination. Some block universe theorists who think that we have perceptual experiences as of time robustly passing argue that this illusory experience is in some way the result of our experiences of motion and change. There are other options. The general point is just that such views appeal to some feature of our cognitive architecture that evolved to represent features of our environment that do exist, such as change and motion, and argue that the functioning of these mechanisms somehow generates a pervasive experience as of time robustly passing.[5]

I don't rule out that a persuasive account of how it is that we are subject to such a pervasive illusion is possible. But I am not overly optimistic. Still, that doesn't mean that I think the argument from temporal phenomenology is a good one. That is because I do not think that we should accept (1): the claim that we have a pervasive experience as of time robustly passing.

This is not as odd as it might first seem. For (1) is not simply the innocuous claim that all our experiences are pervaded by some kind of 'timey' phenomenology that is *like this* (at this point I invite you to introspect how things seem to you right now). To say that (1) is true is to say that our experiences are ones in which it seems to us *as though* a dynamical or tensed theory of time is true, as opposed to seeming to us *as though* a block universe theory is true. If they do seem as though a dynamical theory of time is true, then they seem some way that is incompatible with them seeming as though the block universe view is true. But is the way things seem really incompatible with the block universe view? I don't think it is.[6]

---

4. Something like this argument is offered by Hoerl (2014).
5. Paul (2010) and Le Poidevin (2007) take this approach.
6. Deng (2013) makes this point.

Ask yourself: how would things seem if we lived in a block universe? In a block universe, each of us exists at multiple times. You are located in a piece of spacetime eating breakfast; you are located, now, reading this; and you are located at some other piece of spacetime eating lunch. At some of those locations, you remember how things were at other locations: you now remember having breakfast, but not lunch. You are now perceiving different things to the things you perceive when you are eating breakfast and to the things you perceive when you eat lunch. That's because you are in causal contact with oats when you are having breakfast and toast when you are having lunch. That's why you perceive oats at breakfast and toast at lunch: for pretty much the same reason I perceive Sydney and you perceive Birmingham.

Think of the 'you' that existed just after breakfast. That self—that *part* of you, as we might call it—is located nearer to lunch than the part of you eating breakfast. Similarly, the self that exists now is located closer to lunch than either of those two past selves. As each self accumulates new memories, that self is correspondingly closer to lunch.

If our world is a block universe world, then it is certainly one that contains temporally asymmetric processes. I'll have much more to say about this in section 7. For now, we can just note that each of us remembers the past, but not the future. We age towards the future and away from the past. We deliberate about the future and not the past, no doubt in part because causes tend to be earlier than their effects, and so what we do at one time tends to have causal consequences at later times, but not earlier ones. So, we can causally intervene in the world at future, but not past, times. Our later selves are closer to future events than are our earlier selves. And so on. So, we would expect that, if ours is a block universe world, it would seem to us as though time has a direction: that it 'points' from the past, towards the future. We would expect it to seem as though our later selves are closer to what are, now, future events than are our current selves. We'd expect it to seem as though the future is open to us in a way that the past is not.

That, I submit, is exactly how things do seem to us. But things seeming that way is not the same as them seeming as though time robustly passes. For, in order to seem that way, it would need to seem to us as though the things that exist at this very moment are not only present to us now, but, in addition, they are metaphysically special by being present in some absolute metaphysical sense. They are special in a way that other events in spacetime are not. Moreover, it would need to seem as though there is some change in which events are special like this. I see no reason to suppose that this is how things seem to us. To be sure, I experience the things that exist at this time in a way that I do not experience the dinosaurs, which exist at a different time. But that's really not very different from the way in which I experience the things in Sydney in a way that I do not experience the things in Birmingham. It doesn't follow from that, that I experience the world as containing a metaphysically special 'here', which moves with me as I travel the world! I see little reason to think that things seem to us as though there is a metaphysically special 'now', which travels with us. Rather, we should think that things seem exactly as we would expect if the block universe view were true. In fact, we have veridical temporal phenomenology: it seems to each of us as though we are in a block universe.

Of course, we don't always describe the ways things seem using language that conjures up the image of a block universe. We sometimes describe the ways things seem by saying that we are *moving* closer to lunch, or that lunch is *moving* closer to us. We might even sometimes say that we can *feel* time passing. That, in turn, might lead us to come to mistakenly believe that it seems to us as though time robustly passes. But it's worth noting, first, that recent empirical evidence suggests that people are less inclined to describe their temporal phenomenology using this kind of 'dynamical' language than one might have expected.[7] Moreover, insofar as we do sometimes use this kind of language, it can hardly be surprising. We have selves located at different times that bear different relations to events in spacetime. A very natural way to express how things seem to each of these selves is to use language that allows us to pick out our current self and to talk about how things were with past selves, or will be with future selves. And that very naturally will lead us to use tensed language and to use language that allows us to say how things are different with different selves located at different places.[8]

So, although we might sometimes say that we can feel time passing, this is really just an easy way of describing that it seems to each of our current selves a certain way. Namely, it seems as though they have accrued more memories than their earlier selves; that they are now located later in spacetime than our earlier selves and hence are closer to certain future events than those earlier selves; that they are causally connected to different events than our earlier selves; that they can remember events that were future relative to earlier selves and which were open to those earlier selves to deliberate about but which are, relative to a current self, past and closed to the current self, and so on.

> In sum, there is a 'timey' way that things seem to us to be, phenomenologically. Dynamists think that it seems to us as though time robustly passes. They think that the fact that we have experiences with this content is a reason for us to conclude that time does, in fact, robustly pass. Illusionists agree that it seems to us as though time robustly passes, but they think that, since time does not robustly pass, this is an illusion. Other block universe theorists hold that it does

---

7. See Latham, Norton and Miller (2020).
8. For an extended discussion of these issues, see Miller, Holcombe and Latham (2018) and Latham, Norton and Miller (2020), who argue that it does not seem to us as though time robustly passes.

not seem to us as though time robustly passes at all. On the view I have argued for here, it seems to us as though we are living in a block universe. We have veridical phenomenology as of our world being a block world. I've argued for this view on the grounds that it is a much more attractive view than the view that we are subject to a pervasive illusion. If that view is correct, then we should reject the argument from temporal phenomenology. Since it does not seem to us as though time robustly passes, we clearly have no reason to conclude that time does, in fact, robustly pass on the basis of our having such experiences.

6. Arguments Against the Block: Free Will

Here is another argument against the block universe view.

> (1) Our world contains free action.
> (2) If our world is a block universe, it does not contain free action.
> (3) Therefore, our world is not a block universe.

It seems to be the case that sometimes we act freely. I do not take myself to be free to jump 100 feet into the air or to increase my IQ by 100 or to turn my neighbour into a large boil. But I take myself to be free to choose to have toast rather than porridge for breakfast; to give a student a credit rather than a distinction; to buy a new television rather than give money to charity; and so on. Arguably, most of the banal decisions we make, and the actions we take on the basis of those decisions, are free actions. So let us grant (1). (Of course, one could deny (1): there are free will sceptics who think we lack free will. But for present purposes, I am inclined to accept (1).)

Why think (2) is true? Well, consider your future lunch. You haven't decided what you want for lunch. Perhaps you would like a sandwich, or perhaps soup. But according to the block universe view, the event of you eating lunch exists out there in spacetime, in the same way that your breakfast does (albeit in two different temporal directions from your current location). There you are, out there, eating, say, soup. But if it is already the case that you are eating soup out there in the future, then you are not in a position to, instead, eat sandwiches for lunch. Your lunch is already dictated for you: you will eat soup. If this reasoning is correct, then the block universe view is incompatible with there being free action, because it is simply not possible for you to succeed in eating anything other than soup for lunch.

Let's suppose for a moment that this reasoning is correct. If it is, then the block universe theory is incompatible with there being free choice or free action. For either you will choose to have something other than soup for lunch, but you will find yourself unable to enact that choice, or there is only really one choice you can make: to eat soup. In either case your action is not free.

The reasoning here might look powerful, but, in fact, it's not. At first blush, the argument looks something like an argument offered by incompatibilists about free will. Incompatibilism is the view that determinism is incompatible with free will.

> **Incompatibilism:** Determinism is incompatible with free will.

Determinism is the thesis that the complete way things are, at some time, in conjunction with the laws of nature, logically entails the way things are at every other time. So, for instance, if determinism is true, and if you know all of the facts about the universe at, say, t_5, and if you know the laws of nature, then in principle you can know everything about how things are at every other time.

> **Determinism:** A world w is deterministic iff the complete state of the world at one time, in conjunction with the laws of nature, logically entails the complete state of the world at every other time.

Here is one argument for incompatibilism. Suppose determinism is true of our world. Then what you ate for breakfast this morning was logically entailed by the combination of the laws of nature and the initial conditions of the universe. You, however, had no say in what the laws of nature were going to be, nor in what the initial conditions of the universe would be like. So, things over which you had no control determined what you ate for breakfast. Hence you were not free with respect to your breakfast choices.

It might seem very natural to think that determinism and the block universe theory go hand in hand. If that is right, and if determinism is incompatible with free will, then so, too, is the block universe theory incompatible with free will. We can put the argument as follows:

> (1) The block universe theory entails determinism.
> (2) Determinism is incompatible with free will.
> (3) Therefore, the block universe theory is incompatible with free will.

I am inclined to reject both (1) and (2) of this argument. For now, though, let's just focus on (1).

Consider on some arbitrary time within a block and call it t_7. Does the fact that t_7 is a time within the block entail that the way things are at t_7, in conjunction with the laws of nature, determines the ways things are at every other time in the block? No. Suppose that quantum mechanics is best interpreted as an indeterministic theory. Then, according to that theory, there are genuinely chancy events. This means that the way things are at some time, in conjunction with the laws of nature, *does not* logically entail the way things are at every other time. Is the theory of quantum mechanics incompatible with the block universe theory? If (1) is true, then it must be; for quantum mechanics is an indeterministic theory, and so it cannot be true in a block universe world if the block universe theory entails determinism. But the block universe theory is compatible with quantum mechanics and indeed any other indeterministic theory.

To see this, we should notice that, in the block universe world in question, the ways things are at t_7 do not determine the ways they are at, say, t_9. Chance plays some role in how things turn out to be at t_9. That can be so even though the whole block exists, and hence so does t_9. The *existence* of t_9 is compatible with its being true that the ways things are at t_7 do not *determine* that t_9 is the way it is. This will be true if, for instance, God can look at t_7 and the laws of nature and not be able to predict just on that basis exactly how things are at t_9. What is important is that two times can exist, and yet neither time determines what occurs at the other. This will be true in any block universe that is not deterministic.

In fact, we can perhaps make even clearer the connection between determinism and the block universe theory by noting that it is not simply that the block universe theory is compatible with indeterminism, but also that determinism is compatible with non-block views of time. Once we see this, we see that the issue of whether a world is deterministic or not is completely orthogonal to whether it is dynamic or static.

Let's take presentism as an example. You might initially think that presentism is incompatible with determinism. After all, presentism is the view that past and future things do not exist. Remember, though, that determinism is not a thesis about what exists. It's a thesis about whether what exists at one time, plus the laws of nature, *determines* what exists at other times. Presentism can be true, and yet our world be deterministic. That will be the case if the way things are, in the present, plus the laws, determines the way things *were* in the past and the way things *will be* in the future. That can be the case even if those ways no longer exist or do not yet exist. The fact that past and future events don't exist doesn't mean that they were not or will not be determined by the present moment. Presentism is compatible with determinism.

What this tells us is that, if there is some special problem for free action presented by the block universe view, that problem is not that the block universe view is deterministic. For some block universes are indeterministic and some, deterministic, and equally, some dynamical universes are deterministic and some, indeterministic. So, if determinism is a problem for free action, it is, as it were, everyone's problem, not just a problem for the block view.

Is there some other reason to think that the block universe view is incompatible with free action? Consider again your lunch. What appears to be problematic about the block universe is that it is now (prior to lunch) *already true* that you will have soup for lunch. But if it's already true that you will have soup for lunch, then how can you be free with respect to choosing something other than soup? We can put the argument as follows:

(1) If, at time t, every claim about what happens at some time t^* is eternately true or is determinately false, then there are no free actions at t^*.
(2) According to the block universe view, for any time t, every claim about what happens at some time t^* is determinately true or is determinately false for every t^*.
(3) Therefore, according to the block universe view, for any time t^*, there are no free actions at t^*.

This argument looks quite compelling. When we think about past times, it seems to get things right. All claims about any past time are, now, determinately true or determinately false.[9] Either Penny the dinosaur weighed exactly 700kgs, or she did not, even if we don't know which. Moreover, it seems clear that there's nothing we can do to change how much Penny weighed. So, the inference from its now being true that she weighed 700kgs to its now being the case that she (and everyone else) lacks any capacity for free action with regard to her weight seems to be a good one. By analogy, we might think that the same is true for your eating soup for lunch. But should we draw this conclusion? Is (1) true? I see no reason to think so.

Suppose we ask ourselves the question: why is it that at that piece of future spacetime you are drinking soup and not eating sandwiches? There are two

---

9. Setting aside semantic indeterminacies. For instance, perhaps it's not determinately true whether Bruce, at some past time, is bald. That's not because it's not determinate how any hairs are on his head, but because it's indeterminate how many hairs he needs to have in order to count as being bald. I set aside all these kinds of indeterminacies for present purposes, since they are irrelevant to the issue at hand.

possible sorts of answers. We might answer that you are drinking soup because you really felt like soup for lunch, you had soup handy, you decided to make soup, and then you successfully did so. Or we might answer that, despite your having decided to eat sandwiches, someone broke into your house and, at gunpoint, forced you to drink soup. The former captures the sorts of conditions under which we normally suppose someone to be free with regard to their actions; namely, we typically judge someone to have acted freely when they deliberate about what to do and when they decide what to do on the basis of their own reasons and desires and beliefs and then succeed in doing the thing they decided to do. The latter captures the sorts of conditions under which we typically judge someone to be unfree. These are conditions under which someone does not act on their own reasons, beliefs, and desires.

Let us suppose that you, in fact, felt like soup, and on the basis of your desires and reasons, you chose to have soup for lunch. Normally, we would conclude that you acted freely with respect to lunch. Should we conclude otherwise, simply because the event of your drinking that soup exists somewhere in spacetime? To answer this question, consider what would have happened if, after reflecting on your lunch preferences, you had instead decided that you really felt like sandwiches. There are two possibilities: first, it could be that, if you had felt like sandwiches and had reason to prefer sandwiches (for instance, you are not on a soup-only diet), then you would have made and eaten sandwiches for lunch; second, perhaps, regardless of what you felt like eating and regardless of your reasons, you would have ended up eating soup.

If the second of these possibilities is true, then it seems fitting to say that you lacked free choice with regard to your lunch. *Regardless* of what you decided to eat and how you felt about these things, you were going to drink the soup no matter what, even if, all the while as you were drinking it, you were wishing that you were eating sandwiches. Indeed, if being free is about acting on your own reasons, then we should conclude that you are not free if, despite wanting to have sandwiches for lunch, you would nevertheless have ended up having soup.

Which of these possibilities describes the ways things are in a block universe world? The first. To be sure, the event of your eating soup is out there in spacetime. That does not mean that *that* event would have been out there in spacetime regardless of what you felt like for lunch and regardless of your reasons to have soup or sandwiches for lunch. If, instead, you had felt like sandwiches and had decided to have sandwiches, then you would have chosen to make sandwiches and the event of your eating sandwiches would, instead, be out there in spacetime.

That is because future events are the causal product of earlier events. Suppose it is now true that, in 20 years, the koala will be extinct. Why is that? It's because we will eliminate much of its habitat and introduce new predators. There are no koalas out there in future spacetime in 20 years because of what we do over the next 20 years. If we did different things, then there would be koalas out there. So, according to the block universe view, the future is out there, but what the future is *like* is the direct result of what we are doing here and now.

So (1) is false. The mere fact that every claim about t^* is, now, determinately true or determinately false does not mean that there are no free actions at t^*. For what makes actions at t^* free is that they are appropriately connected to the reasons, desires, beliefs, and so on, of the people whose actions they are. If the reason t^* is as it is, is because of the reasons, desires, and beliefs of the chooser, then we should say that those actions are free. For then, had the chooser had different reasons, desires, and beliefs, they would have made different choices, and the future would have been different.

So far, in the last three sections, I have considered three sorts of arguments against the block universe view and tried to show that none of them is compelling. In the next section, I turn to offer another positive argument in favour of the view. I will argue that, despite appearances to the contrary, the view is actually better able to explain certain phenomena that we want to explain than are dynamical views of time such as presentism. I call this the argument from explanation.

> I have argued that there is no problem of free action arising from the block universe view. First, I argued that, even if determinism is incompatible with free will, it does not follow from the fact that our world is a block universe world that it is a deterministic world. Second, I've argued that compatibilism about free will is true. What matters for free will is that we act in accordance with our reasons and desires. But the fact that our future actions exist is no reason to suspect that those actions are not the product of our reasons and desires. The future is 'out there', but the way the future is, is the product of what we do in the here and now.

7. The Argument From Explanation for the Block

The last three arguments we encountered against the block universe view all try to show that there is some way the world is that cannot be accounted for if our world is a block universe. In this section, I want to turn the tables on the dynamist and argue that there are ways the world is which cannot be explained by dynamical theories of time.

One notable way things seem, in our world, is that time has a direction. Given where you are located, it seems as though breakfast is past and lunch is future and that time's "arrow" points from one to the other. In what sense does time's arrow point in a particular direction? Well, all around us, we see a lot of processes that seem to have a direction. We *remember* the past, but not the future. Indeed, we know about the past by noticing *traces*, or *records*, of the past. But we do not know about the future by looking for traces of the future, since there are no such traces. We *deliberate* about the future, but not the past. We *age* towards the future, not the past. *Causes* seem to have their effects later (i.e., in the future), which means that we can causally influence the future, but not the past.

Let's focus on two of these asymmetries: the *epistemic asymmetry* and the *asymmetry of influence*. The epistemic asymmetry is the asymmetry in our knowledge of the past and future. Or, perhaps better, it's the asymmetry in the way in which we come to know about the past and future. In particular, it's a reflection of the asymmetry in traces that we find at any moment; namely, we find traces of the past, but not the future.

> **Epistemic Asymmetry:** An asymmetry in how we come to know about the past as compared to the future as a result of the fact that, at any time, there are traces of the past but not of the future.

We witness the asymmetry of traces all around us. Our shelves are full of books that are records of the past, but not the future. Our computers, diaries, and heads all contain records of the past, but not the future. Light travels from a source and can be seen at times later than when it was emitted, but not at times earlier than when it was emitted. So, it is possible to see the past (as we do when we see stars that are many light years away) but not to see the future. Likewise, it is possible to hear the past, but not the future, and to smell the past, but not the future. The past leaves traces of itself in the present, but the future does not.

The asymmetry of influence is that we can causally influence the future, but not the past. Causes typically precede their effects rather than the other way around, which means that, by intervening on the world at one time, one can intervene on the world at a later, but not an earlier, time.

> **Asymmetry of Influence:** An asymmetry in how we can causally influence the world; namely, that we can causally influence the future, but not the past.

We see this asymmetry all around us. Each of can causally influence what we have for breakfast tomorrow morning. We can wake up and make toast (if we have bread and a toaster) and thereby causally intervene on bread to make it toasted. We can causally intervene on raw oats to make them porridge. We can, tomorrow, shampoo our hair (or not) and trim our nails (or not). We cannot, it would seem, causally intervene on yesterday in any of these (or any other) respects. None of us can make yesterday's oats cooked (or not) or its bread cooked (or not). We cannot cause our nails, yesterday, to be trimmed or our hair, yesterday, to be shampooed.

It seems plausible that these two asymmetries explain the *deliberative asymmetry*: the fact that we deliberate about the future and not the past. After all, first, there seems little reason to deliberate about things you already know to be the case, whether they are past or future. If I know that I will, in fact, thump the table, then there is no point my deliberating about whether or not to thump the table. Since we often have records of what happened in the past but do not have such records about the future, it makes sense that, in general, we would deliberate about the future; for those are events about which we are less likely to have information about what we will do. Second, it only makes sense to deliberate about things that are within our control. There's little point deliberating about whether to move the sun from its current orbit, since that's not a thing that you or I can do. Since we cannot causally affect the past but we can causally affect the future, it makes sense that we would deliberate about the future and not the past.

Given this, in what follows, I set the deliberative asymmetry aside, since plausibly it can be explained by the two asymmetries just mentioned.

Then here is the argument I will offer in favour of the block universe view.

Temporal Asymmetries Argument

(1) We have reason to adopt that theory of time which best explains the epistemic asymmetry and the asymmetry of influence.
(2) Dynamical theories of time cannot explain the epistemic asymmetry or the asymmetry of influence.
(3) The block universe view can explain the epistemic asymmetry and the asymmetry of influence.
(4) Therefore, we have reason to adopt the block universe view of time.

The remainder of this chapter will be spent arguing for (2) and (3) of the temporal asymmetries argument. Let's begin with (2).

7.1 Dynamical Theories Cannot Explain the Asymmetries

On the face of it, you might think that dynamical theories of time have a ready-made explanation for the two temporal asymmetries. That is because these are all theories on which time has a direction. On any dynamical theory, the direction of time is given by the direction in which time passes. On the growing bock theory, for instance, the entire universe grows as time passes. More things come into being at one end of the block. So, the growing block universe theory has a very clear answer to the question of which end of the block is the first moment and which is the last and, hence, a very clear answer to the question of which direction along the block is towards the past and which is towards the future. The future is that direction towards which the block is growing and the past is that direction away from which it is growing.

Matters are a bit less obvious when it comes to presentist worlds when it comes to specifying whether non-existent states of affairs are ones that did obtain, but no longer do, as opposed to being ones that will obtain, but do not yet. What are non-existent states of affairs? Well, the presentist thinks that I went swimming yesterday. My going swimming is *a state of affairs*. It's a complex thing made up of objects, properties, and relations. So, there's a state of affairs of Annie sitting on the couch and of you receiving a Christmas gift, and so on. Presentists think that some states of affairs did exist (or obtain) but don't anymore (such as the state of affairs of the dinosaurs going extinct) and she thinks there are states of affairs that will exist, but don't now (such as the state of affairs of our all being made into slaves by the robot overlords). We can think of these as *non-existent states of affairs*. The presentist thinks there are lots of non-existent states of affairs. The question is, which of them have *already been* present, and which of them are *yet to be* present?

We can get a sense of how presentists might think about this by imagining a presentist world from a God's eye perspective outside of ordinary time and space. Imagine God is looking down on a presentist world. She sees a single moment of time changing. Let's suppose the world changes from being red to being green to being purple. God watches the changes. It seems that the change itself gives time a direction: the time at which the world is red is earlier than the time at which it is green, which is earlier than the time at which it is purple. Time is directed from the red moment to the purple moment. Or so the presentist will say.

So, dynamical theories are ones on which time has a direction, where that direction is a function of the direction in which time passes. Given this, one might assume that dynamical theories have good resources to explain temporal asymmetries, resources to which the block universe theorist cannot appeal. If so, this would be reason to reject both (2) and (3) of the temporal asymmetries argument. According to the sort of reasoning the dynamists try to offer, what explains the epistemic asymmetry is the fact that time robustly passes and that it passes *from* past *to* future. Unsurprisingly, we have special access to the past, by way of traces of the past on the present, but no such traces of the future. The robust passing of time also explains the asymmetry of influence. Unsurprisingly, past events cause future ones and not the other way around because the direction of causation is inextricably linked with the direction of time's passing. It is practically written into the growing block universe theory that causation proceeds from past to future, since it is the process of new being coming into existence—a causal process, surely—which constitutes the passage of time. Similarly, the presentist holds that the passage of time consists in the changing of the present moment. It seems plausible that the changing of the present moment just is causation in action. If that is so, then causes must precede their effects.

But is this really an explanation? Let's consider the epistemic asymmetry first.

Imagine a presentist world. When we imagine that world, it's natural to imagine a world much like our own, in which the changing present moment is a bit like a snowball. As a snowball rolls, it picks up bits and pieces of its environment. So, the snowball contains within it a record (albeit incomplete) of where it rolled. When we imagine a presentist world, we naturally imagine one in which, as the present changes, it is like a snowball: the present bears traces of the past—records of how things were.

But imagine a presentist world that is like a reverse snowball. To get a feel for what this would be like, imagine watching a snowball move backwards in time. You would see the snowball get smaller and lose traces of where it had been. When we translate this idea into the presentist context, we are imagining a presentist world in which there is a single moment that changes, but, rather than gaining new traces, instead, it loses traces. It's like watching a world like ours (assuming for a moment ours is a presentist world), *but in reverse*. So, the very first moment, in that world, contains *apparent* traces, or apparent records, of what happened in the past. Remember, it's like watching the snowball in reverse. But in fact, *there is no past, since that is the very first moment*. Indeed, the very first moment contains apparent records of events that will happen in the future. In this world, what appear to be past records are really what we might think of as future records. Earlier moments of time contain 'traces', or 'records', of what will happen at later times. Importantly, then, in the world we are imagining, time robustly passes, but each person's apparent memories are not memories of the past; instead, they are 'memories' or 'precognitions' of the future.

In the presentist world just described, there is an epistemic asymmetry, but it points from future to past, not from past to future. In that world, the present moment bears lots of traces of how things *will be*, but no real traces of how things *were*.

While, in our world, the direction of the epistemic asymmetry seems to align with the direction in which time passes (assuming for a moment that time does pass), in the presentist world we are considering, the direction in which time robustly passes is the *reverse* of the direction of the epistemic asymmetry. This suggests that the mere passing of time does not explain the epistemic asymmetry. The fact that time passes from past to future does not, in itself, ensure that the present moment bears traces of the past but not the future.

What of the asymmetry of influence? Even if we maintain that causes precede their effects in our weird reversed-presentist world, it will still be the case that, in that world, it seems as though events precede their causes. After all, in that world, the present moment is one that bears traces, or at least apparent traces, of future, but not past, events. That world is orderly: if the present moment bears apparent traces of some future event being thus and so, then at some future time, that event will be thus and so. Given that, in this world, we have access to future traces but not past ones, it will be natural to suppose that causation itself is reversed. Why is the present the way it is? Not because of some way the past was; some way that has left no trace at all upon that moment. Instead, clearly, the present is the way it is because of the way some future moment will be! The way that future moment *will be* explains why the present moment is this way; that is why the present moment bears traces of that future moment. Moreover, actions that one undertakes in the present will seem to have no effects on the future: what we do in the present will leave traces on the *past*. If I eat a whole cake now, it will be the case that earlier, I was very sick. It will not be the case that later, I am very sick.

The point is this. Even if, in fact, in this presentist world, causes always precede effects (and one could deny this), it will surely *appear* as though causation is asymmetric and that, in fact, *effects precede causes*. Thus, the appearance of the asymmetry of influence cannot be explained by the robust passage of time; for things could appear the same even if the events in question occurred in the reverse order relative to the passage of time.

The problem the dynamist faces is that there are two separate phenomena. On the one hand, we have the *contents* of time; that is, the stuff in time, such as the distribution of traces (including memories) and the distribution of cooked and raw eggs, babies and elderly folk, causes and effects, and so on. This stuff is, in our world, distributed in time in a particular way: raw eggs come before cooked ones, moments bear traces of past times but not future ones, and so on. On the other hand, we have *time itself* and, in particular, the direction of time. For the dynamist, that direction is generated by the changing of the present moment.[10]

The epistemic asymmetries and, arguably, the asymmetries of influence are products of the contents of time. The contents of time seem to have a direction: they seem to point from past to future. The problem for the dynamist is that the direction that is given by the *contents* of time can come apart from the direction that is given by the *passage* of time. This was illustrated by thinking about a presentist world that is like our world, except in reverse. In that world, the asymmetries point in the opposite direction to the direction in which time, in fact, passes.

At this point, you might reasonably complain that none of this shows that, if our world is a presentist world, then its being so (its containing robust passage) does not explain the temporal asymmetries in our world. At best, it shows that, in some *very weird* worlds, the presence of temporal passage does not explain the temporal asymmetries in those worlds.

---

10. Price (1996) makes this point.

But what if it turned out that the laws of nature of our world are ones that permit our world itself to be pretty weird? The laws of nature are, roughly, the physical laws that govern our world. They are the sorts of laws that are discovered by science. What if the laws of nature in our world permit that, at some locations in our world, *events occur in reverse order?* That is, what if some bits of our world are or could be *just like the weird presentist world?* If our world is or could be like this, then we should conclude that, even if our world contains temporal passage, it cannot be what is explaining the temporal asymmetries in our world, any more than it was explaining them in the weird presentist world. In the next section, I argue that the laws of nature do, in fact, permit our world to be weird in just this way.

7.2 Our World Is Pretty Weird

It is generally thought that science has discovered the laws of nature to be *time reversal invariant*. That means that the laws are not sensitive to the direction of time. What that really amounts to is that there is nothing in the laws themselves which requires processes to go in one temporal direction rather than another. So, for instance, there is nothing in the laws which prohibits eggs going from being cooked to being raw, rather than from being raw to being cooked. The process of eggs going from cooked to raw is *nomically possible*. To say that something is nomically possible is just to say that it is consistent with the laws of nature. For instance, it is nomically possible that I run 10km per hour. It is not nomically possible that I run at close to the speed of light.

> **Nomic Possibility**: X is nomically possible just in case X is consistent with the laws of nature.

If the laws are time-reversal invariant, then, for any process, if that process is nomically possible, then the reverse process is also nomically possible.

This seems very puzzling. If these kinds of reversed processes are nomically possible, why don't we see eggs going from being cooked to being raw? Why don't times contain traces of the future, as well as traces of the past?

Below is a rough diagram of how that might look. On the far left we have a singularity: the Big Bang. As we move away from the singularity, the universe gets bigger across the three spatial dimensions. This is the expansion of the universe. At the other end of the universe, there is another singularity: the Big Crunch. The Big Crunch looks just the Big Bang, but in reverse. The universe shrinks in its spatial extent until it reaches the Big Crunch at the opposite end of the universe. So far, we don't know anything about the content of this

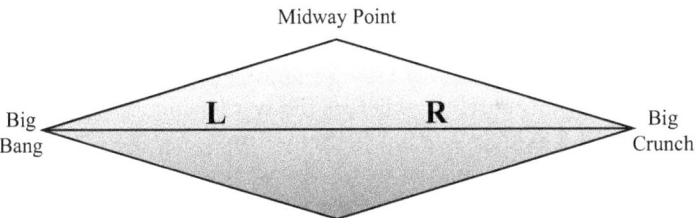

Figure 1.3 The Mirror World

universe. But, in the abstract, it looks symmetrical. The Big Crunch looks like the Big Bang and, in the middle, there is what I have called the midway point. I'll call this the mirror world (Figure 1.3) because the two halves are sort of like mirror images of one another.

Let's call the entire universe from the Big Bang up to the midway point 'L' (for left-hand side) and the entire universe from the midway point to the Big Crunch 'R' (for right-hand side).

Now, let's think about the contents of this universe. Let's suppose, for now, that the Big Bang is the first moment of time. Then, at any time in L, an event is earlier relative to a time t if it lies in the Big Bang direction relative to t, and is later than t if it lies in the Big Crunch direction relative to t. Let's also suppose that the contents of L are just like the contents of our universe around here. In particular, in L, eggs go from being raw to being cooked; people go from young to old; and times bear traces of earlier times, but not later ones. In L, people can influence the future, but not the past. So, in L, there is both an epistemic asymmetry and an asymmetry of influence.

Why are things like this in L if the laws of nature are time-reversal invariant? If it's nomically possible for processes to be reversed, why don't we see any reversed processes in L?

While the exact details of the story vary, there is broad agreement that the answer to these questions has something to do with entropy. Technically, entropy is the measure of a system's thermal energy per unit temperature that is not available for doing work. For our purposes, though, we can think of entropy as a measure of the amount of molecular order or disorder in a system. The two are connected because work is obtained from ordered molecular motion. So, if a system has a high degree of entropy—that is, if it is highly disordered—then the measure of thermal energy per unit temperature that is unavailable for doing work will be high.

> **Entropy:** A measure of the molecular disorder of a system.

For instance, if all of the molecules of various gases are disbursed throughout a room, the entropy of that system is high. By contrast, if the molecules of those gases are clumped together in certain ways, then the entropy of the system is lower. The systems containing the molecules that make up me and you have relatively low entropy, whereas the system containing the molecules floating around my living room has higher entropy.

Roughly speaking, the explanation of why we find traces of the past but not the future is that the past is the direction towards which entropy is decreasing, and the future is the direction towards which entropy is increasing. Why is the direction towards which entropy is decreasing the direction towards which we have traces and the direction toward which entropy increases, the direction towards which we have no traces?

To go some way towards answering this question, we first need to understand why entropy is increasing in L. A natural first thought is that, obviously, entropy is increasing in L because it is a law of nature that entropy increases. That, very roughly, is the second law of thermodynamics. More carefully, the second law of thermodynamics says that entropy in an isolated system never *decreases* and will typically increase until it reaches an equilibrium state (that is, a state of maximum entropy).

The problem is that this is a bad explanation because the second law of thermodynamics is not a law at all. Without even picking up a physics textbook, we know that must be so if the laws of nature are indeed time-reversal invariant. It cannot possibly be a *law* that entropy always increases if, for any process that occurs, the time reversal of that process is nomically possible; for time reversed processes will (often) be ones in which entropy decreases.

In fact, we can explain why entropy tends to increase (that is, on average increases) in L by appealing to nothing more than statistical mechanics and facts about the Big Bang.

Imagine you are given a little beaker full of pink gas molecules (let's suppose the molecules are themselves pink, just for illustration). Each way of arranging the molecules in that beaker corresponds to one *microstate*. There are lots of ways of arranging the molecules in that beaker, so there are lots of possible microstates. Are some microstates more likely than others? No. Each microstate is just as likely as any other. But notice that this does not mean that each *macrostate* is as likely as any other. Macrostates are macro-level states. For instance, suppose we arrange the pink molecules in the beaker in a certain way, so that the beaker appears to contain a series of pink stripes. Then it will have (roughly speaking) a stripy macrostate. Lots of different ways of arranging individual molecules can achieve this same stripy state: we can place Bert the molecule in the right top, the bottom left, or the middle and still achieve that state. But, of course, many ways of arranging the molecules will not be ones in which we get a stripy macrostate.

Some macrostates are more likely than others because some macrostates are realised by more microstates than others. To see this, imagine you are blindfolded and given a bunch of darts to throw at a wall. We let you loose on your task. What do we expect to find? We'd expect to find a bunch of darts sticking out of the wall in no particularly interesting pattern. If, instead, we found that your dart-throwing had created the image of a cat, we would be pretty surprised. Why is that? It is not because that particular arrangement of darts is any more unlikely than any other. Instead, it is because there are lots of arrangements of darts in a wall that fail to make any interesting picture, and very few arrangements that make some interesting picture, and even fewer that make up an image of a cat. So, if we are betting on what will happen prior to your dart-throwing, we shouldn't predict that you will create a picture of a cat; we should predict that you will create a messy arrangement of darts in the wall.

While the idea of order and disorder that applies to microstates is rather different to the intuitive idea that we have when we think about darts sticking out of a wall, we can still learn something instructive by this example. We learn that, for any bunch of molecules in a closed system, there are more microstates in which those molecules are disordered—that is, have high entropy—than there are microstates in which those molecules are ordered—that is, have low entropy.

So, think of your darts as molecules and imagine throwing them at the wall. Then, ask yourself: will the resulting state of darts in the wall be high or low entropy? It is more likely that they will be high entropy than that they will be low entropy. For there are, in effect, more arrangements of darts in the wall that count as high entropy states than that count as low entropy states.

Now, suppose we put the darts into the wall into the shape of a cat and then blindfold you and ask you to move each dart a little, by feel alone. Now we repeat the process again and again. What do you predict about the arrangement of the darts sometime after this process has begun? I'm guessing that you will predict that the nice image of the cat will have largely disappeared, to be replaced by a messy arrangement of darts. That is because you know that there are more ways of arranging the darts that are 'messy' and fewer that are 'non-messy', and so we would expect the dart arrangement to change from being an image of a cat to being an image of nothing at all. We'd predict that the arrangement of darts will go from being more ordered (in the image of a cat) to being less ordered (in the image of nothing at all). While the analogy is imperfect, the same is true of entropy. If there is a state that is low in entropy, we should expect the state to move into a state of higher entropy, simply because there are more microstates that realise high entropy states than there are microstates that realise low entropy states.

So, if we look at the state of the universe at a time and ask ourselves whether that state is likely to move into one of higher or lower entropy, we know that the answer is that it will tend to move into a state of higher entropy, unless that state is already at maximum entropy.

You might think that we now have all we need to explain why entropy tends to increase in L. But, in fact, we don't: we have another puzzle. For let's examine that state of the universe again, but instead of asking whether the state it moves into—that is, the later state—is likely to be higher or lower entropy, let's ask whether the state it moved *out* of—that is, the earlier state—is likely to be higher or lower entropy. The answer is the same: it is likely to be higher entropy. The explanation we've offered is completely time symmetric. We should expect that, at any time, entropy will increase both into the future *and* into the past. That, of course, is not what we find: we find entropy decreasing into the past. Fortunately, in fact, we have all the ingredients we need to explain why this is so, once we notice that the Big Bang is a very low-entropy state.

We'd expect to find entropy increasing away from any low-entropy state. Since the Big Bang is relatively close to each region in L—it's the closest singularity—and since entropy has not yet reached its maximum, we'd expect entropy to increase in L, away from the low-entropy Big Bang. If entropy increases everywhere in L, away from the Big Bang, then that means that, at any time in L, the direction of the Big Crunch is the direction in which entropy is *increasing* and the direction of the Big Bang is the direction in which entropy is *decreasing*.

So, why is it that, in L, we see temporally asymmetric phenomena? Some of these phenomena are straightforwardly explained by increasing entropy. If entropy is increasing, then ice will melt, but water will not turn into ice. If entropy is increasing, then cooked eggs will not become raw again and raw broken eggs will not become whole eggs sitting neatly back in their eggshells. So, at least some of the asymmetries that are present in L are the product of increasing entropy. Or, to put it another way, while the processes of eggs un-cooking or un-breaking are nomically possible processes, they are processes that involve decreasing, not increasing, entropy. And we now have an explanation for why entropy is increasing in L, away from the low-entropy Big Bang.

So far, though, this does not explain why the records in L are of past events but not future ones or why, in L, causes precede their effects. Let's first turn this into a slightly different question. Rather than asking why there are records of *past* events but not *future* ones, let's instead ask why, at locations in which, globally, entropy is increasing, there are records of states in the global direction towards which entropy is decreasing, but not records of states in the global direction towards which entropy is increasing.

The answer to this question is controversial. But here is the idea. Records are, in some good sense, all about correlations across time. If there is a record, now, of something that happened in the past, this is because there is some way things are now which is correlated with the way they were in the past. So, for instance, my kitchen scales measure the weight of eggs that I put on them. They do this by there being some earlier state of the scales in which they were 'zeroed', and then the number the scales displays after I put the eggs on them is the weight of the eggs. In order for the number on the kitchen scales to be a record of how much the eggs weigh, it needs to be that the scales were previously set to zero. This is sometimes called being in a 'ready-to-measure' state.

In order to have records we need to have states that are ready to measure so that other states are ones in which there is a correlation between two things. In the case of the scales, there is a correlation between the number shown on the scales and the weight of the eggs, and this correlation is a record of the weight because the scales were in a ready-to-measure state. In fact, imagine my scales have a 'memory' so that they continue to show the weight of the eggs after I remove the eggs (something I have often wished scales would do). Then this would be a case in which we have a current state—the number showing on the scales—which is a record of the weight of the eggs. This is a record of what happened when the eggs were on the scales, conditional on the scales having been set to a ready-to-measure state prior to having the eggs put on them.

The rough idea is that, when we measure things now, we gain records of events that happened at times closer to the Big Bang than the current time because the Big Bang is like setting the scales to zero. While the Big Bang is the equivalent of setting the scales to zero, some intervening event, such as putting the eggs on the scales, is the event for which we now have a record when we look at the number shown on the scales. Because the entropy of the Big Bang is so low, when we infer what happened at states closer to the Big Bang than the current state, those inferences are relatively constrained in a way that inferences about events in the direction of the Big Crunch (from locations in L) are not. From locations in L, the direction towards the Big Crunch is one in which there are no future states that have set the scales to zero (as it were) and so the state of the universe at a time in L does not allow us to infer what will happen in that direction.[11]

The increase of entropy in L is also thought by some to explain the asymmetry of influence in L. Consider, it is at least in part the case that what it is for one event to cause another is for the presence of the former to make the latter more likely than it would otherwise be. There is a reason we call this

---

11. This explanation is offered by Albert (2000).

the asymmetry of influence, and that is because it is all about the ways in which intervening on some part of the world can result in a change in some other part of the world. Intervening on the world in *this* way makes *that* outcome more likely. What it is to be the cause, rather than the effect, is to be the thing that we can manipulate in order to bring about the effect. The reason causes come before their effects in L is that, in L, the direction of the past just is the direction towards the closest low-entropy state (i.e., the Big Bang) and what we mean by 'the future' just is the direction towards increasing entropy. When entropy is increasing, the manipulation of events at one time raises the probability of events further away from the low-entropy state, but not the converse. So, in L, it will be the case that we can manipulate what we call later events only by manipulating what we call earlier events. The combination of increasing entropy and a low-entropy singularity of the Big Bang are also thought to explain why, in L, there are traces of the past but not the future.

So far, there is nothing particularly weird about this picture of our world. But now, we need to turn our attention to what is going on in R. The Big Crunch is basically the Big Bang in reverse and at the other temporal end of the universe. The Big Crunch, then, is a very low-entropy state. Given the laws of nature in our world, what would we expect the contents of R to look like?

Let's suppose that there is maximum entropy at the midway point. We know there is very low entropy at the Big Crunch. So, we would expect to find that entropy *decreases* from the midway point towards the Big Crunch. Or, to put another way, we would expect to find that entropy *increases* from the Big Crunch towards the midway point. Then, the two ends of the universe are alike in the following sense: entropy is increasing away from each very low-entropy boundary condition. In effect, then, we can expect R to look (in broad brush strokes) rather like L, but in the reverse order.

So, suppose that Figure 1.3 is a representation of a world in which there is temporal passage. Suppose that the Big Bang is the first moment of time and the Big Crunch is the last moment of time. Then, in R, there are traces of *future* events, not past ones. In R, people remember the *future*, not the past. In R, effects *precede* their causes and people manipulate the *past* by manipulating the future. In R, people deliberate about the *past*, not the future. Things in R are very much the way things are in the weird presentist world we considered earlier in this chapter.

Importantly, the world just described has the very same laws of nature as our world. In fact, *that could be our world for all we know*. If there is temporal passage in this mirror world, though, it seems to play no role in explaining the temporal asymmetries that we see in R. For, in R, time is passing in the opposite direction to the direction of the temporal asymmetries. Since the mirror world could be our world, we have every reason to be sceptical that temporal passage explains the temporal asymmetries we see around us.

In Defence of the Block Universe View 51

In these last two sections, I introduced several temporal asymmetries and noted that we want to explain why those asymmetries obtain. I introduced the notion of entropy. I argued that we can explain why entropy tends to increase towards what we call the future, just by appealing to the existence of a low-entropy boundary condition (the Big Bang) and facts about the relative probabilities of ordered versus disordered macrostates. I also argued that the temporal dynamist does not have a good account of the temporal asymmetries. In essence, this is because, for her, the direction of time is given by the passage of time itself, and the passage of time can 'come apart' from things like the increase of entropy. That means there could be worlds in which time, in fact, runs in the opposite direction to the direction it seems to run in. In such worlds, the epistemic asymmetry and asymmetry of influence are not explained by the passage of time. Moreover, I argued, our world could be just such a world. So, I argued, the passage of time is not what explains these asymmetries.

7.3 Can the Block Universe Do Better?

That brings us to (3), the claim that the block universe view can explain the epistemic asymmetry and the asymmetry of influence. To see that this is so, let's revisit our diagram, but this time let's add some arrows to the picture see figure 1.4. Further, let's suppose that this is a diagram of a non-dynamical mirror world: a block-universe mirror world.

How are we to make sense of what is going on in L and R given that there is no temporal passage in this world? Well, the block universe theorist will say that past and future are not only relational—in that they pick out locations relative to one's own—but also that which *direction* they pick out is a relational matter that depends on where one is.

We have already seen that, for the block universe theorist, dinosaurs are past relative to you and me, but they are future relative to the first slime

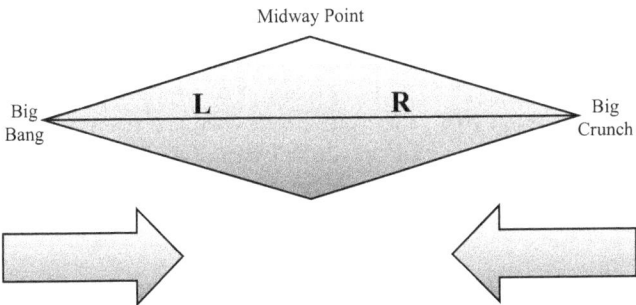

Figure 1.4 The Block Mirror World

moulds. That, of course, is consistent with thinking that there is a fact of the matter which end of the universe is the earlier end and which the later end. The block universe theorist could think that the Big Bang *really is* the first moment of time and the Big Crunch *really is* the last moment of time. She can think this even though she denies that time robustly passes.

But the block universe theorist need not say this. She can instead say that which direction is past and which is future is also a relative matter: it depends on where in the universe one is. For those in L, the Big Bang is the past. That is because, relative to any location, 'the past' is always the direction in which entropy is decreasing. In L, entropy is decreasing towards the Big Bang, so, in L, the Big Bang is past. Likewise, in L, the Big Crunch is future; for, relative to a location, 'the future' is always the direction in which entropy is increasing. In L, the direction from past to future aligns with the epistemic asymmetry and asymmetry of influence.

In R, since 'the past' just is the direction towards which entropy is decreasing and the future is the direction towards which entropy is increasing, it is the Big Crunch that is past and the Big Bang that is future. So, it is not right to say that, in R, people remember the future. They do not; they remember the past. For, in R, the past is the opposite direction to the direction of the past in L. Likewise, in R, effects precede their causes just as they do in L. In R, the temporal asymmetries align with the past-to-future direction in the very same way they do in L. *That is because past and future are reversed in R, relative to L.* Importantly, then, the increase of entropy explains why, in any region, we find the temporal asymmetries we do. Since which direction is past and which is future at a location is determined by the increase of entropy in that location, it will always be the case that the explanation for the temporal asymmetries in any location aligns with the direction of time at that location. It cannot be that the direction of time somehow comes apart from the temporal asymmetries at a location.[12] One way to put this is just that the block universe theorist can say that the direction of time is not something over and above the asymmetries we find in time. Rather, she can say that the direction of time just is, (i.e., reduces to) facts about, say, increasing and decreasing entropy. That is why the direction of time points from the Big Crunch towards the Big Bang in R and why the direction of time points from the Big Bang to the big Crunch in L.

The temporal dynamist cannot say any such things. For she holds that the direction of time is given by the direction of time's passage and that can completely come apart from the asymmetries we are trying to explain. The block universe theorist can and should deny this. And that is why the block universe theorist has a good explanation for the temporal asymmetries, and the temporal dynamist does not.

---

12. Price (1996) offers this explanation.

This chapter introduced the block universe theory of time, which is a view on which past, present, and future exist, and time does not pass. I contrasted this view with dynamical theories of time, such as presentism, on which time does pass. These are views on which there is a fact of the matter as to which moment really is present, and which moment that is changes. I then offered an argument in favour of the block universe view: the argument from special relativity. I argued that the block universe view fits better with some of our best scientific theories (e.g., special reality) and that's a reason to accept it. Then I considered three arguments against the block view: the argument from change, temporal phenomenology, and free will. In all three cases, I argued that these are not very persuasive. They don't give us good reason to think that our world is not a block universe. Finally, I presented another argument in favour of the block universe view: the argument from explanation. I argued that the block universe view is better able to explain the various temporal asymmetries we find in our world when compared with dynamical views, such as presentism. That is because dynamical views tie the direction of time to temporal passage; but temporal passage itself can come apart from the temporal asymmetries, and so it cannot be what explains them. By contrast, the block universe theorist can say that the direction of time is simply given by these very asymmetries, and so it cannot be that the direction comes apart from those asymmetries. In all, I conclude, we have good reason to endorse the block universe view over its rivals.

Chapter 2

In Defence of Presentism

Nikk Effingham

Contents

1. Introduction 54
2. Making Sense of the Debate 56
3. In Favour of Presentism 59
4. Truthmaking 64
5. Being Explains Truth 73
6. Problems for Presentism 75
7. A Proposed Solution 77
8. Objections 78
9. Comparison to Eternalism 81
10. The Open Future 83
11. Presentism and Special Relativity 86
12. Conclusion 94

1. Introduction

Presentism is the theory that only presently existing things exist at all. Given presentism, I exist, you exist, the Eiffel Tower exists, and Billie Eilish exists. Past things, like Genghis Khan, dinosaurs, and Napoleon Bonaparte, do not exist. Nor do future things; for instance, there are no outposts on Mars or as-yet-unborn stars.

Presentism's main competitor is eternalism. *Eternalism* says that things from all times exist, even if they are no longer present or are yet to become present. The eternalist thinks that not only you, me, the Eiffel Tower, and Billie Eilish exist, but so too do dinosaurs, Napoleon, and (should it be that they will come to exist) the outposts on Mars. They don't exist *now*, of course—that would be a strange thing to believe. The eternalist thinks that, just as things may exist even though they don't exist *here* (for instance, the Andromeda galaxy isn't here—it's far away!—yet it nevertheless exists), past and future things can exist even though they don't exist *now*. (Below, I go detail exactly what this is meant to amount to.)

In my sections of this book, I am going to defend presentism. I'm not sure, however, whether I believe it. Some philosophers think there's something intellectually dishonest about defending a principle that one doesn't believe. When faced by a tricky philosophical question, such people look inside themselves, find that they have a strong intuition about what the answer is, and then defend that answer to the hilt. I don't think that this is a bad way to

DOI: 10.4324/9781003105664-3

approach philosophy, but I don't think it's the only way. Whenever I look inside myself, I generally find my intuitions far murkier, far less clear, and far less strong. Moreover, this lack of intuition just gets worse for me the more philosophy I read and the more I get an insight into the pros and cons of competing views. So, I'm not the sort of philosopher who has metaphysical instincts that I defend to my dying breath. Instead, I treat philosophy like a court of law. Philosophers are barristers and the philosophical theories they defend are those accused of crimes. Just as the paradigmatic barrister has to try their best to defend the accused—although never cheating or lying to do so—I think philosophers can (and should!) defend a theory as best they can, just as long as they don't say anything intellectually dishonest in the process. And just as this adversarial procedure of prosecution and defence tends towards producing good results when it comes to justice, I genuinely believe that philosophers defending theories—even when they're unsure whether those theories are true or not—will tend towards us ultimately coming to know which philosophical theory is true. (And just as a barrister might put in their best efforts, but years later agree that their client was guilty, don't be surprised if I put in my best efforts and, outside of this book, admit that presentism is false—that's not dishonesty or academic failure, that's mature philosophical progress.)

That disclaimer in place, let my defence begin! It proceeds in four stages, with an interesting tangent between the third and the fourth.

First: I discuss whether there is any *sense* to be made in asking whether non-present things exists or not? It is not unreasonable to think that questions like 'Does Napoleon exist?' are trivial to answer and any debate about them is a load of nonsense, a manufactured pot of hooey accidentally crafted by metaphysicians. I will argue that the debate *is* intelligible and that we *can* make sense of the disagreements between the presentist and the eternalist.

Second: I argue that, unless you have a good reason not to, you should endorse presentism. Presentism entails that only presently existing things exist and eternalism entails that lots of other things exist besides. If you have two theories where one commits to some things and the other theory commits to a subset of those things, we say that the latter theory is 'ontologically parsimonious' compared to the former. Unless you've got a good reason to think otherwise, you should endorse the more parsimonious theory. Hence, there's some reason to favour presentism.

But that doesn't mean presentism is definitely true, for there might be reasons to think we *need* those extra things—i.e., there might be reasons to think that eternalism is true even though it includes more things than presentism. This is dealt with in the third and fourth stages of my argument. I will discuss the two most common reasons for thinking that we need more things than the presently existing things and I will argue that these reasons are misguided. In the third stage, I discuss 'truthmaking' and whether past things are needed because there are true propositions about the past. I will argue that there is no good reason to think we need dinosaurs (or other past things) to ground truths about there once having been dinosaurs (or other such propositions about the past). In the fourth stage, I consider Einstein's theory of relativity. Many philosophers have taken relativity to be a reason for thinking eternalism is true; I will argue that it is not.

That will complete my argument for presentism. With both reasons for being an eternalist dispatched, and since we have some reason to be a presentist unless you have a good reason not to be, it follows we should believe that presentism is true.

Further to this, I will also—between the third and fourth stages—introduce a second argument in favour of presentism. I will argue that, given the presentist can believe that the future is open (i.e., that facts about the future haven't been settled yet), their theory can be made simpler than the eternalist's theory when we consider the number of fundamental truths in each. Since we should favour simple theories, that is a mark in presentism's favour. So, we have a second argument for presentism, in addition to the motivation from ontological parsimony.

2. Making Sense of the Debate

Start by trying to get our heads around what this debate even means. Some things presently exist—e.g., me, Barack Obama, and the Eiffel Tower. Some things used to exist and no longer exist—e.g., Napoleon Bonaparte, dinosaurs, and the city of Troy. Finally, some things don't exist now but will one day come to be. Obviously, we can't be sure exactly what those things are, for they don't exist yet. But we can assume some examples for the purpose of argument—e.g., outposts on Mars, Barack Obama's great-great-great-granddaughter, or stars from the far future that have yet to form. The study of *temporal ontology* asks which of these things exist. No-one disagrees that the presently existing things exist, but there *is* disagreement concerning the past and future things. Presentists say that only the presently existing things exist. Eternalists say that everything from any time—past, present, or future—exists. (There are also other positions—e.g., the *growing block theory*, which says that things from the past and present, but not the future, exist. I won't discuss such theories in this chapter, since I am limiting my attention just to presentism and eternalism.)

Some philosophers worry that these questions simply don't make sense. And whilst I think they're wrong, I don't blame them for some initial incredulity. Consider the following:

(1) Napoleon Bonaparte does not presently exist, but he does exist.

It's not unreasonable to think that (1) is *obviously* false. Imagine we took the second occurrence of 'exist' in (1) to just mean 'presently exist'; in that case, (1) would clearly be a contradiction (and, like all contradictions, would be false). So, if debates in temporal ontology revolved around which things *presently* existed, then the debate would be trivial and pointless. It'd be trivial that the presently existing things presently existed and trivial that those things that don't presently exist (e.g., Napoleon and the outposts on Mars) don't presently exist.

But I believe debates in temporal ontology are not trivial. So, the second occurrence of 'exist' in (1) must mean something different from 'presently exists'. The phrase 'existence simpliciter' is most often used to capture this different type of existence.

It's easiest to make sense of existence simpliciter by considering the eternalist's point of view. The eternalist will draw an analogy between time and space. Imagine I walk into the New York tourist office and ask for a list of attractions. I'm told there is the Statue of Liberty, there is the Empire State Building, there is the Museum of Modern Art, and so on. I then ask whether there are any pyramids and I'm told that there are not. But, of course, even when I am stood in New York, there still are pyramids! They aren't *in New York*, but they still *exist*—they exist in Egypt and the historic region of Mesoamerica; just because I've entered the city of New York doesn't mean that they've mysteriously vanished! The pyramids might not exist *here*, but they do exist. It's a similar distinction the eternalist wants to draw between present existence and existence simpliciter. Napoleon and the outposts on Mars might not exist *now*, but they nevertheless still exist—that is, they exist simpliciter. They exist, even though they are not spatiotemporally local.

The debate between presentists and eternalists can be cashed out in terms of 'existence simpliciter'. We can define the theories as:

> **Presentism:** Everything that exists simpliciter presently exists.
>
> **Eternalism:** Things that exist in the past, present, and future all exist simpliciter.

Similarly, when we consider (1), the difference between the two occurrences of 'exists' is now made clear: the first occurrence means 'present existence' and the second occurrence means 'existence simpliciter'. So, when we consider (1), what we're really considering is:

(2) Napoleon Bonaparte does not presently exist but he does exist simpliciter.

And the answer as to whether (2) is true or false is *not* trivial.

Having considered how the eternalist interprets the question, consider the presentist's understanding. Even though the presentist disagrees over whether or not the past and future things exist simpliciter, that need not mean that they disagree with the eternalist's explanation of what the concept involves; the presentist can agree that the eternalist's analogical example is instructive when it comes to understanding 'existence simpliciter', even though they disagree over whether past and future things actually exist simpliciter. In general, you can come to understand a concept via examples even when you disagree that those examples reflect reality. Compare to 'phlogiston', which was (wrongly) thought by 18th-century chemists to be a substance in combustible bodies that was released when they were burnt. A scientist can say that they understand the concept 'phlogiston' whilst denying that phlogiston exists—indeed, they must, for how can a scientist say that phlogiston doesn't exist if they are not even sure what it is meant to be? Or consider 'God'. We come to understand what the concept of 'God' involves by reading holy books; even the atheist can agree with that and can do so without believing that those books are veridical. Or consider 'infinitesimals' in mathematics. We might have an idea of what an infinitesimal is meant to be whilst also denying that there are any such things. As it is with those concepts, so it is here: the presentist can agree that the analogues the eternalist is drawing between time and space are coherent, even though they don't reflect reality. So, the presentist can allow for there being a conceptual difference between 'presently existing' and 'existing simpliciter', even though they believe that the only things that fall under the latter also fall under the former.

Of course, you might dig your heels in; perhaps you have not found the eternalist's analogical example instructive; perhaps you remain sceptical that a sensible debate can be had over whether Napoleon exists. Whilst I understand (or, at least, think I understand!) the difference between 'present existence' and 'existence simpliciter', I would not be entirely surprised if you still did not. Indeed, if you are such a sceptic, you will find that there are other philosophers on your side (see the Suggested Readings for some examples). However, I don't need to detain myself too long with such scepticism. If you are truly committed to being unable to make sense of the debate in temporal ontology, then you will think that presentism is *trivially* true. And if it is trivially true, then you won't see any need to argue in favour of the theory—you don't need to offer reasons for believing something if it's trivial that it's true! So, you will find my argument in favour of presentism, presented in section 3, less than interesting. But the problems levelled *against* presentism—which I deal with in sections 4–11 of this chapter—still remain to be dealt with. If there are arguments for thinking that some proposition P is false, then, even if you think that P is trivially true, you still have to deal with those arguments! It is no response to a detailed argument for P being false that you happen to think that P is obvious or trivial or incoherent to deny. Even if you are right to believe that of P, your belief that it is so is not *by itself* an explanation of where the argument against P goes wrong. So, even if you are boggled by the idea that presentism might be false, that doesn't *by itself* get you off of the hook of having to undermine the objections to presentism that I discuss later. So, even if presentism is trivially true, there is much in this chapter that will be of interest to you.

3. In Favour of Presentism

So, the question is whether past and future things exist simpliciter even though they do not presently exist. Now we need to answer that question.

My argument for why we should believe presentism is simple: there is some reason to believe it and no reason not to. This section considers the first of my two reasons in favour of presentism. Before that, though, I start by considering a popular, but flawed, argument for the theory.

3.1 A Bad Argument for Presentism: The Argument From Intuition

It's common in philosophy for intuitions to play a role in deciding which theory is true. For example, one theory in metaphysics is 'mereological nihilism', the thesis that there are no composite objects and only sub-atomic particles. It is widely acknowledged that one problem for that theory is that it rallies against the intuition that *we* exist. Another example: Kant's theory of ethics. Kant says that we should never lie. It is widely acknowledged that one problem for that theory is that it means, counterintuitively, that I am obliged to tell an axe murderer hunting for my friend that the person they are looking for is cowering in the cupboard next to me. A final example: the problem of evil. It is a big problem for believing in God that there is evil in the world. One solution is to deny that there *is* any evil in the world. Obviously, the obstacle to that theory is explaining away what we take as being undeniable—i.e., the existence of terrible things that appear to us to be evil! In short: what we already believe about the world (our 'intuitions') can and should guide us as to what theories we should accept.

Of course, this is not the *only* dimension along which we evaluate a philosophical theory. After all, philosophy is a discipline that explicitly tries to argue that we should believe interesting (and often *counter*intuitive!) things about the world. I am not saying that a theory's adherence to what we already believe is the be-all and end-all when it comes to selecting the correct theory. But it should at least be *a* dimension. If a theory has nothing to recommend it whilst also saying weird and crazy things, you clearly *shouldn't* believe such a theory. A theory's counterintuitive commitments can sometimes be reason enough to ignore it—at least, unless it has some other benefits to outweigh that cost.

In the temporal ontology debate, presentists often say that their theory has the benefit of being intuitive. It just seems sensible that only presently existing things exist, they say. It just seems weird to say dinosaurs and Napoleon exist, they say.

But this is a bad argument and not a good reason at all to favour presentism. The reason it sounds intuitive that only presently existing things exist is because we're reading the second 'exist' as 'presently exists'. And if you read the second 'exist' as 'presently exists' then all you end up with is a truism. And we've just seen in the last section that presentism *isn't* the trivial claim that only presently existing things presently exist. Rather, it is the more contentious claim that presently existing things are the only things that exist simpliciter.

I am deeply suspicious that we can have *any* intuitions about the answer to this more arcane question. As a guide to establishing what counts as intuitive versus what does not, as a rule of thumb I apply a 'What would my mother say?' test. My mother is an intellectually sophisticated adult, but not one who has studied philosophy—I think that means she is a reasonably good guide to what is intuitive versus what is not. If I asked my mother whether dinosaurs exist, she'd presumably tell me that they don't. But that would be because it's only natural for her to read me as asking whether they *presently* exist, rather than the question of whether they exist simpliciter. Were I to explain the idea of existence simpliciter, I doubt she'd have *any* intuitions at all—it's just too esoteric a question. (If you are interested in what people actually say about questions like these, see the Suggested Readings for some sources you might wish to refer to.)

A cannier presentist will try to develop some *intuition pumps* to make us see that, at the end of the day, a belief in presentism underlies some other intuitive belief we have. Intuition pumps are excellent devices and, in general, I approve of their use. For instance, when teaching Gettier problems at the undergraduate level, I sometimes meet students who deny that if you know a proposition then that proposition must be true—such students say that there are cases where we know something even though it's false—e.g., we might know something is true when we passionately believe it. But using an intuition pump, we can demonstrate that, intuitively, one can only know true things. Imagine you're suffering a disease of unknown origin. You're trying to decide who to treat you. Clearly, you should favour the more knowledgeable doctor. Imagine that the choice of doctors has been whittled down to just two. One is a medical doctor from Harvard who says she doesn't know what the disease is, but nevertheless thinks she can trial a new antiviral regime that'll do the trick. When pressed, she openly admits that, whilst she knows a lot about medicine, she doesn't know *everything*—she's not that egotistical! The other candidate is a self-taught 'shaman' who learnt everything from YouTube videos and New Age literature. The shaman says he knows exactly what the disease is—indeed, he claims to know everything about medicine. The self-professed shaman has very few true beliefs about medicine. Nevertheless, if knowledge doesn't require you to be right, then I guess the shaman *knows* a lot more than the doctor. Reason dictates that he is therefore the right person to treat you! This line of reasoning is, of course, madness. And so, the intuition pump has done its work, showing that, underlying your acting in a certain way (in this case, selecting the Harvard professional above the crank), is the intuition that to know a proposition requires that proposition to actually be true.

Similarly, we might try to create an intuition pump for presentism. Focus on death and dying. We're sad when people die because they no longer exist. We're sad that one day we will die because one day we won't exist. And this sadness is not the same as the sadness we feel about people moving far away. If someone I love and care about moves to Ittoqqortoormiit—a remote settlement in Greenland—I might be sad, but I won't be sad in the same way that I would if they died. The presentist might argue that this is an intuition pump showing that not being near me in space is intuitively very different from not being near me in time—that is, that intuitively time isn't like space. Such a presentist will say that, when you have these intuitions, this is because you have an intuition that, when you die, you cease to exist *at all*—i.e., that, when you become a merely past entity, you cease to exist simpliciter. So, the intuition pump would push us towards presentism.

But, at the end of the day, this isn't a very convincing pump. Partially, this is because my imagined sadness is a result of my ability to interact with the person. Even in Ittoqqortoormiit, someone can be interacted with in some sense—it'd be hard to send them post, but not impossible! But if someone was teleported to the other side of the universe by a capricious demon and I knew there was no way whatsoever we'd ever speak again, I might well be as upset as if they died. So that's one reason the pump doesn't work.

But this is only part of the story. We might revise the pump slightly to bring out some more problematic intuitions. I feel bad when someone dies not just because I can no longer communicate with them, but because I feel bad *for them*. Imagine that my loved one is teleported to the other side of the universe where their life continues in a way that it wouldn't continue if they died. Imagine I know this; even though I cannot communicate with them, I would take some solace in that fact. Further, if I found out that they died, then their dying would compound my sadness; my inability to communicate with them is bad, but their being dead makes things worse. So, intuitively, there is something about being dead that is worse than being separated from me. We might think that the 'something' is that they cease to exist in any salient sense—i.e., that they cease to exist simpliciter (and, therefore, that presentism is intuitively true).

However, I can construct a pump of my own which shows that the underlying intuition has nothing to do with presentism. Imagine my loved one travels not in space, but in time, using a time machine to go back to the remote past. Further, imagine that, similar to the situation where they are teleported away by a capricious demon, I know that I will never see them again. In that case, I would be sad, but not as sad as I would have been had they died; I would only be as sad as if they were teleported to the other side of the universe. After the time machine heads off into the past, from my point of view they have ceased to presently exist, yet I would take solace in the fact that, back in the past, they carried on living their life. The sadness I have when someone dies seems *not* to have to do with them ceasing to presently exist; instead, I am sad because their dreams, hopes, and chances to experience and engage with the world have been cut short. Indeed, that best explains why we're sadder when people die young than when they're old and also explains why some people are not bothered by dying when they have led full and vibrant lives. And it matters little where that life is lived, whether near me or in Ittoqqortoormiit, as long as the actual content of that life is good. And, as the time machine example shows, it matters little *when* that life is lived. If the vibrant, full life that my loved one lives takes place in the Cretaceous past (where they enjoy hunting T-Rex), then that's just as good *for them* as them living a full and vibrant life near me in Birmingham (or living a similar life in Ittoqqortoormiit or the other side of the universe or wherever). The intuitions underlying our feelings about people dying have to do with *these* factors and not anything to do with their ceasing to presently exist or not, as the presentist's pump was meant to show. So, the presentist's pump doesn't tell in favour of the idea that intuitively we think things cease to exist simpliciter when they cease to be present.

I want to defend presentism. But I don't want to defend it on poor grounds. So, ignore this argument from intuition; it is unlikely to pay off in the end.

3.2 A Good Argument for Presentism: Parsimony

But I said above that there were dimensions other than intuition that we could adjudicate theories along. One such dimension is how *ontologically parsimonious* a theory is. One theory is ontologically parsimonious compared to another when it entails fewer things existing than the other theory. Consider three examples.

First example: a crude, fictional physics example. The 'standard model' says that there are 17 fundamental types of particles (some of which you'll have heard of—e.g., the photon and electron—and others you probably won't have—e.g., the tauon neutrino or the Z boson). Given these 17 particles, the world around us can be fully explained. Now for the fictional element. Imagine you meet Dr Extraneous who believes in his own model consisting of all 17 particles from the standard model plus an extra particle, the 'pointlesson'. It doesn't do anything, says Dr Extraneous; the pointlesson can't be detected and nor does it interact with the other particles.

Obviously, we should ignore Dr Extraneous's model. And the reason for ignoring it is that it's pointless to add in the existence of some things (in this case, the pointlesson) if we don't have too. Unless there's a reason to include some things, you should not include them. That is, you should select the most ontologically parsimonious theory—i.e., the theory with the least number of things.

Second example: a more sophisticated example from real-world physics. Daniel Nolan (1997) brings our attention to the role of parsimony in the discovery of the neutrino. Physicists investigating β-decay—radioactive decay where beta particles are emitted from nuclei—noted that the mass-energy before β-decay wasn't the same as the mass-energy after the decay. Mass-energy has to be conserved in such processes, so the scientists realised that a previously unknown type of particle was being produced during the process. Enrico Fermi, the architect of the nuclear age, called them 'neutrinos'. The problem was, there was no clear sign as to *how many* of these particles were emitted. Say that the missing mass-energy was equal to m. One theory was that a *single* neutrino was emitted with a mass-energy of m. But it was consistent to describe theories whereby there were two neutrinos, each of mass-energy $½m$, or three neutrinos each of mass-energy $¹/_3 m$, or a trillion neutrinos each of mass-energy of a trillionth of m. The default, however, was to say there was but one neutrino. After all, why add in more? What could be gained by thinking there were more of them rather than just one? Ontological parsimony favoured the singular-neutrino explanation.

A third example. A murder victim has been killed by multiple blows from a bladed weapon. The police start searching and eventually find a knife with signs of the victim's blood. Presumably, the police now *stop* searching, for they have discovered the murder weapon. They don't assume that several weapons were used in the attack and continue looking for them. They posit the *least* number of murder weapons that they can; in this case, just the one. This is, again, ontological parsimony at work: when you can, believe in the fewest things that you need to.

Note that, in each case, the claim is *not* that believing in the least number of things is *always* what you should do. A theory with only three types of particles, instead of 17, would be great. But we don't believe in it because a three-particle model of physics fails to explain the world around us. A theory saying that *no* new particles are emitted in β-decay is more parsimonious than a theory including neutrinos. But believing that theory means giving up on the conservation of mass-energy, so we don't believe it. In the murder case, if the victim showed additional signs of blunt-force trauma or if the wounds were of varying depths and widths indicating that different types of blades were used, then the police *would* have cause to seek out more weapons. So, there can be—and often is—some countervailing theoretical reason to not slavishly use ontological parsimony as the sole method to decide what there is. Exactly how we should weigh up ontological parsimony against the other dimensions is also a tricky question; fortunately, it's not one we need to worry about in this chapter. What is said here is enough to show a minimal demand of parsimony: unless there is *some* reason for including some things in your ontology, you should not do so. That demand is all that is needed in my argument for presentism.

In the context of the current discussion, it's easy to see how this minimal demand favours presentism. Presentists believe in certain things—i.e., the presently existing things. Eternalists believe in other things—i.e., the past, present, and future things. The set of things the presentist believes in is a subset of the things that the eternalist believes in; the eternalist believes in what the presentist believes in *and then adds some more things in*. So, presentism is clearly more parsimonious. And, given the minimal demand, that means we should believe presentism if there's no good reason to add in the extra objects which the eternalist believes in. That in mind, the rest of this chapter examines the two main issues people have levelled against the presentist and explains why they are not a problem. By showing that there are no disqualifying costs attached to being a presentist, we then have an argument for presentism.

> Assume either eternalism or presentism is true. If eternalism is true, then more things would exist than if presentism were true. So, presentism is more *ontologically parsimonious* than eternalism. Presentism has a 'theoretical virtue' that eternalism does not!
>
> Next: We should believe the theory with the best theoretical virtues. So, if presentism has *no* downsides compared to eternalism, then, since it has the upside of parsimony, we should prefer presentism. The rest of this chapter will argue that presentism has no downsides compared to eternalism; thus, presentism is to be preferred.

4. Truthmaking

4.1 Truthmaking Explained

The first difficulty for presentism is a problem concerning *truthmaking*. Consider some propositions:

(3) The Eiffel Tower exists.
(4) The Burj Khalifa in Dubai is 2,716 feet high.
(5) Amal Alamuddin and George Clooney are married.

These propositions are all true. Intuitively, true propositions aren't simply true. Rather, they are true *because* of something about the world; there is a connection between a proposition being true and reality at large; that is, there is something about the world that makes that proposition true. We call those things *truthmakers*.

See how this works in the case of (3). (3) is true because the world contains the Eiffel Tower. So, the Eiffel Tower makes (3) true—i.e., it is the truthmaker for (3). Whenever the Eiffel Tower exists, by necessity, (3) is true.

But it all becomes more complicated when we come to (4) and (5). We might think that (4) is made true by the Burj Khalifa. Similarly, we might think (5) is made true jointly by Alamuddin and Clooney. But—so the argument goes—this can't be right. The Burj Khalifa alone can't make it true that it's 2,716 feet tall because Samsung (who built the building) could've made it taller or shorter. It could, for instance, have had an extra floor and been 2,728 feet tall. So, the mere fact that the Burj Khalifa exists *doesn't* make (4) true; in addition to the Burj Khalifa existing, there must be some other ingredient of reality that makes (4) true. Similarly, Alamuddin and Clooney existing isn't what makes (5) true; for they can exist without it being true that they are married—indeed, for many years this was precisely the case. So, there must be something additional to them existing which is doing the truthmaking work. This idea that the truthmaker for a proposition must *necessarily* make the proposition true is called *truthmaker necessitarianism*. Whilst not every self-avowed truthmaker theorist believes it, the majority do, and, in order to help lay out presentism's truthmaking problem, I'll assume that it's true.

Given that the Burj Khalifa doesn't make (4) true, truthmaker theorists introduce entities belonging to a new *ontological category*. Whilst we are familiar with material objects (e.g., the Burj Khalifa, Alamuddin, Clooney etc.), we've just seen that they won't do the trick in making (4) and (5) true. But ontologists do not always limit themselves to believing in just material objects. They often add that there are other things that exist simpliciter. Examples of such things include numbers, properties, holes, possible worlds, sets, and propositions. All of these things might be thought to exist in addition to the material objects. The truthmaker theorist adds that we should believe in *states of affairs*, an extra category of entity. States of affairs are not material objects. You can't kick them, or pick them up, or weigh them. They don't have a smell, or a mass, or sink in water. Nevertheless, they exist simpliciter, just like material objects do (in the same way that one might think numbers exist, or properties exist, or possible worlds exist). Examples of states of affairs are things like Nikk Effingham being a philosopher, my dinner being hot, or Sydney being 10,587 miles from Birmingham. In the case of (4), the state of affairs that makes (4) true is the state of affairs of the Burj Khalifa being 2,716 feet tall. Whilst the Burj Khalifa might exist and yet not be 2,716 feet high, *the state of affairs of the Burj Khalifa being 2,716 feet tall cannot exist without it being 2,716 feet tall*. So that state of affairs existing *does* necessitate the truth of (4) and that states of affairs *can* be the truthmaker for (4). The same line of thinking applies to other propositions. For instance, in the case of (5), there exists a state of affairs—the state of affairs of Alamuddin and Clooney being married—which is the truthmaker for (5).

We've already seen one principle, truthmaker necessitarianism, which truthmaker theorists tend to believe. They also generally believe another principle: *truthmaker maximalism*. This principle says that, for *any* true proposition, it must have a truthmaker. That is, truthmakers are needed for every truth, not just some truths. It's truthmaker maximalism that drives the problem against the presentist. Consider a proposition about the past:

(6) Napoleon Bonaparte invaded Russia in 1812 AD.

The eternalist will have no problem with finding a truthmaker for (6). The eternalist thinks time and space are relevantly similar. In the same way that propositions true of other places are made true by states of affairs about things existing at those places, a proposition about another time is made true by states of affairs concerning things existing at those times. That is, the eternalist will say that (6) is similar to the following proposition:

(7) Moscow is the capital of Russia.

(7) is made true, not by Moscow or Russia, but by the state of affairs of Moscow being the capital of Russia. Just as some state of affairs about some other *place* makes (7) true, some state of affairs about 1812 AD makes (6) true—namely, the state of affairs of Napoleon invading Russia back in 1812 AD. The eternalist can say this because it's part-and-parcel of their theory that Napoleon is, back in the past, just as real as any military leader alive today. And, there in 1812 AD, he is declaring war on Russia. Thus, the eternalist can straightforwardly believe in the state of affairs of Napoleon declaring war on Russia and has easy access to a truthmaker for (6).

But I'm defending presentism. I deny that eternalism is true and so I cannot make use of this answer. This is because a state of affairs cannot exist unless the things involved in that state of affairs—what are called the *constituents* of the state of affairs—also exist. For instance, there can be no state of affairs of Voldemort invading Hogwarts because neither Voldemort nor Hogwarts exist. Similarly, there can only be a state of affairs of Moscow being the capital of Russia if Moscow and Russia both exist. And this is why the presentist is denied the truthmaker that the eternalist believes in. Where the eternalist says that the state of affairs of Napoleon invading Russia in 1812 AD makes (6) true, this is only possible because the constituents of that state of affairs—crucially, Napoleon!—exist simpliciter. Being a presentist, I don't believe Napoleon exists simpliciter. And if Napoleon doesn't exist simpliciter, then nor can states of affairs about Napoleon exist. So, if the eternalist's states of affairs aren't truthmakers for propositions like (6), the presentist must go and find a replacement truthmaker. The allegation is then that the presentist cannot do this and, thus, eternalism is true.

For any true proposition there is something—a truthmaker!—that makes that proposition true. Some propositions about the past are true—e.g., <Dinosaurs existed>. The eternalist can easily find a truthmaker for those propositions, such as a physically existing dinosaur being located back in the past. Allegedly, the presentist cannot find truthmakers for those past propositions. So, the argument goes, eternalism is therefore to be preferred.

4.2 Truthmaking Is Not a Problem

However, the presentist can respond to this worry about truthmaking. I will put forward not one, but two, arguments to this effect. The first argument (discussed in this section) shows that the truthmaking argument against presentism must be unsound, but doesn't diagnose the problem with the argument. My second argument (discussed in the next section) is more specific, locating the source of the problem.

Start, then, with a demonstration that the argument against presentism must be unsound.[1] Consider how the world actually is. World War II happened. I became a philosopher and not a fisherman. The 2018 Winter Olympics took place in PyeongChang, South Korea. The winner of the 2020 Presidential Election was Joe Biden. Whilst these things are true, they are not *necessarily* true. That 2 + 2 = 4 or that squares have four sides are examples of necessary truths. The truths about World War II, the Winter Olympics, and myself and Biden are instead contingent truths. They could have been false, even though they are actually true. World War II might not have happened. I might have become a fisherman. The Olympics could have been held in Munich, Germany, rather than in South Korea. Finally, consider the following proposition:

(8) It's possible for Dwayne 'The Rock' Johnson to have won the 2020 USA presidential election.

(8) is true. All sorts of things are possible and there are many ways the world could be. Dwayne Johnson being the winner of the 2020 presidential election is just one way the world could have been but didn't end up being. That he won the election is a possibility, even if it isn't an actuality. These propositions, concerning how the world could be (or must be or cannot be) are called *modal propositions*.

---

1. This argument is taken from Trenton Merricks (2007).

Modal propositions like (8) are about what the world *could be* like, whilst (6) is a proposition about what the world *was* like. But whilst modal propositions are of a different character than propositions about the past, consideration of the truthmaker for (8) nevertheless sheds a lot of light on truthmaking theory and presentism.

Start by considering a simpler pair of propositions:

(9) There were once dinosaurs.
(10) There could have been unicorns.

According to the eternalist, (9) is made true by physical, concrete dinosaurs existing back in the past. (10) sounds similar to (9), but concerns something that *could* have existed rather than something that *did* exist. Yet, it's absurd to think that the truthmaker for (10) is anything like what the eternalist thinks makes true (9). If it were, then there would need to exist some physical, concrete unicorns, and that's ridiculous!

Similar worries concern (6) and (8). According to the eternalist, the proposition about Napoleon invading Russia in 1812 AD is made true by a state of affairs concerning something concrete and physical, located within space and time. Napoleon really does exist, says the eternalist; he is made of flesh and blood just as much as presently existing people. But just as it seems bizarre to think (10) has a similar truthmaker to (9), it's bizarre to think Dwayne Johnson's possibly having won the election has a similar truthmaker. If it did, then the truthmaker for (8) would somehow require Dwayne Johnson to win the 2020 Presidential Election—again, a claim that is nonsense! In short, the truthmakers for modal propositions do not concern physical entities being a certain way (e.g., unicorns existing or the Rock winning an election). Here's the point: If modal propositions have truthmakers that don't involve the things they are about being physical entities, then why can't propositions about the past be similar? Whatever the truthmaker for modal propositions like (8) ends up being, why not just say a similar sort of truthmaker makes true propositions like (6)? That is, why isn't the truthmaker for (6) *also* a truthmaker that doesn't require the thing it's about to be a physical thing—i.e., a truthmaker that doesn't require Napoleon to be flesh and blood?

It's worth mentioning that some philosophers double down at this point. They say that there *is* a concrete physical thing that wins the election (and agree that the state of affairs about it makes true (8)). Just as the dinosaurs and Napoleon are removed from us in time, existing back in the past, the concrete things that ground the truth of modal propositions about what could have been are also removed from us—in this case, though, they're not removed from us in time or space but rather they exist in different *possible worlds*. For every way the world could be, these philosophers believe in an entire universe that *is* that way. Since World War II might not have happened, there is a universe at which it doesn't happen. Since I might have been a fisherman, there's a disconnected spacetime at which I am a fisherman. Since Dwayne Johnson could have won the election, there's a concrete, physical portion of reality containing Dwayne Johnson *winning* an election. This theory, sometimes called *genuine modal realism*, has quite the pedigree—David Lewis (1986), one of the most famous metaphysicians of recent years, argued for it. But ultimately, I think it is crackers and most other people agree. That there is an infinite number of disconnected spacetimes out there, at which every possibility plays out, is absurd; this absurdity is doubly the case if we're meant to believe in such things solely on the grounds of philosophical arguments about modal propositions. Certainly, if eternalism must come hand in hand with genuine modal realism then, whilst I would applaud the eternalist's moxy, I take it that few people would find the resulting theory plausible. So, set aside the idea that the truthmaker for (8) in some sense requires Dwayne Johnson to have won the election. Some sort of replacement truthmaker will be needed.

(Note that, if the truthmaker theorist instead said that (8) didn't need a truthmaker—and that modal propositions in general go without truthmakers—then truthmaker maximalism would be false. As we've already seen, if truthmaker maximalism is false then the presentist could add that propositions about the past/future don't need truthmakers either. Again: problem solved.)

As a worked example, consider two possible replacement truthmakers for (8) and see why what is said about the replacement would likewise get the presentist off the hook.

First replacement: imagine that the truthmaker theorist says that what makes (8) true is some 'brute' or 'ungrounded' state of affairs. That is, there exists a state of affairs that makes it true that Dwayne Johnson could have won the election, but that state of affairs does not need President Dwayne Johnson to exist and be one of its constituents. Similarly, we could then say that the truthmaker for unicorns being possible is the state of affairs of unicorns being possible, adding that the unicorns are *not* constituents of that state of affairs and need not exist even though the state of affairs does. But if the truthmaker theorist can say such a thing about the states of affairs making true modal propositions, why can't the presentist say the same of propositions about the past? That is, why can't they say that what makes it true that Napoleon invaded Russia in 1812 AD is just some 'brute' state of affairs that gets to exist without Napoleon having to exist as well?

Second replacement: imagine the truthmaker theorist instead says that the state of affairs that makes (8) true *does* concern Dwayne Johnson. What makes it true that Dwayne Johnson could have won the election is that Dwayne Johnson has the property of being such that he could have won the election. But if that works for modal propositions, the same thing should work for the presentist. *Lucretianists* are presentists who say that the truthmaker for past truths, like Napoleon having invaded Russia in 1812 AD, is our universe having the property of being such that Napoleon invaded Russia in 1812 AD. If we can say the first thing about Dwayne Johnson, what's wrong with saying the second thing about the universe?

And so on and so forth. Whatever truthmaker one suggests for (8) will raise serious questions about why the presentist can't say similar things about allegedly problematic propositions like (6). Thus, we have an excellent argument for why truthmaking isn't a problem for the presentist.

> The eternalist believes that true propositions like <Dinosaurs existed> have truthmakers that are physical beings—in this case, a physical dinosaur located in the past. But they don't think similarly of true propositions like <Dragons are possible creatures>. The proposition about dragons is not made true by some physically existing dragon! So, propositions like that are made true in 'some other way'. Even though we don't know the details of what that way is, presumably whatever we say about the dragon proposition can be said about <Dinosaurs existed>, in which case we *don't* need the truthmaker for <Dinosaurs existed> to be some physically existing dinosaur located in the past

What I haven't provided is an explanation of exactly *why* truthmaking isn't a problem for the presentist. But that's okay, for sometimes it is enough to know *that* an argument is unsound without having to know *why* it is unsound. A good example is Gaunilo's response to the ontological argument for the existence of God. That argument goes thus: God is the greatest thing imaginable; if God didn't exist, then one could imagine something greater than Him (i.e., a deity who did exist!); since it's impossible to accept that there could be something greater than the greatest thing imaginable, it follows that God exists. Gaunilo offered an excellent counterexample: if the greatest island imaginable didn't exist, then there could be an even greater island that *did* exist; since it's impossible for there to be a greater island than the greatest island imaginable, it follows that the greatest island exists. You can rinse and repeat this reasoning for all sorts of things. There's a greatest dragon. A greatest Jedi. A greatest flying carpet. All of this is clearly absurd and so Gaunilo does a good job of showing *that* the ontological argument is unsound. But I don't think Gaunilo diagnoses exactly where it goes wrong—indeed, as the abundance of literature on the ontological argument shows, there's a lot more to say about exactly *why* the argument doesn't work, even if you're already confident *that* it doesn't work. The same thing is going on here. This discussion shows that the truthmaking argument against presentism won't work and that somewhere it must go wrong. However, I haven't as-yet suggested what exactly it is that makes it go wrong.

4.3 Where Truthmaking Goes Wrong

My second argument remedies this omission. I argue that there's no reason to believe the principles of truthmaking theory in the first place; that is, truthmaking is a bum deal we never should have thought about buying into to begin with.

Restate the main claim of truthmaking theory:

(11) For any true proposition, there exists some entity that necessitates that proposition's truth.

Here's the problem: What reason is there for thinking that (11) is true? Few truthmaker theorists have an explicit argument for (11) beyond an appeal to intuition. For instance, Austin says:

> When a statement is true there is, *of course*, a state of affairs which makes it true.
> (Austin 1950, 23)

And Armstrong, when specifically arguing for truthmaker maximalism (although the idea applies more generally to (11)), says:

> What, then, is my argument for Maximalism? I do not have any direct argument. My hope is that philosophers of realist inclinations will be immediately attracted to the idea that a truth, any truth, should depend for its truth for something 'outside' it, in virtue of which it is true.
> (Armstrong 2004, 7)

So, the reason to think (11) is true is, more or less, an appeal to intuition. But (11) isn't intuitively true. What I admit is that the following is intuitively true:

(12) For any true proposition, something makes that proposition true.

(12) is eminently reasonable, at least to my ear; when the truthmaker theorist says something along the lines of (12), I agree that it is correct. But we should not think that (11) follows from it *even though it sounds very similar*. To see why, consider people who have difficulty walking.[2] It sounds true enough to say:

---

2. This example is, again, from Trenton Merricks (1999).

(13) For every person who has difficulty walking, there's something that makes it difficult for them to walk.

But something sounds wrong when I say (13) entails:

(14) For every person who has difficulty walking, there exists some entity that necessitates it being difficult for them to walk.

The leap from (13) to (14) is a torturous and unnatural one to make; in cases where (13) is true, it would be just *weird* to think that (14) is also true. Imagine I have difficulty walking because I have a limp. It seems bizarre to move from that claim to saying that there exists some entity that is a limp. That's ludicrous! It is crazy to think that—in addition to all of the material objects that exist—there exist 'limps', floating around and snagging unsuspecting healthy legs. When someone says that limps exist or someone says that there's something that makes it difficult for me to walk, they don't mean to commit to the existence of an extra *entity*. When I say 'Limps exist', that's best interpreted *not* as a commitment to the existence of an extra thing, but instead as a short-hand claim for saying that there are people who limp and have trouble walking. Similarly, believing (13) doesn't commit us to the *existence* of limps either; to believe (13) isn't to believe in the *existence of* anything other than human beings; rather, to believe (13) is to believe the world *is a certain way*—i.e., something about the world (inflammation in someone's joints, or their being infected by a disease, or the cold weather) causes them to limp. When, in (13), one says 'there's something that makes it difficult for them to walk', that's just elliptical for saying that the person who has difficulty walking has some feature or property that hinders their mobility.

The same thought applies to the leap from:

(12) For any true proposition, something makes that proposition true.

to:

(11) For any true proposition, there exists some entity that necessitates that proposition's truth.

(12) sounds plausible, intuitive, and true. But you've gone wrong if you think it leads to (11). There's no reason to think that the 'something' in (12) is some kind of *entity*, like a state of affairs. More plausibly, like talk about limps, (12) is just a short-hand way of conveying the more trivial claim that, when a proposition is true, the world is a certain way—i.e., a way which is as the proposition describes.

In short, we have a second reason to think the truthmaking argument against presentism doesn't work, since there's no good reason to believe that the underlying principle of truthmaking is true in the first place.

5. Being Explains Truth

5.1 Metaphysical Explanation

I have denied that (12) demands that there exist truthmakers—i.e., denied that, for every proposition, there must be entities that necessitate the truth of that proposition. But I've conceded that (12) is nevertheless true. So, I accept that there's *some* connection between a proposition being true and reality being a certain way; there is *some* relation between the world and true propositions. This section details what that relation might be and then offers a 'new and improved' problem for presentism, one not entirely dissimilar to the problem with truthmakers. I then, of course, go on to explain how the presentist can nevertheless overcome this difficulty.

To understand what the correct connection between truth and reality is, we must introduce the idea of *metaphysical explanation*. To understand metaphysical explanation, first consider causal explanation. For example, my food being hot might be causally explained by my having put it in the oven. This example shows that there can be propositions such that the truth of one explains the truth of the other one. In this case, the *type* of explanation is causal explanation. But some metaphysicians believe there is also a brand of explanation that isn't causal. Consider the true proposition that Obama is 6'2". That proposition's being true seems to be explained by the atoms that compose Obama being arranged in a certain way. But it sounds bizarre to say that the arrangement of his atoms *caused* that abstract proposition to be true, in the same way that an atom might cause another to move by transferring energy to it in a sub-atomic collision. How could a physical thing *causally interact* with a merely abstract object like a proposition? So, when we say that Obama's atomic arrangement *explains* that proposition being true, the explanation cannot be a *causal* explanation. It is instead what we can call a 'metaphysical explanation': just as the proposition that my food is hot is causally explained by the proposition that I put it in the oven, the proposition that Obama is 6'2" is metaphysically explained by his atoms having a certain arrangement.

(Another example: If you were a Platonist about properties, you would say that an object instantiating the property *Red* explains—metaphysically explains!—why the object is red. A last example: If you believed in possible worlds you might explain—metaphysically explain!—some proposition being possible in terms of that proposition being true at some possible world.)

Some philosophers have worried that the very idea of peculiarly 'metaphysical' explanations makes no sense and that discussions involving metaphysical explanation are therefore intellectually bankrupt. For the rest of this chapter, I will assume that 'metaphysical explanation' does make sense, even though I cannot give any further elaboration or analysis of how to better understand it. I contend that the above examples of propositions being true in virtue of how the world is (or objects being a certain way in virtue of instantiating certain properties or propositions being true in virtue of being true at some world etc.) make clear that we do, in fact, understand the notion of metaphysical explanation. The concept is a natural one, not a strange one; it is readily intelligible, rather than something that threatens to make philosophical discussion intellectually bankrupt.

Some die-hard refuseniks will continue to deny that this makes sense, remaining unconvinced by my (admittedly exceedingly brief) explanation of what 'metaphysical explanation' is meant to be. Fortunately, this isn't a problem. In this book, my aim is only to defend presentism. At this stage in the discussion, we are considering the problem of how presentism can account for the connection between truth and reality. I've argued that this question amounts to asking what metaphysically explains propositions about the past being true. Therefore, if you are truly set against understanding what metaphysical explanation is, then you are truly set against understanding this problem *in the first place*. That is, those sceptical of the idea that we can make sense of metaphysical explanation should likewise be sceptical that presentism has a difficulty with accounting for truths about the past. If you think there's no such thing as 'metaphysical explanation', presentism can more easily get off the hook, for then there isn't even a difficulty to begin with! So, by assuming that we can make sense of metaphysical explanation, I'm making a charitable concession on behalf of the eternalist. All that said, I will set aside worries about metaphysical explanation and proceed as if we can make sense of the notion.

> **Truth Supervenes on Being**
>
> If you read the literature on presentism, you will come across the phrase 'truth supervenes on being'. This box explains what that involves.
>
> Supervenience is a modal relation. A collection of facts supervenes on some other collection of facts if and only if there cannot be any change in the first collection without a change in the second. For instance, the facts about someone's height supervene on facts about their atomic structure. Obama is 6'2" and has a specific 'atomic structure'—i.e., those atoms which are a part of Obama are arranged in a certain way. Obama cannot change his height without changing that structure. Thus, his height supervenes on that structure. More generally, all facts about the height of something supervene

on facts about the arrangement of the atoms composing that thing. (Note that it doesn't run the other way around; since Obama's atoms move around, his atomic structure is constantly altering but his height remains the same—his atomic structure does *not* supervene on his height.)

To say that truth supervenes on being is to say that facts—that is, any old fact, no matter what it's about—supervene on facts about what exists *and what existing things are like*. The italicised bit is what makes it different from truthmaking theory. If you're a truthmaker theorist, then, if some proposition is true in one case and false in another, then *what things exist* must differ between those cases; in the case of truth supervening on being, the truths can change even though what exists does not change. For example, when Obama became President, the truthmaker theorist will say that there was a change in what things existed—e.g., that the state of affairs of Obama being President came into existence when he became President. Those who believe truth supervenes on being do not need to say this. They can instead say that what existed did not change; all that happened was that Barack Obama changed. In 2008 AD, he was one way—namely, he wasn't the president of the USA. In 2009 AD, he was a different way—namely, he was such that he was President of the USA. What *existed* did not change; the only thing that changed was *how those things were*.

This idea that truth supervenes on being is effectively an alternative way of understanding the relationship between truth and reality. In section 5, I say that this relationship is instead one of 'metaphysical explanation'; those who believe truth supervenes on being tend to think rather that it is one of 'supervenience'.

In this book, I won't give a detailed discussion of why I prefer to talk of 'metaphysical explanation' instead of 'supervenience'. It will suffice just to explain what supervenience is and to note that these two things are somewhat similar (and, indeed, the problem for presentism I lay out in section 5 can be cashed out in terms of supervenience rather than metaphysical explanation, if you wish!).

6. Problems for Presentism

Once you're comfortable with the idea of metaphysical explanation, we can set about trying to better capture the relationship between truth and reality in a way that truthmaking failed to do. Using metaphysical explanation, we can introduce the following principle, which I will dub Being Explains Truth:

(15) The facts about reality are metaphysically explained by the facts about what exists and what properties are exemplified by the things that exist.

This seemingly pins down the correct relationship between reality and truth. For instance, the proposition

(16) Obama is 6'2".

is true. Given Being Explains Truth, its being true is metaphysically explained by Obama existing and having a certain atomic structure (or—equivalently—by Obama 'exemplifying' some atomic structure). We need no longer believe that there exist 'states of affairs' in addition to Obama that play that explanatory role. So Being Explains Truth is weaker than the theory of truthmaking; the demands it places on what must exist are not as stringent.

Let us have a brief recap. Intuitively, there is some relation between truth and reality. If that relation is truthmaking, the presentist has a problem. But we have seen, truthmaking is *not* that relation. Yet, *some* relation must play that role. I have said that the relation is metaphysical explanation, and that the relation between truth and reality is captured by Being Explains Truth.

This is not the end of the matter, though. Once you accept Being Explains Truth, it's not all smooth sailing because a problem case for the presentist can still be constructed. Consider again:

(6) Napoleon Bonaparte invaded Russia in 1812 AD.

Imagine a world at which nothing existed at all until a few minutes ago when an omnipotent Evil Demon came into existence. Being capricious and all-powerful, this Demon decided to create a universe of confused beings who believe all kinds of falsehoods. Indeed, the Evil Demon created a universe that was an exact duplicate of our universe at some point in time in 2021 AD. Just as, in our world, we're living our lives and believe that Napoleon invaded Russia, the people of this other world likewise live their lives believing that Napoleon invaded Russia. Of course, we're right and they're wrong. Add one further fact: to ensure that the deception is perfect, the Evil Demon wipes himself out of existence in order for reality to leave no trace that any deception took place.

(6) is true at our world and false at the Evil Demon world. Given Being Explains Truth, something about reality must explain why (6)'s truth varies between the worlds. If you're an eternalist, this is easy. Given eternalism, the worlds *aren't* duplicates of one another. Whilst the present moment at each world is a duplicate, the eternalist thinks there's more to reality than just the present moment. At our world, there exist billions of years of history—a history that explains why (6) is true. Whereas, at the Evil Demon world, the past is only a few minutes old and includes an Evil Demon cackling to himself as he dupes us into believing that there was once a Napoleonic Empire. So, the eternalist has the resources to easily explain why the truth of (6) differs between the worlds.

But the presentist cannot say this since, for them, the past does not exist. I've stipulated that the present moments of both worlds are qualitatively the same; thus, all that exists at those worlds is qualitatively the same. Now we have the problem for presentism. Presentists need (6) to be true of our world and not of the Evil Demon world. But, given that every truth is explained by what exists (and how it is), then, since what exists (and how it is) is exactly the same at both worlds, what is true should be the same at both worlds. If (6) is true of our world then it should be true of the Evil Demon world too. But it isn't! It's false! Since the presentist thinks (unlike the eternalist) that our world and the Evil Demon world *are* exact duplicates of one another, they seemingly don't have the resources to explain why (6) is a fact at one world but not the other.

For any true proposition, some other proposition 'metaphysically explains' why that proposition is true. When it comes to propositions like <Dinosaurs existed>, the best explanation for why that proposition is true is that there exist dinosaurs located back in the past—i.e., that eternalism is true.

7. A Proposed Solution

To solve this problem, the presentist must find some sort of difference between the two worlds. I'm going to take a line of attack that once again returns to the original intuition Being Explains Truth was trying to capture: namely, that what's true is explained by how reality is. It seems natural, at least to my ear, to add that facts about what is presently the case are explained by other facts that are presently the case. Similarly, facts about what was once the case— e.g., (6)—are to be explained, not by what's *currently* a fact (why would we believe that!), but by other facts that *used to be* the case. Present facts explain other present facts; past facts explain other past facts. Since the fact that Napoleon invaded Russia in 1812 AD is not a fact about how the world presently is, but instead is about how it used to be, the fact(s) which explain its truth should likewise be facts about the past—i.e., facts about what used to exist and what those things used to be like. Whilst the facts that are presently true of our world and the Evil Demon world are the same, the facts that *used* to be true at the two worlds are different. At our world, it was once the case that Napoleon existed and was once the case that he invaded Russia. At the Evil Demon world, this was never the case. It is this difference over what facts *were once true* that explains why (6) is true at our world and false at the Evil Demon world. Specifically, (6) is explained by a fact like:

(17) It was the case, 209 years ago, that Napoleon Bonaparte invaded Russia.

Since (17) is a fact only at our world (at least, at the time of me writing this book in 2021 AD), and not at the Evil Demon world, we have a difference between the two worlds.

That means we must tweak Being Explains Truth. Above, I cashed that principle out as:

(15) The facts about reality are metaphysically explained by the facts about what exists and what properties are exemplified by the things that exist.

Given what's just been said, it should instead read:

(18) The facts about how reality is (/was/will be/could be . . .) are metaphysically explained by the facts about what exists (/did exist/will exist/could exist . . .) and what properties are exemplified (/were exemplified/will be exemplified/could be exemplified . . .) by those things.

(6), since it's a fact about how reality used to be, is explained by what used to exist and how those things used to be. The presentist's problem is solved.

8. Objections

This section considers two objections to this response.

First objection. My theory is that (6) is explained by (17). But we might suspect that they aren't two different facts but are the *same* fact. Recall (6):

(6) Napoleon Bonaparte invaded Russia in 1812 AD.

At first glance, it looks a lot like (6) and (17) are the same fact. Were this so, I'd have a problem because no fact can explain itself. For instance, imagine your house has burnt down. You are looking for an explanation. Was it an accident? Did you leave the oven on? Was it arsonists? Was it a spurned lover seeking revenge? Imagine I said that the explanation for your house burning down was that your house burnt down. How ridiculous that would be! Thus, nothing explains itself. So, if (6) and (17) are the same fact, I would be wrong to think that (17) explains (6).

But this objection is a non-starter. (6) and (17) are manifestly different. (6) has been true since 1812 AD and will forever remain true. But (17) wasn't true back in 1812 AD. 209 years earlier than 1812 AD was 1603 AD and, in 1603 AD, Napoleon wasn't born yet, never mind conquering the world. (17) will also stop being true. In 2022 AD, it will be false. Instead, in 2022 AD, a somewhat similar fact will explain (6)—i.e., the fact that *210 years ago* Napoleon invaded Russia. Since there are times when one is true and the other false, clearly (6) and (17) are different propositions; since a fact is just a true proposition, (6) and (17) must therefore be different facts.

Second objection. The two facts may be different but are still worryingly similar. The concern is that my proposed explanation is merely 'moving the bump around underneath the carpet'; that is, the explanation is unsatisfactory because I've explained one problematic fact (i.e., (6)) with another fact (i.e., (17)) which is just as problematic in exactly the same respect we were originally worried about. After all, whilst we may have explained (6), what explains (17)? That is, what is it about reality that explains why it was the case that, just over two centuries ago, Napoleon invaded Russia? Isn't *that* question just as tricky to explain as explaining why Napoleon invaded Russia back in 1812 AD? And, if it is, surely I've failed to answer the spirit of the challenge we were originally facing?

This is a more vexing objection. To see how to reply, we should first consider what would (metaphysically) explain a *presently existing* military leader invading a contemporary country. The metaphysical explanation for that invasion would be something roughly like the combination of: (i) there existing a military leader; (ii) that military leader engaging in certain activities (e.g., signing declarations of war, issuing commands to troops); and (iii) the troops engaging in certain activities (e.g., following those orders).

Focus on one part of that explanation; namely, the existence of the military leader. What metaphysically explains their existing? The metaphysical explanation would presumably be something like there being some atoms which are arranged in a certain way, such that their intrinsic properties and the interactions between those atoms, results in there existing a particular person; namely, the military leader. And this would apply to every type of object. The existence of the table in the corner of my room is explained by the existence of atoms arranged a certain way—i.e., being arranged 'table-wise'. The existence of a car is explained by certain atoms existing and being arranged a certain way—i.e., being arranged 'car-wise'. More generally, if some F exists, its existence is explained by there existing atoms arranged F-wise.

But what explains *that*? What explains the atoms existing and being arranged in a certain way? Eventually, explanation must come to an end. Any chain of explanations will eventually 'bottom out', resulting in an ultimate explanatory fact (or set of facts) which explains all of the others but which, itself, has no explanation. We call facts that have no explanation *fundamental facts*. When it comes to metaphysical explanation, there will be a set of facts that are fundamental and which metaphysically explain all of the other facts. For instance, there will be fundamental facts about there existing atoms, fundamental facts about the properties they have, and fundamental facts about what position they have. In light of these facts, all other facts are explained—not only the existence of the dictator, but also what activities they engage in, the existence of their troops, and the troops engaging in certain activities as well (and, therefore, the fact that a country has been invaded is likewise explained).

There's nothing wrong with there being fundamental facts. They're inescapable. Only a small minority of metaphysicians think the world might contain *no* fundamental facts, so I will assume that thinking there are at least *some* fundamental facts is acceptable. Given that assumption, the principle of Being Explains Truth needs another tweak. That principle currently reads:

(18) The facts about how reality is (/was/will be/could be . . .) are metaphysically explained by the facts about what exists (/did exist/will exist/could exist . . .) and what properties are exemplified (/were exemplified/will be exemplified/could be exemplified . . .) by those things.

Having added that there are fundamental facts with no explanation, we should now modify that principle so it instead reads:

(19) The *non-fundamental* facts about how reality is (/was/will be/could be . . .) are metaphysically explained by the facts about what exists (/did exist/will exist/could exist . . .) and what properties are exemplified (/were exemplified/will be exemplified/could be exemplified . . .) by those things.

Given this discussion of fundamental facts, and what the metaphysical explanation would be for contemporary dictators invading a country, we can then turn back to the metaphysical explanation for:

(17) It was the case, 209 years ago, that Napoleon Bonaparte invaded Russia.

In the same way that there would be a fundamental explanation for a contemporary dictator invading a contemporary country, there will be a fundamental explanation for (17)—i.e., there will be some fundamental facts which together jointly explain (17). And, just as the fundamental explanation for the contemporary dictator invading another country concerns facts about there being atoms with certain properties and being in certain locations, we can mirror that for the case of (17). What explains (17) is that, 209 years ago, there *used to be* certain atoms, located in a variety of places, which had certain properties. That is, (17) is explained by a collection of fundamental facts like:

> 209 years ago, it used to be the case that atom a_1 was located at region r_1 and was F.
> 209 years ago, it used to be the case that atom a_2 was located at region r_2 and was G.
> 209 years ago, it used to be the case that atom a_3 was located at region r_3 and was H.
> . . .

Together, these propositions explain (17), which in turn explains (6) and Napoleon having invaded Russia in 1812 AD. When we try and run the second objection again, worrying that we have to explain why those fundamental facts are true, it's now obvious why there's no explanation. Those facts are fundamental! Nothing explains why fundamental facts are true! They are the bedrock of explanation. And, since explanation must come to an end somewhere, it is no slight against the presentist to say that, according to their theory, such facts are fundamental.

In general, then, the presentist can say the following. For any proposition about the past, that proposition is explained by a collection of facts, each of which is of the form:

> n years ago, it used to be the case that some atom, x, was located at region y, and was X.

where n is some number, x is the name of some atom, y is the name of some place/region, and X refers to some predicate characterising the atom—e.g., that the atom is charged, or that it has a certain mass, etc.

9. Comparison to Eternalism

This talk of fundamental facts might make you think the presentist is trying to run a con job, giving special pleading for why some part of their theory is relieved of the explanatory burden we were trying to discharge in the first place. But a comparison of this theory to eternalism shows that if an appeal to fundamentality is a theoretical embarrassment, it is at least one that both theories face. Eternalists must also say that there are fundamental facts. Indeed, the eternalist will say that the fundamental facts explaining (6) are very similar to the fundamental facts I say the presentist should accept.

Again, recall the proposition we are looking to explain the truth of:

(6) Napoleon Bonaparte invaded Russia in 1812 AD.

The eternalist's explanation will be:

(20) Napoleon exists simpliciter. He is located in 1812 AD. There, he is engaging in the act of invading Russia.

However, just as the presentist had to further explain (17), the eternalist must further explain (20). And their metaphysical explanation for (20) will be basically the same that we would use for the contemporary dictator invading a contemporary country. The fundamental facts explaining the contemporary dictator's invasion are that there exist certain atoms in certain (presently existing) places and which (currently) have certain properties. Similarly, the eternalist's explanation for (20) is more or less the same, except we instead care about atoms that are exactly located back in 1812 AD. Since, for the eternalist, places in 1812 AD are just as real as those at the present moment, they can say that there are atoms occupying places from the past just as present atoms occupy present places. So, for the eternalist, the facts explaining (20) would be facts like:

Atom a_1 is located at region r'_1 and was F
Atom a_2 is located at region r'_2 and was G
Atom a_3 is located at region r'_3 and was H
. . .

where the regions $r'_1, r'_2, r'_3, \ldots$ are all places from back in 1812 AD. (In the lingo of metaphysics, we'd say that those places were *instantaneous space-time regions*, existing only at that instant in 1812 AD.)

More generally, eternalists will explain propositions about the past being true in terms of a collection of facts, each of the following form:

Atom x is located at region z, where x is X.

Where x is the name of an atom, z is the name of a place/region from the past, and X refers to a predicate characterising how x is.

It should now be much clearer why there isn't anything wrong with the presentist's proposed explanation for past truths. Take that collection of facts that the eternalist says explains some past truth. Each fact is of the form:

Atom x is located at region z, where x is X.

For every fact of that form, the presentist instead says that there's a fact of the very similar form:

n years ago, it used to be the case that some atom, x, was located at region y and was X.

And that applies for *every* eternalist fact. So, the presentist will believe in the same number of fundamental facts as the eternalist; no more, no less. They disagree only on the specific form those facts take, and even in that case there's very little difference between them.

Let us recap where we have ended up. I said the presentist's explanation for:

(6) Napoleon Bonaparte invaded Russia in 1812 AD.

is the fact that:

(17) It was the case, 209 years ago, that Napoleon Bonaparte invaded Russia.

The worry was that this didn't help, because (17) still stood in need of explanation. That explanation is a collection of fundamental facts (of the form 'n years ago, it used to be the case that some atom, x, was located at region y, and was X'). Those facts, in being fundamental, have no explanation. And this isn't a problem if we're comparing the theory to eternalism, because the eternalist *also* believes in fundamental facts, where those fundamental facts are basically the same as those the presentist believes in—the only difference is that the eternalist concerns themselves with where some atoms that do exist *are* located, whereas the presentist concerns themselves with where some atoms that did exist *were* located. The two theories commit to the same number of inexplicable, fundamental facts; when it comes to metaphysical explanation they therefore appear to be on an equal footing. Thus, the presentist *can* explain why propositions about the past are true. Presentism has no problem with this objection to their theory.

> Some true propositions don't have *any* metaphysical explanation; they are 'fundamental truths'. A theory is more theoretically virtuous than another if it commits to fewer fundamental truths.
>
> The eternalist's fundamental truths are propositions about partless atoms being located at different points in space and time. The presentist believes in fundamental truths as well. For every fundamental truth the eternalist believes in, the presentist believes there is a fundamental truth saying that there *was* (or *will be*) some atom located somewhere. (Because those truths don't say there *is* an atom, the presentist isn't committed to the atoms from the past or future existing—they only say that the atoms *used to* exist or *will come to* exist.)
>
> So, presentists believe in the same number of fundamental truths as the eternalist. Both theories are on a par when it comes to the fundamental truths! And both theories are as good at metaphysically explaining the true propositions about the future and past (e.g., <Dinosaurs existed>). Conclusion: Issues concerning metaphysical explanation are no reason to prefer eternalism.

10. The Open Future

I've already introduced one motivation for presentism; namely, its parsimony. Having introduced the idea that some facts are fundamental, we can turn to a second argument in favour of presentism: it makes for a simpler theory than eternalism because it can leave the future 'open'. The future is open if and only if there are facts about the future that have not yet been settled; that is, they are neither true nor false. Consider:

(21) In 5045 AD, there are outposts on Mars.

If the future is open, (21) is neither true nor false. It's unfixed. It's indeterminate. Only when 5045 AD rolls around will it acquire a truth-value: if, at that point, there are outposts on Mars then it will become true; if there are not, then it will become false.

Not everyone believes the future is open. Some people believe the future is closed—i.e., that propositions about the future are—right now!—either true or false. The eternalist is generally thought to be just such a person. The eternalist doesn't think that the future is any different from the past. Just as things in the past exist simpliciter, all of the things in the future exist simpliciter. That said, for the eternalist, 'the way reality is' already fixes (21) one way or another. If the outposts exist in 5045 AD, then (21) is (presently!) true. If the outposts do not exist, then (21) is (presently!) false. Either way, (21)'s truth-value is fixed. It is not indeterminate. It will never change. And what goes for (21) goes for all propositions about the future. So, the eternalist's future is closed, rather than open. Given eternalism, that I will die on some given day is now a fact. That the human race will last millions of years (or not) is now a fact. That tomorrow I will eat a pizza (or not) is a fact. We may not *know* whether these propositions are true or false but, given eternalism, they *are* true or false.

Some presentists get quite het up about whether the future is open or closed, favouring it being open. The stereotypical motivation for the future being open is to do with free will. The general idea is that, if it's presently true that tomorrow I will eat pizza, then I don't have any *choice* about whether to have the pizza or not. If this is true, then, assuming we have free will and can choose what to do tomorrow, the future must be open rather than closed.

I am not a stereotypical presentist. I'm unmoved by this sort of motivation for the future being open. I don't think these concerns about free will are all that worrisome. If it's true that tomorrow I will eat pizza, I have free will if the *reason* I eat the pizza is because I chose to eat it. And nothing we've said about the future being closed means that the reason for me eating it tomorrow won't be the choice I will eventually make. The debate on this issue is far more complex than what this short explanation makes out, but since I mean to ignore that debate, I will press on.

I ignore the debate about free will, because whilst I am not enamoured of the stereotypical motivation for thinking that the future is open, what we've said about fundamental facts gives us a new motivation for thinking the future is open. That motivation is this: (i) if the future is open that leaves us with fewer fundamental facts than if it is closed; and (ii) we should favour theories with fewer fundamental facts.

Take (i) and (ii) in turn. For purpose of example, imagine an uncomplicated possible world. It consists of only two atoms, a and b, where the former is charged and the latter is uncharged. Imagine that the laws of physics at that world are simple, yet indeterministic. The laws determine whether an atom is charged or not such that, for any time t_n, if an atom was charged at t_n then there's a 90% chance of it being charged at t_{n+1}; if it was uncharged at t_n then there's a 10% chance of it being charged at t_{n+1}. Imagine it is time t_1 and both atoms are uncharged. The presentist who allows for an open future believes the following two facts are fundamental:

Atom a exists and is uncharged.
Atom b exists and is uncharged.

Imagine further that, at time t_2, a has become charged and b has become uncharged. Then the following would be the fundamental facts:

Atom a exists and is charged.
Atom b exists and is uncharged.
It was the case, one unit of time ago, that a existed and was uncharged.
It was the case, one unit of time ago, that b existed and was uncharged.

Now there are four fundamental facts. And, as time continues, the fundamental facts will continue to accrue. And, keeping with the spirit of this simple example, the number of facts will always be finite, two facts for every unit of time that has passed.

Compare this to the eternalist. They will instead say that the future is closed. If the universe continues for eternity, then there will be an infinite number of times. And, at each time, there will be a fact about whether the atoms are charged or uncharged. So, even at t_1, the eternalist will say that there are an *infinite* number of fundamental facts dictating what the future will be like as well as the past. So, if the future is closed, then we need more fundamental facts than if the future is open. That completes the argument for (i).

Turn to considering (ii): that we should prefer a theory that has fewer fundamental facts. This is a common belief within metaphysics. Remember, a fundamental fact is a fact that has no explanation. It seems intuitive that it's a bad thing for a theory to commit to there being inexplicable things. Whilst we must allow that *some* facts are inexplicable (and that there is some fundamental bedrock), we should favour the *least amount* of such inexplicability. In short: Maximise explanation by minimising fundamentality! Thus, when comparing theories, one way to adjudicate which theory is best is by seeing which theory is committed to the least number of fundamental facts.

We should incline towards the theory with the fewest fundamental facts. In this case, that's the future being open. Since eternalism demands that the future is closed whilst presentism allows for it being open, we should favour presentism. This talk about fundamental facts thus gives us a second motivation for presentism.

> The open future argument for presentism says that, all things being equal, we should prefer the theory with the fewest fundamental truths. The eternalist believes there are fundamental truths for every time, past, present, and future. Presentists can believe that the future is 'open' and that there are no truths at all about the future; only about the past and present. So, the presentist can believe in fewer fundamental truths than the eternalist, since they will only believe in fundamental truths about the past and present. So, all things being equal, we should prefer presentism over eternalism.

11. Presentism and Special Relativity

This final section turns away from purely philosophical concerns to those involving physics. It is commonplace for philosophers to think that the work of Einstein on the theory of relativity indicates that eternalism, not presentism, must be true. This section argues otherwise.

11.1 Physics and Philosophy

If you talk to physicists, they certainly say things that seem to assume an eternalist view of the world. They talk of spacetime, rather than space and time, as if the two cannot be separated. They talk of a 'four-dimensional manifold', which assumes that reality extends in the temporal dimension just as it does in the spatial. Einstein wrote, in a letter to the widow of Michael Besso about the death of her husband:

> Now he has departed from this strange world a little ahead of me. That means nothing. People like us, who believe in physics, know that the distinction between past, present and future is only a stubbornly persistent illusion.

All these things assume some sort of eternalist view of reality. Indeed, as a sociological observation I suggest that this is why so many philosophers are inclined towards eternalism in the first place. Because they came into contact with this way of seeing the world at an early age (e.g., during one's teenage years whilst reading popular science books), it then just seems natural to start seeing the world in that fashion when one encounters the presentist/eternalist debate at the university level.

But the mere fact that scientists talk as if eternalism is true is not reason enough to favour eternalism. Whether or not such scientists are *right* in talking in eternalist terms is what's at stake. What we need to know is what reasons there are for thinking physics favours eternalism, rather than simply appealing to the treatment physicists commonly give of the subject. It's difficult to see how a straightforward empirical experiment could determine whether dinosaurs still existed in the past (how would that work?), so presumably the scientists are instead reading eternalism off of their theories. Many different theories in physics have been argued as indicating that eternalism, not presentism, is true. In this chapter, I focus on just one: Einstein's theory of relativity. I argue that nothing in the theory entails anything that the presentist cannot accept.

11.2 The Special Theory of Relativity

To get to grips with the argument, we first need to understand some of the physics involved. This won't be in that much depth—this is, after all, a book on philosophy rather than physics. To understand relativity, it's best to start with the everyday fact that how things are to an observer may vary from one observer to another. For instance, relative to someone close to it, the Eiffel Tower is nearby whilst, relative to someone else, it might be far away. Simply put, from one observer to the next, facts may sometimes be different.

Relativity makes the following claim about how what is simultaneous may vary between observers:

(22) Whether two events are simultaneous differs for observers who are in different inertial frames of reference.

There's a piece of terminology in there that needs explaining: *inertial frame of reference* (or 'inertial frame' for short). A crude definition will suffice: You are in a different inertial frame from someone if and only if they are moving at a different velocity relative to you. If I am on a train platform and you are on a train moving past it, we are in different inertial frames. If you are in a car travelling at 40mph down the road and I'm in a car travelling 70mph down the road, we are in different inertial frames. If we are both travelling 40mph towards one another, then we are in different inertial frames, for whilst our speed is the same, our *velocity* is different (since our direction of travel differs); whereas, if we are both sat on a train next to one another, or both stood unmoving on a train platform, we are both in the same inertial frame.

That terminology in place, we can see how weird (22) ends up being. Normally, we think that if an event is simultaneous for me, it's simultaneous for you. Imagine we are both enthusiastic breeders of the short-lived mayfly. Further imagine that we're in the same inertial frame of reference, but spatially distant from one another. For instance, imagine that we are both in the same inertial frame of reference but that I live in Birmingham and you live in Sydney (given that the Earth rotates, we wouldn't be in precisely the same inertial frame, but ignore that detail). One evening, we are talking to one another via our phones when, coincidentally, my favourite mayfly from my collection, and your favourite mayfly from your collection, die simultaneously with one another. Here's where it gets weird. Given (22), someone travelling faster than us—that is, in an inertial frame different from our own—will report something different. Imagine someone zooming along in a spaceship which is going at almost the speed of light. They would see that the mayfly in Sydney died *after* the one in Birmingham (or, if they were travelling in the opposite direction—and therefore with a different velocity—that the one in Sydney died before the one in Birmingham). And here's the rub: (22) doesn't simply say that *it seems like* these things aren't simultaneous for the person on the spaceship. This is no illusion; this is not a trick of measurement. Far from it. (22) is the claim that *it is literally true that* the mayfly deaths aren't simultaneous for the person on the spaceship, even though it's equally literally true that they are simultaneous for us. If you don't think that's weird, I don't think you've understood what I've just written. It's bonkers! It is nevertheless what physics appears to indicate.

The detailed explanation of *why* physicists think this is true won't overly concern us here. Nevertheless, very briefly, I sketch why physicists tend to think (22) is true. (22) explains, in an elegant manner, weird observations in physics concerning light's constant speed. No matter how fast you are going, were you to measure the speed of light in a vacuum, you would find it has the same speed no matter what—i.e., ~300,000kms^{-1}. And this speed never varies, no matter what inertial frame you are in. And that's *really* weird. Imagine the spaceship is going almost at the speed of light from our point of view—e.g., ~299,999.999kms^{-1}. Were the ship to fire a photon from its prow, we'd watch that photon shoot out, with the ship behind it quickly following it up. From our point of view, after one second, the photon would only have managed to advance one metre away from the prow of the ship. But we've said the speed of light is constant in every inertial frame. So, from the point of view of everyone on-board the ship, after one second, the photon would have managed to advance nearly 300 million times as far! How can *both* of those things be true? How can it, in one second, advance *both* one metre *and* 300 thousand kilometres? That seems like a contradiction!

The solution is to say that, were we to look carefully at the fast-moving spaceship, we'd see that the clocks on that spaceship had slowed down—indeed, all processes on the ship (including everyone's thought processes) will slow down. Further, the tape measures and metre rules that they use to measure distance would have contracted, becoming shorter (at least, from our point of view). The distance we see the photon covering in one second, is—according to those on the spaceship—covered in a far shorter period of time, both because their clocks are ticking more slowly and because their metre rules are shorter. These two factors always conspire to make it the case that, from the point of view of those on the spaceship, the photon will have moved roughly 300 thousand kilometres further than the ship in one second, whilst we think the two are going almost exactly the same speed.

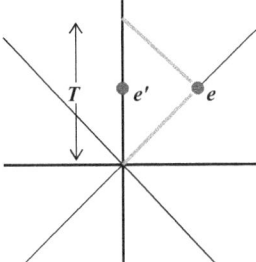

Figure 2.1 Coma Formation Relative to Earth's Inertial Frame of Reference

Einstein's insight was in explaining this 'slowing down'. He did this by *redefining* simultaneity. See Figure 2.1: the x-axis represents space; the y-axis represents time; the diagonal lines represent two beams of light moving in opposite directions (so anything travelling at 45° on my diagram would be travelling at the speed of light). Imagine that a comet is forming its coma as it approaches the sun; call that event of coma formation '*e*'. I am stood on Earth. I shine a super-powerful torch to illuminate the comet, hitting the comet with my torch beam just as *e* occurs. The beam then bounces back, so I get to see *e*. Between my firing the beam and seeing it return, a certain amount of time elapses according to my watch; call that interval *T*. Now, imagine I'm trying to calculate at what time, according to my watch, *e* took place. Einstein defines simultaneity such that *e* occurs when my watch reads ½*T*. Where *e*' is the event of my watch reading ½*T* then (given Einstein's definition) *e*' is simultaneous with *e*. And this makes a lot of sense—after all, if light travels the same speed in both directions, wouldn't that be the obvious thing to say?

Having defined simultaneity in these terms, it follows that things moving faster than us will appear to 'slow down' from our perspective. The details to show this are slightly complicated and needn't detain us here. Here, it is enough to show that—given this new definition—simultaneity varies depending upon your inertial frame. See Figure 2.2. One line represents the movement of the spaceship, almost going at the speed of light. The two dots are the different mayfly deaths—Birmingham on the left, Sydney on the right. The dotted lines represent two beams of light shined from the ship. As is clear, the beams return to the ship after different intervals. Thus, if simultaneity is defined in terms of those intervals, then those two different events are—from the reference frame of those on the spaceship—not simultaneous. So, (22) ends up being true! Given Einstein's redefinition of simultaneity, we can explain the disagreement over which things are simultaneous to which other things when in different inertial frames of reference.

That ends my explanation of why physicists think (22) is true. I won't give any more details; for our purposes, it is enough to know that physicists almost uniformly accept that (22) is true. Certainly, every test we've ever

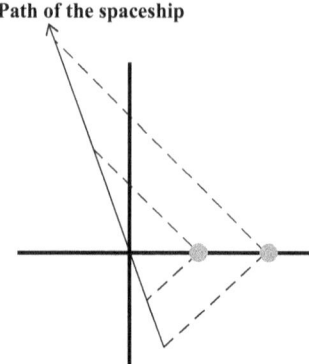

Figure 2.2 The Spaceship Seeing the Mayflies

conducted appears to have proved that Einstein was correct that (22) is true. Admittedly, you might take issue with the physics. Perhaps, you might think, things only *appear* to slow down when you're on board the spaceship. Perhaps the demise of the mayflies really are simultaneous with one another and the person on the spaceship has just got it wrong because the laws of physics mean they end up making incorrect and misleading observations. All of this might be true, and some physicists and philosophers have defended this line of argument. But I won't pursue this line of argument, since it is more interesting to focus on the metaphysical aspects of the problem than get bogged down in a (probably losing battle) with traditional physicists as to what the correct interpretation of our observations is meant to be. So, I will presume that (22) is correct and focus instead on undermining the eternalist's move from (22) being true to presentism being false. Having thus far said nothing about that move, let us turn to it now.

11.3 Relativity and Presentism

If you change what it is for one thing to be simultaneous with something else, you change what it is to be present. This is because, by definition, if some events are all present then those events are all simultaneous with one another. After all, it would be bizarre for me to think that some event was present but claim that it will happen ten minutes *after* the moment I'm at! Given this definition of presentness, if follows from (22) that not only which things are simultaneous, but which things are present will vary from one observer to another. If you and I are in the same inertial frames when we're watching our cherished mayflies die, then we can agree that both deaths occur at the present moment. But if you were to communicate with the person on the spaceship, then they will tell us that a totally different collection of things is present. For instance, they'll say that your mayfly may have just died, but will go on record as saying that mine died earlier.

Now add in presentism. Presentism says that the presently existing things are all and only the things that exist simpliciter. Now we appear to have a contradiction. From your point of view, there is no time at which your mayfly exists simpliciter whilst mine does not, but from the viewpoint of those on the spaceship this isn't the case—if they are presentists, they will say there is a point in time at which one existed simpliciter when the other did not. So, if we imagine that such a time is present, we get a contradiction about what exists simpliciter. Does my mayfly exist simpliciter? You say it does; those on the spaceship say it does not. And if this disagreement is not some sort of illusion—that is, if we are taking seriously that (22) is true—then we get the contradiction that the mayfly in Birmingham both does and does not exist simpliciter. We have arrived at the problem for presentism!

But I doubt there's any real problem here. What we should say is that existence simpliciter is relative to an inertial frame of reference. When someone tells me whether or not something exists, they can really only tell me whether or not it exists *in some specific* inertial frame.

> The special theory of relativity says that the relation of simultaneity is relative to one's inertial frame of reference—i.e., two things moving at different velocities will differ over which events are simultaneous with which other events. But that means that which things are present will differ in different inertial frames (since what is present with x is just what is simultaneous with x). So, presentism is committed to the bizarre belief that *what exists* varies depending upon what velocity you are going. And that's absurd!
>
> The eternalist thinks that things exist *regardless* of whether they are present or not—i.e., regardless of whether they are simultaneous or not, and so regardless of what inertial frame of reference you are in. So eternalism does not have the absurd upshot that presentism does when combined with the special theory of relativity.
>
> Because presentism says something absurd and eternalism does not, we should favour eternalism.

11.4 Metaphysical Completeness

We can cash out this idea in terms of *metaphysical completeness*. Imagine you have a phoneline to God, who you can call and ask questions of. Some questions are easy for God to answer. 'What is the square route of 81?', you ask; '9', God replies. But some questions are harder. Imagine you ask, 'Which is the correct side of the road to drive on?' God would be rightly befuddled. 'You haven't asked a proper question', He would say, 'You need to fill it out a bit more. Which side of the road you drive on is an incomplete question—you have to ask *relative to a specific country* which side of the road is it correct to drive on? Relative to Britain, it's the left. Relative to the USA, it's the right. Without that addition, you've not asked a proper question.'

Or imagine you ask how fast you're going. If you're in a car going at 70mph, you might think that's an easy question to answer. But again, when you ask the question, God is perturbed. 'What do you mean?', He complains, 'This question is again incomplete. You need to ask how fast are you going *relative to something*? Relative to the surface of the road, you're going at 70mph. But you're going at different velocities relative to different things. Relative to the car next to you, also travelling at 70mph relative to the road surface, you're not moving *at all*. Whilst relative to the Andromeda galaxy, which is hurtling towards you through interstellar space, you're going at 68 miles per second.' So even this question, where you think the answer is obvious, turns out to be incomplete. You only think it's a complete question because, when you ask 'How fast am I going?', this gets charitably interpreted to be asking 'How fast am I going relative to the surface of the Earth?' And *that* question, in relativising your speed to the planet Earth, is a complete question.

So, some questions are complete and some questions are incomplete. In some cases, there is a serious philosophical dispute about whether a question is complete or not. Consider colour. If I see a red ball and my colourblind friend sees it as green, we might ask the question:

(23) Who is correct? Is the ball red or green?

Answering (23) is a quintessentially philosophical activity; much ink has been spilt on what the answer to (23) is and, more importantly, whether it even *has* an answer—i.e., whether we can even make sense of some person being 'correct' about the colour of the ball, with the colourblind person being objectively 'wrong'. There are many different views on the matter. We shall contrast just two such views.

The first view says that there's a fact about which one of us is correct—presumably me and not my colourblind associate. In this case, the ball is red. I am correct and he is wrong. The question is complete and sentences of the form 'The ball is red' are also complete.

The second view takes a different tack, treating (23) as being an incomplete question rather than a complete question. It is incorrect to ask what colour the ball is and leave it at that; we can only ask what colour the ball is *relative to a given observer*. This is a conciliatory approach to the problem, for when I say the ball is red and you say it is green, we are, in a sense, both correct. Assertions of the form 'The ball is red' are incomplete and, noting this incompleteness (and thinking that colour assertions are more like assertions about velocity than assertions about square routes) is part and parcel of this second theory concerning colour.

So, there can be a philosophical debate about whether some question/answer is complete or not. My claim that existence simpliciter is to be relativised to inertial frames of reference can be best understood in terms of metaphysical completeness. Usually, we think claims about what does or doesn't exist simpliciter are complete; my claim is that, having come to believe relativity, it turns out that they are incomplete. Contrary to what you would normally think, we need to relativise existence claims to our inertial frames of reference. It is only having relativised such claims to an inertial frame that we get a metaphysically complete statement.

Having relativised the claims about what exists simpliciter, we no longer have a conflict between presentism and physics for there is no longer a contradiction concerning the mayfly's existence. Relative to our inertial frame, you are correct to say that the Birmingham mayfly exists simpliciter. Relative to the spaceships's inertial frame, observers are correct to say that it doesn't. And just as it makes no sense to ask who is 'really' correct about how fast something is going or which side of the road you should drive on, it makes no sense to ask whether you are 'really' correct about the mayfly existing simpliciter, as opposed to not existing simpliciter.

This claim that existence simpliciter is relativised to inertial frames is deeply weird. Imagine I'm on the phone to God again. It seems natural for Him to request more information when I ask what side of the road to drive on, or how fast the Earth is going, or, perhaps, even what colour an object is. But when I ask things like 'Do you exist?' or 'Does the Eiffel Tower exist?', it seems very weird for God to come back with 'I don't know—how fast are you going and in what direction?' Intuitively, my speed and direction of travel should make no difference to what things exist! But, if I am correct, then only once God has those facts to hand can He determine my inertial frame and answer my question.

So, the theory we end up with is utterly bizarre—so bizarre that you might worry that it isn't believable. Given that, above, I said we shouldn't believe genuine modal realism because it was so absurd, you might accuse me of hypocrisy; for here I am, mooting a theory that entails absurdities, yet, on this occasion, I suggest you should accept it. In short, the worry is that, if I am correct that presentism requires existence to be relativised to inertial frames, then perhaps presentism is too peculiar to be believable?

But I am not being a hypocrite. I admit that it *is* peculiar. I admit that it *is* weird. Indeed, I think it comes *close* to being unbelievable. But don't blame me. Don't blame presentism. Blame Einstein! It's *his* fault that we're saying really weird things. I above said that thinking that simultaneity is relative (i.e., endorsing (22)) is a deeply weird thing to believe. Similarly, that we might watch a photon slowly outpace the prow of the spaceship whilst everyone on the spaceship watches that photon zoom off at 300 thousand kilometres per second is *prima facie* absurd. But, having assumed that physics has told us that these crazy, hard to believe, things are true, I don't think we should then baulk at believing that existence simpliciter is relative to inertial frames. The presentist believes that what exists simpliciter is intimately connected with presentness; as Einstein changes our understanding of what presentness is, we should likewise change our understanding of existence simpliciter. It's not the fault of *presentism* that you end up believing that unrestricted existential claims are incomplete; it's the fault of *relativity*. To draw the line at believing that existential claims are incomplete without relativisation to an inertial frame seems unjustified if you are already in the business of taking the physics seriously.

So, I have not argued that physics is misguided or wrong. Nothing that physicists say about relativity is incorrect. Rather, those who think presentism is inconsistent with relativity have merely failed to take the physics as seriously as they should. Einstein's lesson needn't just be one about simultaneity, but—if you're a presentist who accepts the physics—it is also one about the nature of existence. If Einstein is correct, it is unsurprising that both should be relativised to inertial frames of reference.

> It is *not* absurd to believe that whether something exists or not depends upon what velocity you are travelling at—i.e., existence *can* be relativised to inertial frames of reference. It's weird, certainly, but the weirdness is the result of believing in the special theory of relativity. Once you accept that theory, it should be no surprise—and not be strange at all!—to believe that the existence of things is relativised to inertial frames of reference.

12. Conclusion

In this chapter, I have argued that presentism is true. It proceeded by carrying out a *cost-benefit analysis* of presentism and eternalism. The benefits of presentism are that it is: (a) ontologically parsimonious, committing only to the presently existing things rather than committing to things from all times existing simpliciter; and (b) it can allow that the future is open, thus committing to fewer fundamental truths than the eternalist theory.

I have then argued that there are no appreciable costs attached to presentism. One cost which is often thought to threaten presentism is that it cannot meet the demands of the correct relationship between truth and reality. *Vis-à-vis* that cost, I argued that the correct relationship was not truthmaking but metaphysical explanation. I then argued that presentism could nevertheless respect that relationship.

The second threat to presentism is from Einstein's theory of relativity. I argued that the correct lesson of relativity is that we should relativise existence simpliciter to inertial frames. That's weird, but no weirder than accepting the relativity of simultaneity in the first place.

Since presentism has benefits compared to eternalism and incurs no costs, we should endorse presentism and believe that only the presently existing things exist simpliciter.

This chapter has defined two theories:

Presentism: Only presently existing things exist simpliciter.
Eternalism: Things that exist in the past, present, and future all exist simpliciter.

The main argument of this chapter is that you should believe presentism because (a) it is to be preferred because it commits to fewer things than eternalism (i.e., only the presently existing things rather than things from all times) and (b) there is no reason to prefer eternalism.

In defence of (b), I have argued that the truthmaking argument is not a reason to prefer eternalism; nor are issues regarding metaphysical explanation. Finally, I have laid out the standard argument for preferring eternalism in light of the physical theory of relativity. I agree that, given relativity, presentists have to say weird things, but place all the blame for that on the theory of relativity, not presentism. So, relativity is not a reason to prefer eternalism.

I have also advanced a second argument for presentism. Presentists can believe the future is 'open' and indeterminate; eternalists cannot. If you believe the future is open, then you can believe in fewer fundamental truths than someone who believes the future is closed. Believing in fewer fundamental truths is a good thing, so a presentist who is an open-future theorist is on better footing than an eternalist. So, we should prefer an 'open-future' presentism to eternalism.

Part II

First Round of Replies

Chapter 3

Past and Future Do Not Exist
Reply to Kristie Miller

Nikk Effingham

Contents

1. Introduction 99
2. Change 100
3. Direction, Asymmetry, and Explanation 109
4. A Bad Presentist Explanation 114
5. A Better Presentist Explanation 115
6. Back to the Open Future 119
7. Conclusion 122

1. Introduction

Like many philosophical debates, the debate in the ontology of time can be divided up in different ways. In Chapter 1, Kristie divided it up one way; in Chapter 2, I divided it up in another. I compared presentism to eternalism; Kristie compared dynamic views of time to the block universe theory.

Both theories bear on the question of this book as to whether tomorrow exists. The block universe theory entails eternalism—indeed, traditionally, the eternalist accepts that time isn't dynamic and that the block universe theory is true. So, if either eternalism or the block universe theory is true, then the outposts on Mars and Barack Obama's great-great-great-great granddaughter all exist (as do the dinosaurs and Napoleon and so on).

Similarly, there are dynamic theories whereby presentism is false and things from the past/future exist. There is 'growing block theory', whereby the past and present exist simpliciter but not the future. And there is 'moving spotlight theory', whereby eternalism is true, but some time is nevertheless 'metaphysically privileged' in some fashion.

But little is lost by treating this debate as being just between the dynamic-presentist and the block universe theorist. So, for the sake of simplicity, I will assume that the only dynamic theory in town is presentism and that the only eternalist theory we should consider is a block universe theory. Henceforth, I will only talk of presentism vs. block universe theory.

This chapter cannot discuss all of the arguments put forward in Chapter 1 in favour of the block universe theory. However, in some cases, no discussion is needed, since I broadly speaking agree with Kristie. For instance, I don't think

DOI: 10.4324/9781003105664-5

our phenomenology indicates that the world is tensed or that presentism is true—we experience happiness, joy, and loss, but it seems bizarre to me to think that I 'experience' the flow of time. Similarly, I don't think there is any conflict between free will and the block universe theory (and I think this for, roughly, the same reasons as Kristie).

That said, this chapter focuses on just two of the arguments presented in Chapter 1. The first is the response to the *basic change argument* that the block universe theory is incompatible with there being change. I argue that the block universe theory can indeed allow for change, but that it doesn't allow for the right flavour of change; where our intuitions call for Pepsi, the block universe theory delivers only a supermarket own-brand. The second argument I will discuss is Kristie's *argument from the explanation of asymmetries*. I will argue that presentism can explain the asymmetries just as well as block universe theory—indeed, in precisely the same way that the block universe theory does.

2. Change

2.1 The Basic Change Argument

The basic change argument against the block universe theory is straightforward:

(1) If the block universe theory is true, things would not change.
(2) Things change.

Therefore:

(3) The block universe theory is false.

Given my assumption that either presentism or the block universe theory is true, it follows that presentism is true and tomorrow does not exist.

Miller's response is a solid one: distinguish two different definitions for 'things change' such that, given one definition, (1) is true and (2) is false whilst, given the alternative definition, (2) is true and (1) is false. Either way, the argument is unsound and it only proves convincing to those who miss the equivocation.

It's worthwhile recapping the two definitions. Start with the definition whereby, given the block universe theory, nothing changes. Given this definition, things only change when the entirety of what unrestrictedly exists differs from one time to another. I introduced *states of affairs* in my opening chapter and they are an excellent device for cashing out what this involves. Recall the idea: In addition to material objects existing (e.g., the Burj Khalifa or Barack Obama), there are states of affairs (e.g., the state of affairs of the Burj Khalifa being 2,722' tall or Obama being 6' tall). This first understanding of 'things change' is that there is change if and only if the states of affairs that exist simpliciter change over time:

(4) 'Things change' is true if and only if there are two distinct times, t^- and t^+, such that the states of affairs which exist simpliciter at t^- are different from those states of affairs that exist simpliciter at t^+.

There are two types of states of affairs: those about tensed matters and those about tenseless matters. Tensed states of affairs are states of affairs like:

S_1: The state of affairs that Barack Obama is presently 6' tall.
S_2: The state of affairs that Barack Obama was 4' tall 53 years ago.

Presentists say that the only states of affairs are tensed states of affairs. (Or, at least, they say that the states of affairs about the physical universe are all tensed; perhaps there are tenseless states of affairs like 2 and 3 adding up to 5, but we can set aside such states of affairs as being beside the point for our purposes.) The presentist will say that, as of the time that I am writing this book, S_1 and S_2 exist. But they did not always exist. Earlier, there were different states of affairs. For instance, 53 years ago (in 1968 AD), the following states of affairs existed instead of S_1 and S_2:

S_3: The state of affairs that Barack Obama will be 6' tall in 53 years' time.
S_4: The state of affairs that Barack Obama is presently 4' tall.

Given presentism, at one time, S_1 and S_2 exist and S_3 and S_4 do not; at an earlier time, S_3 and S_4 exist and S_1 and S_2 do not. So, what states of affairs there are changes—if they didn't change, then both S_1 and S_4 would exist at the same time, which would be contradictory (for, unless Obama has used a time machine to visit his younger self, he cannot be *both* 4' and 6' tall at the present moment of time). Thus, given (4), things change according to presentism. (Note that those presentists who think the future is open will deny that S_3 existed 53 years ago. This is also beside the point, since such a presentist nevertheless agrees that the states of affairs are changing.)

The block universe theorist will deny that what states of affairs there are changes. The block universe theorist believes only in tenseless states of affairs—e.g.,:

S_5: The state of affairs that, in 1968, Barack Obama is 4' tall.
S_6: The state of affairs that, in 2021, Barack Obama is 6' tall.

The block universe theorist will say that S_5 and S_6 both exist simpliciter (and, unlike with S_1 and S_4, there's no contradiction in that). That they exist simpliciter is an unchanging fact: right now, S_5 and S_6 both exist; next year, S_5 and S_6 will both exist; last year, S_5 and S_6 both existed. At *any* time you care to mention, S_5 and S_6 both exist. And the same will be said of all of the other tenseless states of affairs. Thus, given the block universe theory, which states of affairs there are will never alter. Given (4), things don't change according to the block universe theory.

There is then a second definition of 'things change', one that allows for things to change even if the block universe theory is true:

(5) 'Things change' is true if and only if there is something, x, some predicate, F, and two distinct times, t^- and t^+, such that x is F at t^- and x is not F at t^+.

It's not hard to see how (5) allows for things to change, even given the block universe theory. Everyone agrees that how things are at different regions of *space* varies from place to place. For instance, the planet Earth is grass-covered in some areas (e.g., my local parkland) and sandy and arid in other areas (e.g., the red sand dunes of the Gibson desert in Australia). So, the Earth's properties vary from place to place. Block universe theorists are driven by the belief that time is a lot like space. So, the block universe theorist will say that, if things are spread out across time and have varying properties at those different times, then their properties vary from time to time. And properties varying from time to time *just is change*, given (5). For example, consider Barack Obama. He is spread out across time and has different properties at different times. At 1968, he is 4' tall. At 2021, he is 6' tall. So, the block universe theorist believes that the right-hand side of (5) is true; given (5), things *do* change, according to the block universe theorist. (Things will also change, according to the presentist, who likewise agrees that the properties of things are different at different times.)

So, which of (4) and (5) is the 'correct' definition of 'Things change'? I think that's a bad question, and the block universe theorist will probably agree. Sometimes what words mean is *contextual*. Consider the word 'tall'. What that word means can change from context to context. If I'm trying to get onto a roller coaster ride that my five-year-old niece is too short to go on, then I *am* tall. If I try out for the Los Angeles Lakers basketball team, I am *not* tall. It seems quite reasonable to me that 'Things change' is contextual in the same way; in some cases, (4) is the correct definition whilst in others it is (5). The block universe theorist will say that, in any context where you believe things change, then (5) is the salient definition, not (4). Certainly, it's wrong to think that (4) is somehow obviously true and wrong to think that there's something obviously defective about (5). Think back to what I said in my first chapter about one way to decide whether something is intuitive or not: Imagine what my mother would say. If I asked her to tell me which of (4) and (5) was true, I doubt that she would have a firm belief either way that one of them is the 'correct' definition and the other one is 'incorrect'. (Feel free to try this on your own mother, father, or other person you trust to have common-sense views unsullied by studying academic philosophy.)

I agree with Kristie that this response to the basic argument from change is sufficient. We should not believe that the block universe theory has a problem with change on these grounds. But that does not mean there are not more sophisticated reasons in the same ballpark for thinking that the block universe theory has a problem.

2.2 Disparate Types of Change

I concede that things change, given the block universe theory. My worry is that, whilst things change, given the block universe theory, they nevertheless don't change *in the right kind of way*. It is not the intuition that 'things change' which the block universe theorist fails to respect, but a *different* intuition, namely:

(6) Spatial change and temporal change are disparate—i.e., they are different in some metaphysically relevant way.

Before moving on to why the block universe theory fails to respect (6), first consider two arguments in favour of believing (6).

The first argument is an *appeal to intuition*. To show that (6) is intuitively true, I will give examples of some types of change and compare them to one another in order to show that spatial and temporal change are disparate. Consider four such examples.

The first example is:

(7) Barack Obama changed from being 4' tall in 1968 to being 6' tall in 2020.

(7) is a case of temporal change (that is, a case where something 'changes over time').

But it is not the only type of change. There can be cases where things change in the merely spatial dimension. Consider my second example. Imagine a river that starts out thin as it descends down the mountain it is sourced from. It meanders its way across the land and then opens out into the sea. Where the river mouth meets the sea, it widens. In such a case we might say:

(8) The river changes from being thin to being wide.

Turn to a third example. Australia is an arid desert in some places and an urban sprawl in others. We might say:

(9) Australia changes from urban sprawl to arid desert as you move across it.

Spatial and temporal change are not the only types of change. As a final example, consider the natural number series—i.e., 1, 2, 3, 4, 5 . . . As you move along that series, you will encounter prime numbers. At the start of the sequence, the prime numbers are quite common. As you progress, the frequency of prime numbers decreases as more and more numbers tend to separate them. For instance, there are just over 78,000 prime numbers in the first million numbers, but only around 70,000 in the next million, and fewer than 68,000 in the million after that. And this decrease continues as you consider greater and greater numbers. So, a mathematician might say:

(10) The natural number series changes such that there are fewer and fewer prime numbers as you progress along it.

(7)–(10) are all true propositions about change. But it's clear that they deal with different *types* of change. Certainly, (8), (9), or (10) are not propositions about temporal changes; for instance, given (5), 'Things change' would not be true in virtue of any of (8), (9), or (10), whilst 'Things change' is true in virtue of (7) being true. So, by their own lights, the block theorist should think that, if those propositions are about change, then they are about different types of change than the change involved in Obama getting taller. And that seems right to me; it seems weird to think that the sort of change that is described by (10), whereby the abstract number sequence changes as you move along it, is the same sort of phenomenon described by (7), whereby Obama changes height over time. Whilst these things may be *related*, they are *disparate*. And once you have accepted that there are different types of change—that is, accepted that temporal change is different from the change in frequency of prime numbers in the natural number series—I think it's intuitive that (8) and (9), which concern spatial change, are similarly disparate from (7).

I can bolster this with my second argument in favour of (6). The uses of 'change' in (8)–(10) are *polysemous*. To understand polysemy, first we should understand 'homonyms'. One word is a homonym of another word if they express different concepts but correspond to the same vocal sound. For example, the word 'bank' refers to two different things—i.e., a place where you stick your money, as well as the edge of a river. Other examples of homonyms include 'bat' or 'Pole'. In the case of these examples, the concepts picked out by the homonyms are distinct concepts and (presumably) it is an accidental fact that 'Pole' refers both to a wooden rod and a person from Poland. They are 'accidental homonyms'. But not every homonym is like this. Some homonyms refer to related concepts and there is an explanation for why those concepts are both expressed by the same vocal sound. Call such (non-accidental) homonyms 'polysemous'. Consider two examples of polysemous words.

> *Example one:* 'Face' can refer to the front of a creature's head and it can refer to a side of a cube or the front of a building.

Example two: 'Mouth' can refer to the hole in my face which I use for eating and talking as well as a portion of a river or the entrance to a cave.

In both examples, whilst the same vocal sound is being used to refer to different concepts, those concepts are nevertheless related (in a way that wooden rods and Polish people, or places to store money and places where stoats live, are unrelated). Indeed, that's *why* we've ended up using the same word for both things. We call the face of a building its 'face' because we recognise that the building is similar to a creature in some respect, such that the side facing the pavement is relevantly similar to a creature's face. It is precisely because of that similarity that both get called 'face'. Similarly, the English language has developed such that a cave mouth is a 'mouth' because we recognised that there was a similarity between caves and creatures, and a similarity between their entrances and the gaping holes we use for eating and breathing.

In cases of polysemy, one usage of the word is the 'literal' usage. When we use 'face' to apply to a part of a creature's head, or 'mouth' to apply to the orifice it eats with, that is the literal usage of that term. It is what we originally dubbed those things—they are 'literally' faces and mouths. Those words can then also be used metaphorically, in the polysemous usage, whereby that second usage is parasitic on the literal usage. When we use 'face' to apply to buildings or 'mouth' to apply to cave entrances, that is a metaphorical use of 'face' and 'mouth'; we only use those words in that way because we believe building sides and cave entrances to be analogous to the face and mouth of a creature.

(7)–(10) all feature the word 'change', and they are all picking out somewhat similar phenomena—in (7)–(10), 'change' is functioning polysemously. In (7), 'change' is picking out the concept of 'temporal change'; it is this usage that is the 'literal' usage. To say Obama changed his height is to say that he has *literally* changed his height. In the other examples, this is not the case. This is starkest in (10), where the frequency of prime numbers change. It seems obvious to me that this is a metaphorical use of the word 'change', rather than a literal use. Whilst Obama literally changes, the number series is 'literally changeless'. The properties of the number series are timelessly fixed and static; how they were last week, they are this week; a mathematician in ancient Greece will find the number series to be exactly as we find it today. At best, the number series can only *metaphorically* change and alter. So, on pain of contradiction, 'change' cannot be referring to the *same* concept in (7) and (10). It is instead referring to a related concept. 'Change', as it appears in (7) and (10), is polysemous; its appearance in (10) is parasitic on its appearance in (7); it is its appearance in (7) which is the literal use and its appearance in (10) which is the metaphorical use.

Now turn to (8) and (9). 'Change' features in both of them. Again, though, I contend that, whilst they mean a concept *similar* to that picked out by the occurrence of 'change' in (7) (and, indeed, similar to the concept referred to by the occurrence of 'change' in (10)), it *is not the same* concept. The sort of change we are talking about in (8) and (9) is not the same sort of change we are talking about in (7). And, again, it seems to me that the 'change' we are talking about in (8) and (9) is a metaphorical spin on the literal change that Obama undergoes by getting taller. Australia's changing to become arid as you move from east to west is *similar to* Obama's growing taller over time. It is analogous to it. But—make no mistake—it is not the same phenomenon.

It is the phenomenon of polysemy that best explains why these sentences are similar, rather than its being the case that there's a single univocal concept of 'change' that they all share. Once we are acquainted with the idea of polysemy (as we are in cases involving the words 'face' and 'mouth') it seems to me unshakeable that (7)–(10) involve exactly such examples. This bolsters the appeal to intuition for thinking that (6) is true.

Having made my case for thinking that (6) is true, I can turn to explaining why the block universe theory conflicts with (6). To get our heads around that argument, we first need in place the idea of the block theoretic universe being a *spatiotemporal* whole, rather than a *spatial* whole. Our universe has three spatial dimensions (up/down, left/right, backwards/forwards). It also has one dimension of time (past/future). Spatiotemporally speaking, it therefore has four dimensions; from some imaginary God's-eye view of the cosmos, God would see it as a four-dimensional whole.

It's easiest to get your head around this idea by first considering a universe with fewer spatial dimensions. Such universes are called flatlands. A flatland universe has two, rather than three, spatial dimensions. It is a flat plane. If sentient creatures lived upon it, they would be two-dimensional beings, such as circles or squares. Nevertheless, a flatland universe is three-dimensional; for, whilst it only has two dimensions *of space*, it also has one *of time*. From the God's-eye view outside of the cosmos, God would see flatland as an extended three-dimensional object.

A further flatland example will help. Consider one of the inhabitants of flatland, Prof Circle. Throughout her life, she is—spatially speaking—circular. Like a human, who starts off small and grows larger, she starts off life as a dot and then grows to be an ever-bigger circle. But whilst she is spatially circular, from God's viewpoint, Prof Circle is a cone; she is stretched out across time, such that every slice of her is a circle. (Similarly, Mr Square would be spatially a square at every point in his life but, from the God's-eye view, would be a pyramid.)

The block universe theorist says the same can be said of our world. It's impossible for us to picture it in our minds, since we cannot picture four-dimensional shapes in our heads. But in the same way that Prof

Circle could figure out what, in theory, it would mean for God to see her as a cone, we should be able to get our heads around what it is for the world to be a four-dimensional object, even if we can't literally picture it in our minds.

(If you think that it's impossible to understand something without picturing it in your head, bear in mind that some people have a condition called 'aphantasia' and cannot picture *anything at all* in their minds—such people are, in fact, quite common and you are likely to know a handful. People with aphantasia nevertheless still manage to understand the same concepts as everyone else. So, even if you can't *picture* four-dimensional objects in your mind's eye, you should nevertheless be able to still come to understand what it is to be one.)

Keep with the metaphor of what God sees from outside of the cosmos. Think of how God sees me. According to the block universe theorist, I am a four-dimensional object, stretched out across time as well as space. From God's view, this object has varying qualities at different places in spacetime. Just as Prof Circle varied across time, such that at each time her slices were increasingly bigger circles, I vary across time such that at each time my slices are different. My slices from 1980 are childlike and small; my slices from the 2020s are older, taller, and come with a beard.

But this means there's a new type of change. Not only is there temporal change and spatial change (and abstract change) but there is also *spatiotemporal change*. God sees the spatiotemporal whole that is Nikk Effingham and further sees that—in one spatiotemporal direction—that whole changes from being childlike to being adultlike; whereas, if God focuses just on one slice of Nikk Effingham—e.g., the slice of my head that currently exists—He will see that it goes from being almost hairless on the scalp to being fairly hairy on the chin. Both such changes are just variations in spatiotemporal wholes; both such changes are spatiotemporal changes. The first change is also a temporal change; so, temporal change is just a species from the genus of spatiotemporal change. The second change is a spatial change; so, spatial change is also a species from the genus of spatiotemporal change. Metaphysically speaking, they are not disparate; they are just the same phenomenon (i.e., spatiotemporal change), differently conceived. The only difference is the direction along which we trace the change. Temporal changes are traced along one direction of spacetime and merely spatial changes are traced along another. In the same way that spatial variation in an east-west direction is no different, metaphysically speaking, from spatial variation in a north-south direction, if temporal and spatial change are as described, then they are not metaphysically disparate. In conclusion, given block universe theory, (6) is false.

The presentist, however, will say no such thing. Keep with the God metaphor. A God's-eye view of a presentist cosmos is not that of a four-dimensional spatiotemporal manifold. Instead, God would see only a three-dimensional universe as it presently is; God would see nothing of the past and future states of the universe. With spatial change, God would be able to simultaneously see the different states of the object. God could see that my head changes from being hairless to hairy. And when God sees this, He would simultaneously see a hairless scalp and a hairy chin; in attending to one, He wouldn't be unable to see the other. But with temporal change, things would be very different. God has seen me grow from being childlike to adultlike, but, attending to my current adult state, He cannot see my childlike states. On the presentist picture, temporal change is radically different from spatial change.

This concludes my argument against the block universe theory. To recap: I agree with Kristie that we cannot simply say that there is no change, given the block universe theory. However, intuitively we believe that temporal change and spatial change are quite different things. The block universe theorist says that temporal and spatial change are ultimately very similar things. Thus, whilst the block universe theory might allow for change, it nevertheless rallies against some intuition we have about change. Since presentism does not rally against that intuition, that's a point in presentism's favour and a black mark against the block universe theory.

I am *not* saying that this argument is, by itself, decisive. Something which is intuitively true may nevertheless turn out not to be the case. Our intuitions are not sacrosanct! Philosophical arguments (and physical evidence) may convince us that things we intuitively believe are false. So, this discussion about the block universe theory and change does not 'seal the deal' in favour of presentism; the block universe theorist could simply accept that (6), whilst intuitive, is false.

But (6) being false is nevertheless a *cost* that must be taken into account when trying to decide which theory is true. Moreover, it bears noting that exactly the same could have been said about the *original* basic argument from change. If the block universe theory had entailed that there was no such thing as change, the block universe theorist could have 'taken it on the chin' and accepted that, counterintuitive as it sounds, we live in a changeless universe. So, if the block universe theorist was worried about the original argument, I don't see why they wouldn't also worry about (6) being false.

> I agree that the block universe theorist can allow that things change. But the block universe theorist says that things changing over time is the same sort of phenomenon as things varying their qualities across space. Intuitively, these things are *not* the same sort of phenomena; intuitively, they are 'metaphysically disparate'. Presentism correctly says that these types of change are of a different character and that changing properties over time is very different from changing properties across space. So, presentism better captures change than eternalism does.

3. Direction, Asymmetry, and Explanation

The second of Kristie's arguments from Chapter 1 to which I will respond is the *argument from explanation for the block*. I briefly recap the argument and then argue that it's not a problem for the presentist, for reasons very similar to those I advanced for thinking that relativity is not a problem.

There are certain temporal asymmetries. For instance, there is an epistemic asymmetry. We can know things about the past and present, but not the future—or, at least, what we know about the future we clearly know in a different way from how we know things about the past and present. There is also a causal asymmetry. We can influence and causally affect what will come in the future, but—unless you have a time machine—we cannot affect the past.

With those asymmetries in mind, Kristie argues in Chapter 1 that:

(11) Nothing about time being tensed explains these asymmetries.

(12) The block universe theory has the resources to explain these asymmetries.

Given (11) and (12), Kristie says that we should favour the block universe theory.

I deny neither (11) nor (12). (11) is true. Nothing about time being tensed or presentism being true explains why I might only know about the past and present or why backwards causation is not routinely possible. Similarly, I agree that (12) is true. The block universe theorist *does* have the resources to explain the asymmetries. Nevertheless, this is no argument for the block universe theory. This is because the presentist/dynamic theorist *also* has the resources to explain the asymmetries—it's just that the explanation has nothing to do with time being tensed. Similarly, the block universe theorist's explanation of the asymmetries ultimately has nothing to do with time being tenseless!

Consider an analogous argument. Imagine you meet two scientists who believe they can explain gravity. They are both football fans (that is, 'soccer fans'). One scientist believes that Manchester United will win the season; the other scientist believes that Liverpool FC will win the season. Two things are true: first, nothing about Manchester United winning the football season explains how gravity works; second, the scientist who believes Liverpool FC will win the season can explain gravity. Nevertheless, it would be clearly erroneous to conclude anything about the likelihood of who will win the football league. After all, the scientist who believes Manchester United will win the season can *also* explain gravity—indeed, they presumably have the *same* explanation as the other scientist. Exactly the same sort of thing goes on with the presentist and the block universe theorist. A presentist can explain the asymmetries in time using the same machinery as the block universe theorist; it turns out that the explanation is neutral with regards to whether one is a presentist or not.

3.1 Entropy and Direction

To see why, consider Kristie's proposed explanation as to why there are such asymmetries around us. There, the explanation was given in terms of entropy. Entropy is a measure of how disordered a system is. For instance, if all your cutlery is in the appointed compartments in your kitchen drawer, then they are highly ordered; they are in a state of low entropy. Whereas, if I chuck your cutlery into the air and it scatters everywhere, then it is highly *dis*ordered; they are now in a higher entropy state.

The laws of nature say that the world tends to increase its entropy over time, going from low entropy states to high entropy states. It is this increase in overall entropy that explains the asymmetries. As a heuristic for this, consider the following metaphor. Imagine that God has set a compass that points in the temporal direction that causation flows. When an angel wants to know whether an event at one time causes an event at another time, they check the compass; if the compass says the first event is earlier than the second, the angel fixes causation so that the earlier event causes the later event. So, in this metaphorical story, the compass explains the causal asymmetry. (We could also tell a similar story about the epistemic asymmetry.) One day, an Evil Demon maliciously spins the compass around so now no-one knows which way is which. Now the angels are lost. Which way does causation go? One plucky angel goes to God and asks how they should figure it out for themselves. 'Aha,' says God, 'It's not too hard. Each slice of the universe has an associated amount of entropy; just point the compass so it points in the direction where you find higher entropy slices.'

So, the angels sit down and calculate the amount of disorder in each slice. In physics, entropy is measured in joules per Kelvin, or JK^{-1}. So, imagine three slices: one has a bajillion JK^{-1}; another has 2 bajillion JK^{-1}; the third has 3 bajillion JK^{-1}. In that case, the angels would know that the compass should point from the first slice, through the second slice, and to the third slice.

The compass metaphor is particularly apt here. If you pick a compass direction, walk in that direction, *and keep going*, then you will eventually arrive in a place where your compass *reverses direction*. For instance, if you take the northwards direction and keep walking in that direction, never once consulting the compass again, then, once you have gone past the North Pole, you will now be heading south. So it might be with time. As explained in Chapter 1, physics says that the universe might be such that, from *our point of view*, the future is one way, but, in the future, there exist strange people who appear to live their lives in reverse. From the point of view of those people, futurewards is in the opposite direction, and it is *we* who are living backwards. If time's direction is like a compass, then *both* people are correct, from their own point of view; we just have to understand that which direction counts as the future is a fact relative to the people in question.

(As a note, *some* physical processes might not be reversible in this way. They are obscure processes you probably haven't heard of, such as 'neutral kaon decay'. In this book, I will set aside discussion of them. If you are interested in those processes and why some philosophers think they don't help with the debate, then I suggest reading Maudlin (2002).)

In this chapter, I will assume that Kristie is correct and that it is because of entropy that we observe the asymmetries that we do. That we remember the past and not the future is just a function of the fact that the future is more highly disordered than the past. Similarly, that we can influence the future and not the past is also a function of the variation of entropy across spacetime. I won't recap Kristie's argument for this. This is not because it is uncontroversial—some people believe the asymmetries are a result of other things—but I am not going to pursue such lines of argument here. Instead, for the purpose of argument, I will assume that Kristie is correct and that the entropic explanation of the asymmetries is likewise correct.

In the remainder of this chapter, I will explain why my presentist theory *agrees* that the asymmetries are the result of increasing entropy. Indeed, my presentist theory will ape everything that the block universe theorist has to say.

3.2 Two Block Theoretic Explanations

Before turning to that presentist theory, we must first consider a second block theoretic view, one that tries to explain the asymmetries but without using entropy.

Consider a world consisting of just four instants—i.e., four 'slices' of spacetime. (In reality, spacetime consists of infinitely many such slices, but for simplicity, we will consider a world with just these four; similarly, relativistic physics makes it difficult to talk about spacetime being made up of 'slices', but we will ignore that detail as well—things are tricky enough as they are without having to factor relativity into the mix!) Call the four slices of spacetime s_1, s_2, s_3, and s_4. Rather than roping in entropy, the block theorist might just say that the instants are related by tenseless earlier-than and later-than relations. The fundamental facts describing such a world would be something like:

Slices s_1, s_2, s_3 and s_4 exist simpliciter.
s_1 is earlier than s_2, s_3, and s_4.
s_2 is earlier than s_3 and s_4.
s_3 is earlier than s_4.

These facts would, indeed, explain the asymmetries—no mention of entropy is required! Going back to the angel metaphor, the angels could see which way the compass was pointing: when the angel is on the first slice, from their point of view, the future lies towards s_2, s_3, and s_4 (in that order). That is where they point the compass, and that is how they decide which way causation flows.

But something is wrong with this explanation. The above fundamental facts contain an *asymmetric component*. The relation 'earlier than' is an asymmetric relation; for, if x is earlier than y, then y is not earlier than x. If this asymmetric temporal relation appeared in the fundamental facts that explained the causal asymmetry, then it would not be a satisfying explanation, for all that would have happened is that we would have moved the bump around under the carpet. We may have explained the asymmetry of influence and the epistemic asymmetry, but we would have done so only by inserting a third one—i.e., the asymmetry of the tenseless relations between instants. We'd be left with the further question of explaining *that* asymmetry.

So, a more sophisticated block universe theorist must avoid talking about tenseless relations like 'earlier than' and 'later than'. They will instead talk about a more 'neutral' relation; call it the relation of *temporal separation*. Where the cruder block universe theorist says that an instant in 1066 AD is 955 years earlier than some instant in 2021 AD, the more sophisticated theorist instead says that, at the fundamental level, they are 955 years separated—and that is all they say of the *fundamental* level.

To see why this helps, consider spatial separation and spatial direction. Imagine a table that is one metre away from a chair. To what extent is the table spatially separated from the chair? The answer is easy: the chair and the table are one metre apart. But now consider the following question: Is the table to the left or the right of the chair? Unless I give you more information, that's an absurd question to ask; after all, if one is stood on one side of the pair of objects, the table is to the left, whilst if one is stood on the other side, it's to the right. So, facts about spatial direction are (a) relative to an agent and (b) derived from facts about where that agent is stood, in combination with facts about spatial separation. Spatial separation itself doesn't come in 'left and right flavours'; it has no 'innate direction' to it.

When it comes to time, we intuitively think time is quite unlike space in this regard; that is, we think time does have an innate direction, a 'forwardness' and 'backwardness' to it. But—as Kristie explained in Chapter 1 and as the possibility of strange people from the future who live their lives 'backwards' shows—physics has apparently shown us that we are wrong. The 'pastwards/futurewards' of time is precisely like left and right in the spatial case. Physics has shown that temporal separation lacks any innate direction, just like spatial separation.

So, like spatial separation, temporal separation is not asymmetric. Once you have the facts about temporal separation, you only get the *order* of the different slices of the universe. For instance, in our toy example, the fundamental facts would be:

> Slice s_1 is temporally separated from s_2 by one unit, from s_3 by two units, and from s_4 by three units.

Slice s_2 is temporally separated from s_1 by one unit, from s_3 by one unit, and from s_4 by two units.
Slice s_3 is temporally separated from s_1 by two units, from s_2 by one unit, and from s_4 by one unit.
Slice s_4 is temporally separated from s_1 by three units, from s_2 by two units, and from s_3 by one unit.

So, we know the order of the slices is:

$s_1 \quad s_2 \quad s_3 \quad s_4$

But those facts don't give the series any *direction*. That is, we could equally represent the order as:

$s_4 \quad s_3 \quad s_2 \quad s_1$

For the series to have a direction, entropy must enter the picture and we move to the block theoretic explanation that Kristie proposes. Each slice has a certain amount of entropy. So, there are facts like:

Slice s_1 exists simpliciter and has an entropic value of 1 bajillion JK^{-1}.
Slice s_2 exists simpliciter and has an entropic value of 1 bajillion+1 JK^{-1}.
Slice s_3 exists simpliciter and has an entropic value of 1 bajillion+2 JK^{-1}.
Slice s_4 exists simpliciter and has an entropic value of 1 bajillion+3 JK^{-1}.

Now the block universe theorist can explain in which direction time runs. Stood at s_1, time runs towards s_4, for that is the direction in which entropy increases. Where > marks the direction of time from one individual slice to another, the series can (from s_1's point of view) be represented as:

$s_1 > s_2 > s_3 > s_4$

Thus, the combination of facts about temporal separation and facts about entropy jointly explain why time appears to be moving forwards, why it's impossible for me to meet Napoleon but not impossible for me to meet Donald Trump, and why I know the name of my first girlfriend but don't know the names of my great-great-grandchildren.

This completes my version of the block theoretic explanation of the asymmetries. The take-home message is that a simple version of block universe theory—one which holds that the universe consists of slices connected by the asymmetrical tenseless 'earlier than' relation—must be supplanted by a revised block universe theory relying on a symmetric relation of temporal separation. The asymmetry of one thing being earlier than another is not fundamental, but is instead a derivative fact that drops out of the facts about entropy. This insight will be crucial when we come to consider the presentist version of this theory.

We explain the different asymmetries (the asymmetry of influence and the epistemic asymmetry) using entropy. At different times, there are different levels of entropy; 'the future' lies in the direction in which entropy increases whilst 'the past' is just the temporal direction in which entropy decreases. These entropic facts explain the asymmetries we see around us—e.g., why past events cause present events and not vice versa, or why we cannot know about future events but can know about past events.

The block universe theory can allow for this. Presentism (allegedly) cannot. The allegation will be that presentists have to think there is some special objective fact about which temporal direction is the future—a fact that holds regardless of anything to do with entropy. Were that the case, presentism would commit to facts that go beyond what our best physics tells us. That extraneous commitment is a bad thing and so we would have a reason to prefer eternalism.

4. A Bad Presentist Explanation

Before I begin my discussion of how presentism can escape this problem, a quick disclaimer: For the time being, I will assume that the future is closed—i.e., that propositions about the future are either true or false, rather than being indeterminate. In Chapter 2, I toyed with the idea that the future is open and that propositions about the future might be indeterminate. I will return to toying with that idea below. But to get to that stage, we first need to simplify things and so I will assume that the future is closed. This section and the next explain how presentists who believe the future is closed can account for the asymmetries and the direction of time. This section details a presentist explanation that doesn't work; the next section improves on it, giving an explanation that does work.

My overall claim is that the presentist can ape whatever the block universe theorist says about explaining the asymmetries. They cannot, however, say exactly the same since, given presentism, the non-present slices do not exist simpliciter and, thus, they cannot believe in the fundamental facts about temporal separation that the block universe theorist accepts. But they get to say something suitably similar.

Both theories agree that one of the slices exists simpliciter; namely, the presently existing slice of the universe. Unlike the block universe theorist, the presentist denies that past and future slices exist simpliciter. They don't deny, though, that there are facts concerning what those slices were like or will be like. For instance, if slice s_2 was present, then my imaginary presentist might believe the following were fundamental facts:

It was the case (one unit of time ago) that s_1 existed and had an entropic value of 1 bajillion JK^{-1}.
Slice s_2 exists simpliciter and has an entropic value of 1 bajillion+1 JK^{-1}.
It will be the case (in one unit of time) that slice s_3 exists and it will have an entropic value of 1 bajillion+2 JK^{-1}.
It will be the case (in two units of time) that slice s_4 exists and it will have an entropic value of 1 bajillion+3 JK^{-1}.

These facts are just the block universe theorist's facts parsed into a tensed way of speaking rather than a tenseless way of speaking (which—for the presentist—is the more metaphysically perspicuous way of speaking). Were these facts true, they would explain the two asymmetries of epistemic access and causal influence.

But this presentist theory is just as bad as the original version of the block universe theory we discussed in the previous section. If these were the fundamental facts, then we would be explaining those two asymmetries only by relying on facts which themselves encoded a temporal asymmetry into the fundamental nature of the universe. Just as the asymmetric 'earlier-than' relation cannot feature in the fundamental facts, the presentist is making a similar error by using asymmetric components in *their* fundamental facts. The presentist's asymmetric components are the bits reading 'It was the case that . . .' and 'It will be the case that . . .'. Given that they feature in the fundamental facts, there would be some metaphysically deep division between things having once been the case and things going to be the case. By building them into the fundamental facts, the presentist is inserting temporal asymmetry at the fundamental level. Since the aim of the game is to avoid doing exactly that, this theory is a bad theory.

5. A Better Presentist Explanation

But the presentist can deliver a better theory and avoid fundamental asymmetry by copying the block universe theorist's solution. The block universe theorist's initial, flawed, theory contained asymmetrical components; namely, the 'earlier-than' relation. Looking for a theory without such asymmetrical components, the block universe theorist revised their theory, swapping out that asymmetrical component for a 'symmetrical' component; namely, the relation of temporal separation. The presentist must do likewise, swapping out their asymmetrical components for a more pleasing symmetrical component.

The presentist's asymmetric components are 'It was the case that . . .' and 'It will be the case that . . .'. Unlike the 'earlier-than' and 'later-than' relations, those components are not relations. They are more properly called *operators*, in that they 'operate' on other propositions to result in a further, different, proposition. Consider the (presently false) proposition:

(13) Barack Obama is President of the USA.

Applying the 'It was the case that . . .' operator to it, we generate a new proposition:

(14) It was the case that Barack Obama is President of the USA.

(14) is a different proposition from (13). Indeed (14), unlike (13), is true.

The presentist must replace the 'It was the case that . . .' and 'It will be the case that . . .' operators with a new operator, one that does not have the same problems of imbuing reality with a fundamental asymmetry. We can use the 'occasionally' operator. You are already familiar with that operator. Consider propositions like:

(15) Occasionally, wars happen.
(16) Occasionally, people are born.
(17) Occasionally, people die.

(15), (16), and (17) are all true. And they are not true because the events they concern specifically lie in the future nor because the events they concern specifically lie in the past; they are true because the events they concern lie in either direction. For instance, (15) is true because there are wars in the pastwards *or* the futurewards direction.

That said, give a first pass 'formal definition' to help understand the 'occasionally' operator. Where φ stands for any proposition you care to mention, ↔ stands for the biconditional ('if and only if'), and ∨ stands for disjunction ('or'):

Occasionally φ ↔ It was the case that φ ∨ φ ∨ it will be the case that φ

Admittedly, this sketch does not quite match how we use the word 'occasionally' in natural language. For instance, in natural language, to say that something occasionally happens standardly indicates that it has happened and that it will happen again. To say 'Occasionally, the Romans invade countries' sounds strange because it will never again be the case that Caesar storms another nation. And to say 'Occasionally, the planets in our solar system are destroyed' sounds strange because it's never happened as yet that a planet nearby has been destroyed (though it will happen in a few billion years' time). But, in giving the definition that I do, I don't think we are stretching the word 'occasionally' too much and it's not that bad that those strange-sounding sentences end up being true.

Indeed, I will stretch my use of the word 'occasionally' even further. The 'It was the case that . . .' operator can be given a 'metric' whereby we say how long ago it was since the relevant proposition was true. 'It was the case 955 years ago that the Battle of Hastings took place' is (as of the time of writing) true, whilst 'It was the case 2 years ago that the Battle of Hastings took place' is not true. Similarly, the block universe theorist's relation of temporal separation has a metrical element (whereby 2021 AD and the Battle of Hastings are temporally separated by 955 years). This metrical element can be added to 'occasionally'. Call the resulting operator the 'OCC_n:' operator, where n is the metrical element (measured in years). For instance, the following is (as of 2021 AD) presently true:

(18) OCC_{955}: The Battle of Hastings is taking place.

(18) expresses, not just that the Battle of Hastings happens at some time or another, but that it happens at a point 955 years separated from the present moment. Note, though, that it doesn't say whether that's 955 years *into the future* or 955 years *into the past*. The OCC_n operator is blind when it comes to direction; it is *not* an asymmetric component.

The OCC_n operator does not quite correspond to how we use the word 'occasionally' in English; it is *similar*, but certainly not the same. That is why I have switched to using the more 'logicy-looking' presentation of 'OCC_n', rather than using some word from English. Indeed, I don't think *any* word in the English language quite expresses what OCC_n expresses. You might worry that this is a problem. But whilst the OCC_n operator doesn't exactly mirror any part of the English language, this isn't problematic for two reasons.

First, whilst the 'OCC_n' operator may be new to you, I nevertheless think you can easily get your head around it. Sometimes, philosophers ask people to understand an alien piece of terminology that has no easy explanation as to what it is. We might have in mind concepts like Heidegger's 'Dasein', Derrida's 'deconstruction', or perhaps even the concept of 'existence simpliciter' that I introduced in my original chapter. It is right to be suspicious of such concepts and make the philosophers introducing those terms work hard to explain what they mean (as I hope to have done with 'existence simpliciter'!). And if such concepts are not properly introduced, it is right to be so suspicious of them think that they should be shunned. But that is *not* what is going on with 'OCC_n'. We can straightforwardly define what 'OCC_n' means:

OCC^n: φ ↔ It was the case n years ago that φ ∨ it will be the case in n years' time that φ.

(Notice that, whilst I am helping you *understand the concept* by defining it in terms of 'It was the case that . . .' and 'It will be the case that . . .' operators, I am not suggesting that the operator itself is *reducible to* those facts. Whilst *in English*, we learn of OCC_n via those operators, at the fundamental level of metaphysics, the OCC_n operator is what is primary.)

Secondly, we should not think that the operators that feature in the fundamental facts of metaphysics must necessarily be those that feature in English. To do so would be remarkably parochial. In George Bernard Shaw's *Saint Joan*, one of the funniest exchanges is between the Inquisitor and the English chaplain pressing him to prosecute Saint Joan:

> THE CHAPLAIN. [Joan of Arc] has actually declared that the blessed saints Margaret and Catherine, and the holy Archangel Michael, spoke to her in French. That is a vital point.
> THE INQUISITOR. You think, doubtless, that they should have spoken in Latin?
> CAUCHON. No: he thinks they should have spoken in English.
> THE CHAPLAIN. Naturally, my lord.

It's funny—at least, *I* think it's funny—because it's ridiculous to think that God would necessarily speak English over and above some other language. The same thought applies here. To think that English somehow captures the fundamental nature of reality is the height of prejudice. Even if 'OCC_n' does not feature in English, that is no reason to think it cannot play a crucial role in the fundamental facts of reality.

Having established the credentials of the OCC_n operator, we can turn to how its introduction helps the presentist. Recall the position that the block universe theorists found themselves in. They had to remove the asymmetric 'earlier-than' relation and replace it with the symmetric 'temporally separated' relation. The presentist can make an analogous move. The presentist starts with the 'It was the case that . . .' and 'It will be the case that . . .' operators. They are asymmetric components of facts and must be removed. The OCC_n operator is *not* an asymmetric component and so we can solve the problem by replacing those operators with the OCC_n operator. What's sauce for the goose is sauce for the gander; if the block universe theorist can retreat to talking about temporal separation, the presentist can drop the problematic tense operators and replace them with the OCC_n operator.

Where (in the toy example of four slices) the original presentist believed the fundamental facts were facts like:

> It was the case (one unit of time ago) that s_1 existed and had an entropic value of 1 bajillion JK^{-1}.
> Slice s_2 exists simpliciter and has an entropic value of 1 bajillion+1 JK^{-1}.
> It will be the case (in one unit of time) that slice s_3 exists and it will have an entropic value of 1 bajillion+2 JK^{-1}.
> It will be the case (in two units of time) that slice s_4 exists and it will have an entropic value of 1 bajillion+3 JK^{-1}.

this new and improved presentist will say the fundamental facts are:

OCC_1: s_1 exists simpliciter and has an entropic value of 1 bajillion JK^{-1}.
Slice s_2 exists simpliciter and has an entropic value of 1 bajillion+1 JK^{-1}.
OCC_1: s_3 exists simpliciter and has an entropic value of 1 bajillion+2 JK^{-1}.
OCC_2: s_4 exists simpliciter and has an entropic value of 1 bajillion+3 JK^{-1}.

Those facts do not have any asymmetric components. And they can explain the asymmetries in exactly the same fashion as the block universe theorist. In the toy example, slice s_2 was the presently existing slice. At s_2, we can say that s_1 lies in the past because s_1 has lower entropy than s_2. Whereas s_3 lies in the future, followed further into the future by s_4, those things are true because those slices have a higher entropy. This is, more or less, *exactly* what the block universe theorist says explains the asymmetries. The presentist is just hijacking that explanation.

And, through all of this, the presentist still remains a presentist. Only the presently existing things exist simpliciter, they shall say. The things that only occasionally exist at other times do not exist simpliciter. So, slices s_1, s_3, and s_4 do not exist simpliciter (when s_2 is present) even though there are true facts about those slices. (And what makes those facts about those slices true? Well, that just takes us back to the issues of truthmaking, and of dependence of truth on reality, from Chapter 2!)

You might think it's weird to believe in a presentist theory where there's no fundamental fact of the matter about which way time is flowing. And I agree, it *is* weird to believe such a thing. But it's not weird because of anything *I've* said. It's weird because we have assumed (i) that physics says there is no empirically accessible fact of the matter about which way time 'really' flows and (ii) if a fact is not empirically accessible, then there is no such fact. The weirdness is the fault of the *physicists*. BLAME THEM!

This argument effectively mirrors that which I used for relativity. There, I said the presentist should say that what exists simpliciter is relativised to inertial frames of reference. I admitted that this was weird to believe, but then I blamed the physicists for the weirdness. I say exactly the same here. The resulting theory is weird, but that just captures the weird things the physicists tell us to already accept. If you are taking the physics seriously—if you are willing to buy into the weirdness!—then I see nothing wrong with the presentist theory we end up with.

6. Back to the Open Future

But we are not quite done. One issue remains. The prior discussion assumed that the future was closed—i.e., that propositions about the future were either true or false, not indeterminate. But, at least at one stage, I argued in Chapter 2 that the presentist might well be attracted to the future being open. If you believe that the future is open, then it looks unavoidable that reality has a temporal asymmetry at the fundamental level. Some non-present propositions would have a fixed, set truth-value, being either true or false. Other non-present propositions would have no fixed truth-value, instead being indeterminate. That is a clear metaphysical difference!

As an example, consider some propositions:

(19) OCC_{955}: The Battle of Hastings is happening.
(20) OCC_{76}: World War II is coming to an end.
(21) OCC_2: Nikk Effingham exists.
(22) OCC_{500}: There are outposts on Mars.
(23) OCC_{700}: Nikk Effingham's descendent is Galactic Emperor.

As presented in Chapter 2, the open future presentist would (at the time of my writing) say that (19), (20), and (21) are true whilst (22) and (23) are indeterminate. (19), (20), and (21) are true because it was the case, 955 years ago, that the Battle of Hastings took place; it was the case, 76 years ago, that World War II ended; it was the case, two years ago, that I was alive. (22) and (23) are indeterminate, for it might yet be that, 500 years in the future, there will be outposts on Mars, or that, 200 years after that, my great-great-grandson rules the galaxy with an iron fist. Clearly, there is an asymmetry here. If these were the fundamental facts, it would be irresistible to not think that the past corresponded to the direction where solid truth and falsity lay whilst the future was the direction in which lies indeterminacy and unsettledness. As long as we keep assuming that physics says that there is no empirically accessible temporal asymmetry at the fundamental level (and that there can be no such fact if the fact is not empirically accessible) then the open future presentist has a problem because their theory installs into the world exactly such an asymmetry.

One response would be to give up on the future being open (and I would then have to abandon one of my arguments for presentism from Chapter 1). But I think that open future presentism can still be saved, for there is one more option on the table. The presentist can say that not only are propositions about the future indeterminate, but so, too, are propositions about the past; at the fundamental level, all of (19)–(23) are indeterminate! The asymmetry at the level of fundamental reality is now removed.

This is a radical claim. Some people might complain that it is crazy to say that apparently past propositions are indeterminate, which is what this would entail. To say that it is indeterminate whether I will die in 2079 AD has merit. To say that it is indeterminate whether I was alive in 1985 AD is absurd. I was there! I *know* I was alive in 1985! Says the complainant: To think that the past is open is a step too far!

But thinking that the past is open is a natural extension of the open future thesis once you accept the weird lesson from physics that there is no fundamental temporal asymmetry. If you concede the reasonableness of the initial intuition that the future is open (which is a dialectically appropriate concession to make!), then once the physicists convince you that the world is a really weird place that has no fundamental arrow of time, you have two choices. One choice is to give up on the open future and say that the future is as closed as the past. The other choice is to instead give up on the past being closed. Given that we have taken on-board some crazy (yet true!) physical truth about the nature of time, it's not beyond the pale that we should take the second option instead of the first. Prior to accepting the physics, it might be unthinkable that the past is open, but once we have accepted the core physical insight that there is no fundamental arrow of time—once we've internalised what that weird truth really *means*—it's less clear to me that this is a problem. Effectively, physicists have not only discovered that there is no fundamental asymmetry and no fundamental direction of time, but also made the startling discovery that the past is open.

Further, even if there is some theoretical cost to thinking that the past is open, it comes with a huge corresponding benefit. Recall Chapter 2's argument for presentism on the grounds of the open future. I argued that we should be presentists because (unlike the block universe theory) presentism allows for the future to be open, and we should favour that the future is open because it means we can accept fewer fundamental facts than if the future were closed. Now that argument returns with a vengeance! Not only do we not need any fundamental facts about the future, since the past *and* the future are open, we don't need fundamental facts about *any time other than the present*! A version of presentism whereby the past and future are both open whittles the fundamental facts about reality down to just those concerning the present moment. That theory is *exceedingly* parsimonious when it comes to considering how many fundamental truths there are. I suggest that this benefit of parsimony outweighs any alleged cost of the past being open.

> When it comes to explaining asymmetries, the presentist should mimic the block universe theorist. Rather than saying that, at the fundamental level, there are facts about what was (and will be) the case, we need to introduce 'occasional' talk. What is occasionally the case is a 'direction-blind' version of what was/will be the case. At the fundamental level, there are only facts about what is occasionally the case, which includes facts about what the level of entropy occasionally is. Just like the block universe theorist says, these fundamental facts about entropy then explain the asymmetries. So—as physics demands!—there is no direction of time at the fundamental level, and the asymmetries we see and the direction of time we perceive only drop out of facts about entropy.
>
> This means revising the open-future argument for presentism from Chapter 2. We must now say open-future theorists believe that facts about the past *and*

future are open and unsettled, as well as those about the future. That the past is open is weird. But it's only weird because physics tells us time does not have a fundamental direction—if you are taking the physics seriously, you shouldn't think it all that weird at all.

7. Conclusion

There are many arguments against the block universe theory. Kristie is correct that many of these arguments are flawed. I have argued, however, that one of the critiques of the block universe theory—the argument from change—is more or less along the right lines, even if its original formulation is wrong-headed.

Chapter 1 also offered positive arguments in favour of the block universe theory. In the second half of this chapter, I have discussed the one I find most compelling: the argument from explanation. I don't think it works, but the issues concerning temporal asymmetry are nevertheless a problem for a presentist theory that allows for an open future; I've argued that a more radical presentist theory, allowing for an open past as well as an open future, solves that problem.

> I have dealt with two arguments from Chapter 1.
>
> The first argument concerns change. I have allowed that things can change, given the block universe theory. But I have argued that the *type* of change that the block theorist allows for is not in-line with our intuitions. The presentist can allow for it, though, so we have a reason to favour presentism over the block universe theory.
>
> The second argument concerns asymmetries and the direction of time. Physics tells us that, fundamentally speaking, there is no direction to time and the asymmetries that we observe only come about because of entropy. The allegation is that block universe theorists can allow for this whilst presentists cannot. I have argued that the same sorts of things that the block universe theorist says to allow for time to have no fundamental direction can be mirrored by the presentist. So, there is no reason to prefer the block universe theory over presentism in light of what physics says about the direction of time.

Chapter 4

The Past and Future Exist

Reply to Nikk Effingham

Kristie Miller

Contents

1. Introduction 123
2. The Argument From Ontological Parsimony 124
3. Truthmaking and Parsimony 129
4. The Objection From Relativity 140

1. Introduction

Chapter 2 of this book presented one argument in favour of presentism over eternalism, and hence in favour of presentism over the block universe theory (which is committed, remember, to eternalism): the argument from ontological parsimony.

In this chapter, I begin by considering that argument (section 2). There, I focus on the question of whether presentism is indeed more ontologically parsimonious than eternalism. I argue that whether it is depends on how we conceive of ontological parsimony, and that on many such conceptions presentism is not more ontologically parsimonious than eternalism.

In Chapter 2 of this book, Nikk also responded to several powerful objections to presentism: the objection from truthmaking and the objection from relativity. In section 3 of this chapter, I take up the question of whether the account of presentist-friendly truthmaking offered in Chapter 2 does the job required. That is, does the account provide an adequate response to the objection from truthmaking? In section 3.1, I argue that it does not. This is, of course, an independently bad thing for the presentist, since they need to respond to the objection in question. But it is also bad because it spells trouble for the argument from ontological parsimony. I return to this argument in section 3.2. There, I note that the failure of this account of truthmaking undermines one crucial premise (premise 3) of the argument from ontological parsimony; namely, that presentism and eternalism are otherwise equally good theories. In section 3.3, I go on to argue that this account of truthmaking also undermines another premise of the argument from ontological parsimony (premise 2); namely, that

DOI: 10.4324/9781003105664-6

presentism is more ontologically parsimonious than eternalism. Finally, in section 4, I consider the response offered in Chapter 2 to the problem of relativity. There, I argue that this response is not plausible. Presentism fits less well with our best science than does eternalism. So, this gives us yet another reason to reject premise 3 of the argument from ontological parsimony.

I conclude that the argument from ontological parsimony fails, and hence we have been given no reason to endorse presentism over eternalism.

2. The Argument From Ontological Parsimony

Chapter 2 offered a single argument in favour of presentism: the argument from ontological parsimony. According to that argument, all else being equal, we should prefer a theory that is more ontologically parsimonious to one that is not. Presentism is more ontologically parsimonious than eternalism, so we should prefer presentism to eternalism. Here's my rendition of argument:

The Argument From Ontological Parsimony

(1) All else being equal, we should prefer theory T to theory T* if T is more ontologically parsimonious than T*.
(2) Presentism is more ontologically parsimonious than eternalism.
(3) Presentism and eternalism are equally good theories in all other respects (i.e., all else is equal).
(4) Therefore, we should prefer presentism to eternalism.

Of course, the 'everything else being equal' is important here. If (1) were simply the claim that we should prefer theory T to theory T* if T is more ontologically parsimonious than T*, then it would be obviously false. We clearly should not prefer a theory that posits the existence of a single atom and nothing else over a theory that posits the existence of more things, given that we have data that can only be explained on the assumption that more than just one atom exists. So, things are not 'equal' when T and T* are not equally explanatory, or not equal with respect to some other theoretical virtue. If T is more parsimonious than T*, this might give us some reason to prefer T to T*, but unless things are equal with respect to the other virtues, once we take those virtues into account, we might find that we should prefer T* to T.

At any rate, it seems plausible that we should prefer T to T* if they are otherwise equally good theories and T is more ontologically parsimonious than T*.

(3), though, is true only if presentism and eternalism *are just as good in all other respects*. They must be equally explanatory, equally consistent with our scientific evidence, equally simple, equally fruitful, equally ideologically parsimonious (more on this shortly), and so on. It's not obvious that this is so. Indeed, if either the objection from truthmaking or from relativity succeeds, then (3) is false. So, if either of the responses to these objections which Nikk presented in Chapter 2 fails, then we should conclude that (3) is false. I'll turn to consider these responses later in the chapter, where I will argue that neither response succeeds. Hence, I will conclude (3) is false. For now, though, let's focus on the status of (2).

2.1 What Is Ontological Parsimony?

If we list all of the objects, properties, and relations that exist according to a theory, then we have a list of its *ontological commitments*. One way of thinking about the ontological commitments of a theory is to think: if this theory were true, which things would exist? So, for instance, consider the following fairy-ball theory. There are a lot of rubber balls in the garden. According to the fairy-ball theory, this is because there is a family of fairies at the bottom of the garden, who like to play ball. These fairies steal balls from wherever they can find them and leave them in the garden. If this theory is true, then it must be that there exist fairies and, in particular, that there exist a family of fairies at the bottom of the garden; there must also exist a garden and some rubber balls. So, we can say that the ontological commitments of the fairy-ball theory are, say, seven fairies, one garden, and fourteen rubber balls.

What does it take for one theory to be more ontologically parsimonious than another?

One option is that the theory simply has fewer ontological commitments. Or, as we might put it, it posits *fewer things*. On this view, if one theory has a shorter list of ontological commitments than another, then it is more ontologically parsimonious. So, if we had two fairy-ball theories and the second posits only six fairies, (one garden and fourteen balls) then that theory is more ontologically parsimonious than the first. Then, all else being equal, we should prefer the fairy-ball theory that posits only six, rather than seven, fairies. We can express this view about ontological parsimony as follows:

Ontological Parsimony (NUMB): A theory, T, is more ontologically parsimonious than theory T*, just in case T posits a smaller number of entities than does T*.

To move away from fairies, consider two theories. One posits particles a, b, and c. The other posits particles d and e. Since the former posits three particles and the latter, two, all else being equal, on the current proposal (i.e., NUMB) the second theory is more ontologically parsimonious than the first.

Suppose, however, that particles a, b, and c, are all the same kind of particle. Call them *hoovons*. Then the first theory is ontologically committed to the existence of three hoovons. Now suppose that d and e are different kinds of particle. One is a *hoovon* and one is a *gloovon*. So, the second theory is ontologically committed to the existence of one hoovon and one gloovon.

One might think that the first theory is actually *more* ontologically parsimonious than the second. Why? Well, one might think that what makes a theory ontologically parsimonious is not the sheer *number* of things it posits, but rather, the number of different *kinds* of things that it posits. The intuition is roughly this. Once a theory posits a particle of a certain kind—a hoovon—then it is not more ontologically parsimonious if it says that only five hoovons exist, as opposed to seven existing. The thought is that, once we have, as it were, incurred the cost of "buying" hoovons for our ontology, then whether we have five or seven of them makes little difference; but if, in addition, we also have to buy gloovons, then that does make the resulting theory less ontologically parsimonious. On this view, theory T is more ontologically parsimonious than T* just in case T posits fewer kinds of entity than does T*. We can express this view about ontological parsimony as follows:

Ontological Parsimony (KIND): A theory, T, is more ontologically parsimonious than theory T*, just in case T posits a smaller number of kinds of entities than does T*.

A third option is that ontological parsimony should be measured in terms of the number of kinds of *fundamental* entities. To get a feel for the proposal, consider two theories. The first theory posits three different fundamental kinds of particles: hoovons, gloovons, and soovons. In addition, it posits seven different kinds of ordinary, macro-sized objects composed of those fundamental particles. The second theory posits the existence of two different fundamental kinds of particles—hoovons and soovons—and posits the existence of nine different kinds of ordinary, macro-sized objects composed of those fundamental particles. So, the first theory posits ten different kinds of things and the second posits eleven different kinds of things. If we measure ontological parsimony in terms of the number of different kinds of things, then we will say that the first theory is more ontologically parsimonious than the second.

Some philosophers, at least, suspect that this is a mistake. It's true that, when particles come together in certain ways, new things come into existence. For instance, tables and chairs come into existence when particles are arranged in certain ways. Likewise for ducks and dogs. But, they argue, in some good sense the chairs and tables, ducks and dogs, are no addition to being over and above the particles. That is to say, once you have the particles in your ontology, you don't need to add anything more (other than to arrange them) in order to get chairs and tables, ducks and dogs. If you think of ontology as a kind of cost that a theory incurs, then once you've "purchased" all the relevant particles, you don't need to then shell out more money to buy chairs and tables; you get them for free by just having particles that you already purchased, arranged in certain ways. So, goes the thought, when we think about ontological parsimony, we should be focussing on the number of different kinds of *fundamental* things, since these are the things that you need to buy in order to purchase all the things in our ontology. We can express this view about ontological parsimony as follows:

Ontological Parsimony (FUND): A theory, T, is more ontologically parsimonious than theory T* just in case T posits a smaller number of fundamental kinds of entities than does T*.

According to FUND, the second theory just described is more ontologically parsimonious than the first. Even though it contains more *kinds* of entities, it contains only two, as opposed to three, *fundamental* kinds.

2.2 Presentism, Eternalism, and Ontological Parsimony

With these notions of ontological parsimony in hand, let's examine the argument for presentism via parsimony.

Suppose we think that what it takes for theory T to be more ontologically parsimonious than T*, is for T to posit a smaller number of entities than T*. That is, we accept NUMB. Then it looks as though (2) is true. After all, eternalism is ontologically committed to many more things than is presentism: it is committed to all the past things and all the future things.

It's worth noting that this will be the right conclusion to draw, given most ways things could turn out. It is not, however, true, come what may. To see this, suppose that the spatial extent of the present is infinite along (at least) one of its three dimensions. Then, when the presentist tallies up her list of ontological commitments, that list will be infinite. In turn, when the eternalist tallies up her list of ontological commitments, her list will also be infinite.

Then their lists are the same length; that is, they have the same cardinality. So (2) is false.

Indeed, we don't even need to think that one of the spatial dimensions extends infinitely to get this result. Suppose we are substantivalists about space (or spacetime); that is, we think that space/spacetime is a substance. Now suppose, as most substantivalists do, that we also think that space/spacetime is composed of spacetime points. Suppose, also, that we think that space/spacetime is *continuous*. That is, between any two spacetime points there is another point. This is a plausible assumption, and one that underlies all the mathematics of general and special relativity. If we accept all these claims—claims that are each independently quite plausible—then it follows that we are committed to infinitely many things: infinitely many spacetime points. Moreover, we are committed to infinitely many things, regardless of whether we accept presentism or eternalism. So (2) would, in this event, be false.

The point is this. If NUMB were the right characterisation of ontological parsimony (and it is far from clear that it is), then it might well turn out that presentism and eternalism posit the *same* number of things, because they both posit an infinite number of things. So, (2) could turn out to be false.

Few contemporary philosophers, however, think that NUMB is the right way to think about ontological parsimony. Most think that ontological parsimony should be understood in some other way. So, let's consider (2) in light of the other two proposals. Suppose ontological parsimony should be understood as a claim about the relative number of different kinds of things a theory posits. Then, assuming that dinosaurs are a different kind of thing (in this sense) to dogs, (2) is almost certainly true. Eternalism posits all sorts of past and future kinds of things—dinosaurs, sentient robots, and so on—that the presentist theory does not. So, if we think that ontological parsimony should be understood as KIND, then (2) is true.

That brings us to the final proposal: that parsimony is a measure of the number of fundamental kinds. On this view, remember, non-fundamental kinds get a free ontological pass. If we accept this view, then it's likely that (2) is false. Presentism and eternalism posit the same number of *fundamental* kinds of things. They posit, for instance, the same fundamental particles, fields, forces, properties, and so on. It is just that, according to eternalism, these fundamental things are distributed across the past and the future as well as the present.

So, whether (2) is true is going to depend on how we understand ontological parsimony. At the very least, it is not obvious that (2) is true. So, even setting aside worries about (3), it is not obvious that the argument from ontological parsimony shows that we should prefer presentism to eternalism.

In the next section, I will argue that (3) is false. In particular, I will argue that presentism and eternalism are not otherwise equally good theories, because presentists do not have a good account of truthmaking.

> In sum, in these last two sections, I have introduced several different ways we might think about ontological parsimony. The first is parsimony in number of things; the second is parsimony in numbers of kinds of things; and the third is parsimony in fundamental kinds of things. I then noted that whether the argument from parsimony succeeds in showing that presentism is more parsimonious than eternalism is going to depend on which notion of parsimony we are relying on.

3. Truthmaking and Parsimony

One of the most common arguments against presentism is that it does a poor job of providing truthmakers for past-tensed truths. Chapter 2 set out a proposal for solving this problem. In what follows, I will begin (section 3.1) by outlining the problem and remind us how the proposed solution is supposed to go. Then, I will argue that the proposed solution is no solution at all. That being so, it follows that eternalism is a better theory than presentism; for eternalists can provide a compelling account of truthmaking. Thus, premise (3) of the argument in favour of presentism is false.

Perhaps, however, I will not convince you of that. So, in section 3.2, I will return to consider ontological parsimony. There, I argue that if the presentist accepts this proposal for explaining truths about the past, she commits herself to a view that is *less* ontologically parsimonious than the eternalist's. So, by an argument that is analogous to that of the argument from ontological parsimony, we should endorse eternalism over presentism. So, the presentist faces a dilemma. Either she has no good account of truthmaking, and hence premise (3) is false, and so the argument we have been offered in favour of presentism fails, or she has a good account of truthmaking, but that account commits to her to a view that is not more ontologically parsimonious than eternalism, and hence the argument we have been offered in favour of presentism fails. In either case, the argument fails.

3.1 The Objection From Truthmaking

There appear to be lots of truths about the past: truths such as that you ate porridge for breakfast yesterday or that Betty the dinosaur was large. But since, according to the presentist, neither Betty nor the event of your eating breakfast yesterday exist, those things cannot be what makes those claims true. This is what is known as the objection from truthmaking. Here is one way to frame that objection.

> **The Objection from Truthmaking**
>
> A. Past-tensed propositions are about past states of affairs.
> B. Propositions are made true by what those propositions are about.
> C. So, past-tensed propositions are made true by past states of affairs (from A, B).
> D. There are no past states of affairs (assumption of presentism).
>
> Therefore
>
> > CON: No past-tensed proposition is true.

To understand this objection, we need to get a little clearer about some terminology. First, I will suppose that propositions are *representational truth-bearers*. They are *representational* in that they represent that the world is some way or other. Drawings, sentences, and maps are all representational in this sense. The sentence "Annie is sitting on the couch" represents that the world is some particular way; namely, a way in which Annie is sitting on the couch. Propositions are also *truth-bearers* in the sense that they are things that take a truth-value: they can be true or they can be false. Propositions take the value **true** when what they represent about the world is in fact the case. In what follows, I will use the convention of using angle brackets <> to pick out propositions. So, for instance, the proposition that Annie is sitting will be represented as <Annie is sitting>.

Then, past-tensed propositions are propositions such as <Napoleon *crossed* the Rubicon> or <It *was* the case that Napoleon crossed the Rubicon>. A natural way to think about past-tensed propositions is that they are propositions that represent something about the past. Finally, I will take *states of affairs* to be things in the world composed of objects, properties, and relations. So, for instance, at this moment, Annie is sitting on the couch. So, there is a state of affairs of Annie sitting on the couch. That state of affairs is made up of Annie, the couch, and Annie's bearing the relation of sitting-on to the couch. That state of affairs is a perfectly ordinary, concrete thing. We encounter states of affairs all the time: the state of affairs of driving a car; of eating a doughnut; of buying tofu; of sitting in a car eating a doughnut; and so on.

With this in mind, let's briefly examine (A) through (D).

(A) says that past-tensed propositions are about past states of affairs. This is pretty plausible. Consider the past-tensed proposition <Betty the dinosaur was hungry>. This proposition appears to represent a certain past state of affairs; namely, the past state of affairs in which Betty is hungry. So, the proposition is *about* that state of affairs.

(B) says that propositions are made true by what they are about. That is also pretty plausible. We'd expect that if <Betty the dinosaur was hungry> is true, it will be made true by something about Betty and her state of hunger. You'd be pretty surprised if I told you that that proposition was made true by, for instance, the state of affairs of Annie sitting on the couch.

(C) follows from (A) and (B). (D) is entailed by presentism. But (CONC) is clearly false. There surely are true past-tensed propositions. So, one of (A), (B), or (D) must be false. Since (A) and (B) are very plausible, we should reject (D). So, we should reject presentism. Or so goes the objection from truthmaking.

Presentists typically respond to the objection from truthmaking by rejecting (B). They argue that there is some presently existing thing that makes past-tensed propositions true, but which is not what those propositions are about. So, for instance, perhaps what makes such propositions true is the present existence of some special, tensed property of the world (or something in it) such as a *Lucretian property*. Lucretian properties are special properties posited by presentists. Different presentists posit different sorts of such properties. Some think that the world itself has special, past-tensed properties, so that the world has the property of having-once-contained-dinosaurs (say). Some think that certain objects in the world have past-tensed properties, so that I have the property of having-gone-swimming-yesterday. These are all examples of Lucretian properties. They are properties that are had in the present, by present things. In general, then, presentists posit some sort of presently existing things which make true the past-tensed proposition, even though the proposition is about a past state of affairs. For instance, they might say that the fact that Annie has the property of having-gone-swimming-yesterday is what makes true <Annie swam yesterday>.

In Chapter 2, Nikk explored a somewhat different avenue. The account Nikk offered was framed in terms of the idea that to talk of truthmaking is to talk of what *explains* why a proposition is true. But we need to be a little careful here. What explains why <Annie is sitting on the couch> is true? One natural response is that this is true because, earlier today, Annie went for a walk, came home, was tired, and consequently got up onto the couch to snooze. There is *some* sense in which this does explain why it is true that Annie is sitting on the couch. But it's not the kind of explanation we are looking for. After all, it could be true that <Annie is sitting on the couch> is true, even though she did not earlier go for a walk. So, the kind of explanation we are looking for is usually thought to appeal simply to the state of affairs of Annie's sitting on the couch: the one thing that *guarantees* that the proposition in question is true.

Indeed, it is natural to say that truths (i.e., the fact that a proposition is true) are explained by the way the world is and, in particular, are explained by there being certain states of affairs. This is exactly what the eternalist says. She says that past-tensed propositions are made true by the obtaining of the states of affairs that those propositions are about. So <Betty the dinosaur was hungry> is, if true, made true by there being some past state of affairs of Betty being hungry.

Since the eternalist thinks there are past and future states of affairs, she rejects (D) of the objection from truthmaking.

The proposal articulated in Chapter 2 appealed to *past facts*. What, I hear you say, are past facts? That depends on what one means by 'fact'. Some people use that word to mean something pretty much like state of affairs. So, the *fact* that Annie is sitting on the couch is really just the state of affairs of Annie sitting on the couch. It's a piece of the furniture of the world. Others use 'fact' to mean something like *true proposition*. So, when they say that there's a fact that Annie is sitting on the couch, they mean that the proposition <Annie is sitting on the couch> is true.

If the presentist were to think that past facts are states of affairs that exist in the past, then she would be unable to explain the truth of past-tensed propositions by appealing to past facts. For she denies that there are any past facts conceived in this way. That is why the proposal outlined in Chapter 2 instead construed past facts as true propositions. So, it's important to bear this in mind in what follows. Let's call this new truthmaking proposal the *past fact proposal*.

According to the past fact proposal, past facts make past-tensed propositions true. So, what are past facts on this view? Well, I take it there are two options. One could think that past facts are present-tensed propositions *that presently have a past-tensed property of having once been true*. Or, perhaps better, one could think that there is some present state of affairs of a present-tensed proposition having once been true. On this view, past facts are states of affairs of there being present-tensed propositions that were once true (but, often, are true no longer).

A second option is to say that past facts are just true propositions about the past: they are true past-tensed propositions.

On the face of it, both of these options look puzzling. We wanted to know what it is that makes past-tensed propositions true. On the first of these options, what makes them true is that there is some present state of affairs of there being a present-tensed proposition that was once true. That, however, just seems to move the bump in the carpet. For now, we want to know what makes it the case that the relevant present-tensed proposition *was once true*. Answering that question seems no easier than answering the question with which we began. Indeed, a very natural suggestion is that, if <Betty the dinosaur is hungry> is not true, now, but was true in the past, this is made true by the state of affairs, in the past, of Betty being hungry. But of course, the presentist cannot say this.

This leaves the second option: that past facts are true past-tensed propositions. Now, on the face of it, this suggestion also looks pretty odd. We wanted to know what explains why certain past-tensed propositions are true.

It seems odd to say that what explains why certain past-tensed propositions are true is that certain past-tensed propositions are true. That explanation appears to be hopelessly circular.

Certainly, this proposal will be hopeless if we appeal to the very same past-tensed proposition, <P>, to explain why that very past-tensed proposition is true. So, for instance, we clearly cannot explain why <Betty the dinosaur was hungry> is true by appealing to the truth of <Betty the dinosaur was hungry>. Fortunately, the past-fact proposal outlined in Chapter 2 is one on which we explain the truth of one past-tensed proposition in terms of the truth of some other past-tensed proposition. Roughly speaking, the idea is that the truth of <Betty the dinosaur was hungry> is explained by its being true that <29 million years ago, Betty is hungry>.

To be sure, this is a big improvement on explaining the truth of <Betty the dinosaur was hungry> in terms of itself. How much of an improvement is it, though? At first blush, we still seem to have done nothing more than move the problem around. After all, the original problem the presentist faced was to explain in virtue of what past-tensed propositions are true. The past-fact proposal explains the truth of some past-tensed propositions in terms of the truth of others. But what remains to be explained is how those past-tensed propositions that do the explaining get to be true. In this case, what needs explaining is why <29 million years ago, Betty was hungry> is true.

Nikk has something to say here. Here is the idea. Consider Annie, who is sitting on the couch. What makes it the case that she is sitting on the couch? Pretty plausibly, it's because there are various fundamental particles arranged in a certain way, a labradoodle-way (Annie is a labradoodle) and a couch-way, and certain fundamental relations between those particles. There being those fundamental things, arranged in those ways, bearing those relations to one another, is what explains its being the case that Annie is sitting on the couch. In turn, its being true that there are those things, arranged that way, explains why <Annie is sitting on the couch> is true. Or so one might think.

Plausibly then, what explains its being the case that, 29 million years ago, Betty was hungry is that there *were* various fundamental particles located 29 million years ago, arranged in a certain way, bearing certain relations to one another. Let's suppose that's roughly right. Then the idea is that what explains why <29 million years ago, Betty was hungry> is true is some long conjunction of true past-tensed propositions of the form <29 million years ago, particle A was located at L> for all the particles that made up Betty. Jointly, these true propositions explain why it's true that <29 million years ago, Betty was hungry>.

So far, this still has not helped the presentist. She *still* has a bunch of true, past-tensed propositions whose truth we need to explain. It's just that now, the truths she has to explain are ones such as <29 million years ago, particle A was located at L>. What does Nikk say about this? Well, the idea seems to be that these truths are *fundamental*. That is, they require no further explanation. These fundamental truths explain the truth of various other past-tensed propositions, which in turn explain the truth of still other past-tensed propositions.

Is this a good view of truthmaking? (Notice that this could be the best account of truthmaking that the presentist can offer and it still be the case that it's not a very good account, or that it's a worse account than that offered by the eternalist.)

Here is one reason to think that it's both not a very good account and also that it's a worse account than that offered by the eternalist. According to the past-fact proposal, we explain the truth of past-tensed propositions in terms of the truth of still more past-tensed propositions. When it comes to past-tensed propositions, we never at any point connect up truth and world. Every past-tensed proposition is either made true by some other past-tensed proposition or that past-tensed proposition is not made true by anything: it is a fundamental truth. Here's what's odd about that. As I noted earlier in this chapter, propositions are representational. They represent that the world is some way or other. They are true just in case what they represent is the case, and false otherwise. So, we expect an explanation of why some proposition is true to make reference to the way the world is. It's that the world is thus and so, which makes some particular proposition true, because the proposition represents the world as being thus and so. On the proposal under consideration, though, the truth of past-tensed propositions has nothing to do with the way the world is. Those truths do not, in any way, connect up to the world. They are not true *because* of the way the world is. There is, in *some* very good sense, no explanation for why they are true. That's because, at the end of the day, every past-tensed proposition is ultimately made true by a past-tensed proposition or set of propositions which is itself fundamentally true.

This is most mysterious and quite disconcerting. To be sure, philosophers often talk of *fundamental truths*. What this usually means, though, is that there are truths that are made true by some fundamental feature of the world. So, consider <particle P has spin u>. Let's suppose that proposition is true. Further, let's suppose that whether or not a particle has a particular spin is a fundamental matter: it's not explained by anything further. Then we will say that <particle p has spin u> is a fundamental truth. But that's not because that truth has no explanation. <particle p has spin u> is made true by the world being one in which particle p has spin u. That is, the proposition is made true by some particular state of affairs involving particle p having spin u. The truth is fundamental only in the sense that there is no further explanation for why it is that p has spin u.

Contrast that case with the following: <Annie is sitting on the couch>. That proposition is made true by its being the case that Annie is sitting on the couch. So, once again, that proposition is made true by a certain state of affairs: the state of affairs of Annie sitting on the couch. But *that* Annie is sitting on the couch is not itself a fundamental state of affairs. We can explain it in terms of the arrangement of various particles and various physical laws, and so on.

For the eternalist, then, in both cases there is some explanation for *why* the proposition in question is true. It's just that, in one case, the explanation appeals to a fundamental state of affairs and, in the other, it does not. In neither case is the truth itself fundamental, in the sense that there is no explanation of why it is true. For the eternalist, what it is to be a fundamental truth is to be a truth and to be made true by a fundamental state of affairs. It's not to be a truth that is not made true by anything at all. In order to distinguish this sense of fundamental truth from the notion that is being proposed by the advocate of the past fact proposal, let's call that second notion Fundamental Truth (capital letters). While fundamental truths are truths that are made true by a fundamental state of affairs, Fundamental Truths are truths that are not made true by anything at all.

You can see just how weird Fundamental Truths are. Consider <particle p *had* spin u>. According to Nikk, there is *nothing* that makes that true. It's not made true by anything to do with particle p and its spin! That seems deeply counterintuitive and to sever the connection between truth and the world in a most alarming manner.

So, my first objection to the past-facts proposal is that it ultimately appeals to Fundamental Truths and that this is objectionable. Perhaps there are some Fundamental Truths. But it beggars belief that these Fundamental Truths ultimately explain all past-tensed truths. In effect, this is to say that the truth of all past-tensed propositions 'floats free' from explanation since, ultimately, the explanation for all such past-tensed propositions is one that 'bottoms out' in past-tensed propositions that have no truthmakers.

The idea that past-tensed propositions require no truthmakers is one that presentists have explored. Those who defend such a view sometimes call themselves *nefarious presentists*.[1] The proposal under discussion is really a version of nefarious presentism. But we should reject nefarious presentism precisely because it provides no constraints at all on which past-tensed propositions are true. After all, they are not made true by anything. So, it's very hard to see why it cannot be the case that, for instance, <Betty the dinosaur was 1,000 metres tall> is true.

You might respond by saying that this cannot be true because the relevant set of propositions about the locations of particles 29 million years ago are not true. But why is that? Why can't it be that <29 million years ago, particle X was located at L> and so on, in such a manner as to make it true that

---

1. See for instance Tallant and Ingram (2015).

<Betty the dinosaur was 1,000 metres tall>? After all, nothing at all makes true propositions of the form <29 million years ago, particle X was located at L>: they are Fundamental Truths. Since that is clearly ridiculous, we should reject this view.

Hence, I conclude, presentists do not have a reasonable account of truthmaking. As such, premise (3) of the argument for presentism from parsimony is false. Presentism is, in other respects, a worse theory than is eternalism. So, even if presentism is more parsimonious than eternalism, we don't have reason to endorse presentism over eternalism. After all, if a theory cannot account for the truth of past-tensed propositions, then it doesn't matter how parsimonious it is: we shouldn't prefer that theory to a theory that can account for the truth of past-tensed propositions. So, even if considerations of parsimony militate in favour of presentism over eternalism, those considerations do not outweigh the costs that presentism incurs from its inability to provide truthmakers for past-tensed propositions.

But suppose you don't agree with me about this. Suppose you think the past-fact account of truthmaking is good. Then you don't yet have a reason to reject the argument for presentism from parsimony. To see why you should nevertheless still reject this argument, we need to return to earlier discussion of parsimony. In what follows, I will argue that if one accepts the past-fact view of truthmaking, then this undermines the very argument from parsimony that was supposed to motivate presentism in the first place.

> In this section, I argued that presentists do not have a reasonable account of truthmaking. I articulated several truthmaking proposals and noted that the one that was defended in Chapter 2 is a view on which many truths are Fundamental Truths. These are truths that are not made true by anything at all. I argued that it is implausible that there are Fundamental Truths. So, even if presentism were more parsimonious than eternalism, this virtue would be undermined by the fact that presentism does not have a good account of truthmaking.

3.2 Ontological Parsimony Revisited

Suppose you are inclined to think that propositions such as <29 million years ago, particle X was located at L> can be true without anything in the world making them true. Then, the view you end up with is one on which, as time passes, the universe accrues more and more Fundamental Truths.

Fundamental Truths, though, are an addition to ontology. With this in mind, let's revisit the argument from ontological parsimony.

> **The Argument From Ontological Parsimony**
>
> (1) All else being equal, we should prefer theory T to theory T* if T is more ontologically parsimonious than T*.
> (2) Presentism is more ontologically parsimonious than eternalism.
> (3) Presentism and eternalism are equally good theories in all other respects (i.e., all else is equal).
> (4) Therefore, we should prefer presentism to eternalism.

In Chapter 2 Nikk argued that even though the presentist is committed to there being exceedingly many Fundamental Truths, and even though Fundamental Truths are an addition to ontology, the argument from ontological parsimony is still sound. I think this is a mistake.

In order to see this, let's see why one might have thought otherwise. Here is the argument that was offered in Chapter 2 for why presentism is still more ontologically parsimonious than is eternalism, despite the fact that the presentist posits a plethora of Fundamental Truths that the eternalist does not.

Notice that, wherever the eternalist thinks there is some fundamental past state of affairs, the presentist thinks there is some Fundamental Truth. To see this, consider fundamental particle p. The eternalist holds that p exists at some past time t. Let's suppose that the eternalist holds that the state of affairs of p's existing at t is a fundamental state of affairs: it cannot be explained in terms of any other state of affairs. So, the eternalist thinks there is a fundamental state of affairs, and that this fundamental state of affairs explains why the proposition <p existed at t> is true. By contrast, the presentist who endorses the past-fact proposal will say that <p existed at t> is a Fundamental Truth. It lacks a truthmaker.

So, when it comes to the past, we have a straightforward mapping between the ontology of the eternalist and that of the presentist. Wherever the eternalist posits a past fundamental state of affairs, the presentist posits a Fundamental Truth. So, when it comes to the past, the presentist and the eternalist are committed to the same number of fundamental entities.

Presumably the eternalist and the presentist are also committed to the same number of fundamental present entities. But—so goes the argument—the presentist is committed to *fewer* future fundamental things than is the eternalist. After all, the eternalist thinks there are many future fundamental states of affairs. The presentist, though, need not be committed to thinking that every future-tensed proposition takes a truth-value. She can instead think that the future is open. So, she need not think that for each future fundamental state of affairs posited by the eternalist, she should posit some future Fundamental Truth.

Since the presentist and eternalist are committed to the same-sized ontology when it comes to the past and present, and the presentist is committed to a smaller future ontology, the presentist is, overall, committed to a smaller ontology than the eternalist. So, Nikk argues, presentism is more ontologically parsimonious than eternalism.

Is this argument a good one? Well, it relies on us conceiving of ontological parsimony in one of two ways. We could conceive of it as NUMB:

Ontological Parsimony (NUMB): A theory, T, is more ontologically parsimonious than theory T* just in case T posits a smaller number of entities than does T*.

If ontological parsimony is a measure of the number of entities posited, then the argument just offered will go through: presentism will be more ontologically parsimonious than eternalism. But we've already seen that most philosophers think that we should construe ontological parsimony in some way other than NUMB.

There is another way to construe ontological parsimony that will do the work. That is to conceive of it as FUND*:

Ontological Parsimony (FUND*): A theory, T, is more ontologically parsimonious than theory T* just in case T posits a smaller number of fundamental entities than does T*.

FUND* is a new suggestion for thinking about ontological parsimony. It differs from FUND. Recall that FUND says the following:

Ontological Parsimony (FUND): A theory, T, is more ontologically parsimonious than theory T* just in case T posits a smaller number of fundamental kinds of entities than does T*.

FUND says that one theory is more ontologically parsimonious than another just in case it posits a smaller number of fundamental kinds than the other theory. FUND* says that one theory is more ontologically parsimonious than another just in case it posits a smaller number of fundamental entities than the other theory.

To see the difference, consider two theories. The first theory posits the existence of three fundamental particles—a, b, and c. All three particles are of the same kind: they are all hoovons. The second theory posits the existence of two fundamental particles—d and e. D is a hoovon and e is a gloovon. According to FUND*, the second theory is more parsimonious, since it posits fewer fundamental *things* than the first theory. The second theory posits two fundamental things, while the first posits three. According to FUND, the first theory is more parsimonious, since, although it posits a greater number of fundamental things, it posits only one *kind* of fundamental thing (the hoovon), as opposed to positing two fundamental kinds of things (the hoovon and the gloovon).

We can now see why it matters how we construe ontological parsimony. If we accept FUND*, then it is likely that presentism is more parsimonious than eternalism. If we accept FUND then eternalism is either *more* ontologically parsimonious than presentism or, at the very least, it is *as* parsimonious. So, if FUND is the notion we should be using or, at least, if FUND is a better account of parsimony than its competitors, then eternalism might turn out to be at least as parsimonious as presentism.

Given FUND, eternalism will be *more* ontologically parsimonious than presentism if the eternalist does not posit any Fundamental Truths. The eternalist might say that there are fundamental truths, but no Fundamental Truths. All truths, she might say, have truthmakers. To be sure, some of them are explained by fundamental states of affairs, but that is an explanation, nonetheless. If the eternalist says this, then she posits *fewer* kinds of fundamental things than does the presentist. For the presentist posits the existence of fundamental particles and forces and relations. In addition, she also posits the existence of Fundamental Truths. Then, according to FUND, eternalism will be more ontologically parsimonious than will presentism.

Even if the eternalist allows that there are some Fundamental Truths (just not the ones the presentist posits), her view will be *as* ontologically parsimonious as that of the presentist. In either case, (2) is false.

The general point, then, is that whether presentism is more parsimonious than eternalism or the other way around is very sensitive to exactly how we are conceiving of ontological parsimony, and it is not at all clear that we should conclude that presentism is, in fact, more parsimonious than eternalism.

Let's recap. In section 3, I argued that the past-fact proposal is not a good account of truthmaking. If you think I am right about this, then you should reject the argument from ontological parsimony. That is because you should think that premise (3) of that argument is false. All is not equal between the presentist and eternalist theory, since the eternalist has a good account of truthmaking and the presentist does not. So, we have no reason to prefer presentism to eternalism.

I then went on to argue that, even if you do think the past-fact proposal is a good account of truthmaking, accepting that account undermines premise (2) of the argument from ontological parsimony. That is because it commits the presentist to a new kind of fundamental thing: Fundamental Truth. Since the eternalist need not be committed to any such truths, if we accept FUND as the correct account of the nature of ontological parsimony, we will conclude that, in fact, eternalism is more ontologically parsimonious than is presentism.

That leaves one last thing to consider. I argued in Chapter 1 that one powerful objection to presentism is the objection from relativity. Chapter 2 set out a response to this objection. In the next section, I consider whether that response succeeds.

> In sum, in this section, I have argued that, even if you accept Fundamental Truths, it is still not the case that presentism is straightforwardly more parsimonious than eternalism. I argued that, on many views about what parsimony consists in, it will turn out that presentism is not more parsimonious than eternalism, because it commits us to a new fundamental kind of thing: Fundamental Truth. Indeed, if parsimony is about minimising fundamental kinds, then eternalism is more parsimonious, given that it does not posit Fundamental Truths.

4. The Objection From Relativity

Relativity poses a problem for presentism because, according to relativity, there is no absolute simultaneity. That is, there is no fact of the matter as to which events really are simultaneous with one another. But the presentist thinks that only present events exist, and it is plausible to think that events E and E* are present only if E and E* are simultaneous. After all, the presentist surely doesn't think that E and E* are each *present*, and yet they can fail to be simultaneous. So, she wants to say that what exists is present, and all things that are present are absolutely simultaneous. But this is just what she cannot say if relativity is true.

In Chapter 2, in response to this objection, Nikk suggested that the presentist should simply say that existence simpliciter is relative to an inertial frame of reference. One can only, as it were, specify what exists relative to an inertial frame.

It's worth getting clear just how radical this proposal really is. Sometimes, when we talk about what exists, we are deliberately relativising our discussion. We are not talking about the list of absolutely everything that exists;

instead, we are talking about what exists around here: in our house, our neighbourhood, our planet, our solar system. And, of course, roses, say, can exist *around here* and not *around there*. But the notion of existence that the presentist has in mind is one that is meant to encompass absolutely everything. When the presentist says that the past and future do not exist and the present does, they mean that, when we take an absolutely complete inventory of everything that exists, we will not find any dinosaurs on that list. It is surely very intuitive to suppose existence, in this sense, is not relative to anything.

Suppose you and I are asked to put together a complete list of absolutely everything that exists. You list C and I do not. Now suppose you respond to this discovery by telling me that, relative to you, C exists, but relative to me, it does not. I would be deeply puzzled. We are listing absolutely everything that exists. How can something exist relative to you but not me? One might complain: look, if it exists relative to you, *then it just exists*. We are trying to construct the most complete list of everything that exists. So, if something exists relative to anyone whatsoever (who exists) then that thing just exists.

But if we were to take that view, then the present would turn out to be very different than we imagined. Presentism is usually thought of as the view that there is just one three-dimensional object which is our world, and that what that object is like changes as time passes. That three-dimensional object is all there is to the world: there is no past and no future. So, on this view, the present is wafer-thin; it has no temporal extent though, of course, it has spatial extent. All and only the present things exist at the same time.

If, however, we suppose that relativity is true, and we also suppose that everything that exists relative to one inertial frame exists simpliciter, then we would have to give up on this picture of the present. The present would no longer be a single three-dimensional sheet of reality. That is because, for any two events in the *absolute elsewhere* of a point P, there is some inertial frame located on P, at which an observer will see those two events as simultaneous. The absolute elsewhere of P includes all the events that are space-like separated from P; that is, all the events that are such that light cannot travel between those events. (The absolute elsewhere of P includes everything outside of the forwards and backwards light cone centred on P.) If what exists simpliciter at a point P is what exists according to *some* inertial frame located on P, then it will turn out that what exists simpliciter at P is P *and everything in P's absolute elsewhere*. So, the present will look like a giant bow-tie.

To see this, look at the diagram below. The point in the middle is P, and the shaded orange area represents everything that exists (and hence is present) simpliciter at P. For fairly obvious reasons, this view is often known as bow-tie presentism.

Not only does this view commit one to a pretty odd view about what counts as the present (namely all the shaded orange area) but it also requires that one jettison the idea that all and only those things that are simultaneous

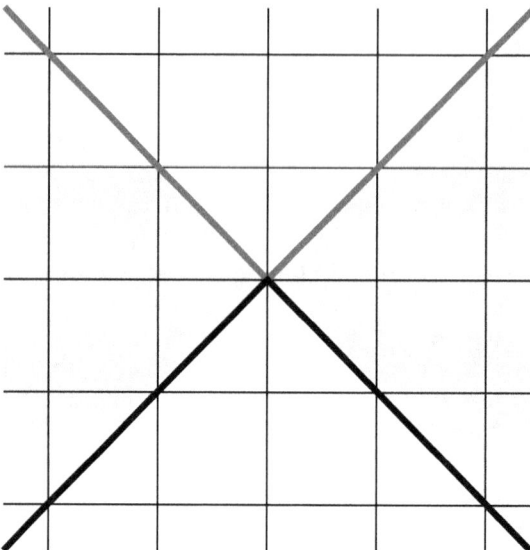

Figure 4.1 Bow-tie Presentism

with one another are present. For, of course, there are many events in the orange shaded area that are not simultaneous with one another relative to many inertial frames.

The alternative is to say that existence is relative; it is relative to an inertial frame. This is the view proposed in Chapter 2. On this view, which events exist and, hence, which are present varies depending on the inertial frame. I've already noted that this is pretty counterintuitive. Now, Nikk suggests that this is indeed counterintuitive but that what we learn from relativity is just that: existence is relative. And, to be fair, since relativity is indeed peculiar, one might be inclined to say that it's bound to result in some counterintuitive consequences.

One problem is that it is no longer clear whether the resulting view really deserves to be called presentist or not. On that view, at a point P and relative to an inertial frame F, there is a three-dimensional plane, and all and only the events on that plane exist and are present. So far so good; that's just what we want presentism to say. The problem is that, at point P, relative to other inertial frames, there will be other three-dimensional planes, such that all and only the events on that plane exist and are present. So, if P is a point in the middle of Figure 4.2, each of the differently coloured lines represents 'the present' relative to different inertial frames located on P.

This is a pretty weird view. We can no longer ask ourselves the question: which events are present simpliciter? We cannot, as it were, bring together all the data from each inertial frame to construct a unified picture of our world

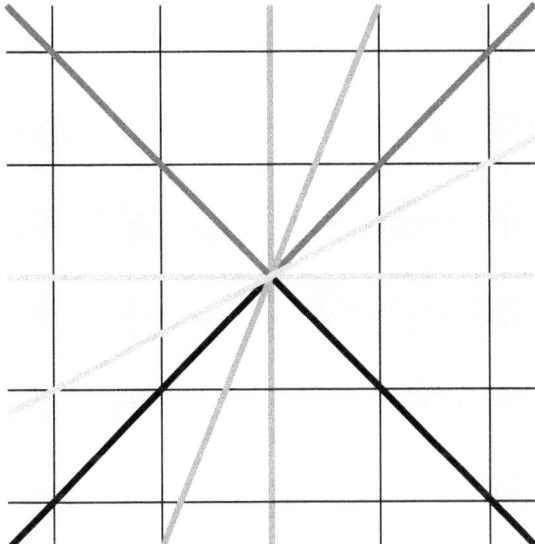

Figure 4.2 The Various 'Presents' Relative to Different Inertial Frames

that depicts which events exist and which are present. For, if we do that, we end up with a diagram that looks just like the bow-tie in Figure 4.1. That's because the 'bow-tie' area will be completely coloured in once we put in every line that corresponds to the present at P, relative to each inertial frame. If we represent things that way, it once again looks as though the present is a big, bow-tie shape. Instead, to avoid that consequence, we need to say that, really, there are many different diagrams, each of which depicts 'the present' at P, relative to an inertial frame. But—and here is the important claim—we cannot put these all together into a single diagram and say that, taken jointly, all these lines are, together, the present. Instead, we can only ever look at one diagram and say that it represents how things are, simpliciter, relative to a particular inertial frame. There is no complete, unified diagram in which we can bring together each present that is defined relative to an inertial frame.

Notice, though, that such a proposal is odd. To see this, suppose that three people go on safari in the same small safari park. Hermione sees an elephant, Ron sees a lion, and Harry sees a zebra. We want to build a picture of which animals are in the safari park. Presumably, we come to the conclusion that there are (at least) lions, elephants, and zebra. We collate our data and come to a single coherent representation of the safari park. It would be weird indeed if, at the end, we said: well, relative to Ron, there are lions, but no zebra or elephants, and relative to Harry there are zebra, but no lions or elephants.

The same is true for constructing a picture of our world. We expect that we can bring together data from different observers to generate a single coherent picture of the world. But if we do that, we end up drawing the bow-tie diagram. If we are not allowed to generate a single representation, but instead can only say how things are relative to an observer, then our world is very much odder than we might have otherwise thought.

It's true, of course, that relativity is weird. But there is no reason to suppose that its weirdness should result in our thinking that there is no single, coherent representation of which things exist simpliciter and which are present. The eternalist has *no reason at all to embrace any such weird conclusion.* She thinks we can bring together the data from observers in different inertial frames; the resulting picture is a representation of a block universe. That should give us pause.

Suppose we had two theories of safari parks. One of the theories entailed that we could only ever represent a safari park relative to an observer, so that we always have to say that there are lions relative to Ron but not relative to Hermione or Harry. The other theory says that we can create a complete representation of the safari park. If Ron observes lions, and Hermione elephants, and Harry zebra, then the theory says that all of these animals are to be found in the safari park. To be sure, it says, depending on where one is and where one is looking, one will see different animals. (Actually, relativity is a little weirder than this, even for the eternalist, but you get the idea.) But the animals themselves have a perfectly ordinary location which is independent of where anyone is looking, and we can represent all of their locations into a single coherent picture of the park (this is true given the block universe view).

Faced with these two theories of safari parks, I suggest that it is very reasonable to adopt the latter over the former. The same is true for eternalism and presentism. The eternalist picture of the world fits very much better with relativity theory than does presentism. That means that, when we combine them together, the resulting theory is very much less peculiar than is the resulting presentist theory. '

If you are with me on this, then you will agree that premise (3) of the argument from ontological parsimony is false. Presentism and eternalism are not equally good theories, setting aside issues of ontological parsimony. Rather, eternalism is a better theory. It is a better theory because it better accords with our best science, and the resulting picture of our world is much simpler and more straightforward than that offered by the presentist. But if (3) is false, then the argument from ontological parsimony is unsound. So, we have been given no reason to prefer presentism to eternalism.

Indeed, quite the reverse is true: we have several reasons to prefer eternalism to presentism. First, we should do so because, at the very least, eternalism provides a much simpler and more elegant account of truthmaking and, at the best, it provides the only reasonable account of truthmaking. Second, we should do so because eternalism provides a simpler and more elegant picture of our relativistic world.

In this chapter, I have argued that, when we put eternalism and presentism into the context of special relativity, we see that eternalism is by far the simpler and more elegant theory. I've also argued that presentism cannot give us a good account of truthmaking, because it cannot make sense of what makes past (or indeed future) tensed claims true. These, jointly, give us reason to think that, even if presentism is more parsimonious than eternalism, it is not overall the better theory. Parsimony cannot trump these other factors that clearly militate in favour of eternalism.

But I've also argued that, on many views of parsimony, it's not true that presentism is more parsimonious than eternalism. On some views of parsimony, they are equally parsimonious, and on others eternalism may even be more parsimonious. So overall, we have reason to prefer eternalism to presentism.

Part III

Second Round of Replies

Chapter 5

Back to the Block
Reply to Nikk Effingham's Reply

Kristie Miller

Contents

1. Change   149
2. Direction, Asymmetry, and Explanation   156

1. Change

Is the kind of change that we see in a block universe the *wrong kind* of change? (Here, I cannot help but to imagine the episode of Wallace and Gromit in which Wallace ends up wearing the *wrong trousers*. But I digress). In Chapter 3, Nikk conceded that there is change on the block universe view. He argued, however, that it's the wrong kind of change.

What undergirds this argument is the idea that spatial change and temporal change are different in some metaphysically relevant way. But, the argument proceeds, on the block view, these two kinds of change are *not* different in any metaphysically relevant way. So, the block view cannot accommodate something important about the nature of change. On that view, temporal change turns out to be just like spatial change. Here's my rendition of that argument:

> **The Argument from Change**
>
> (1) Spatial and temporal change are different in a metaphysically relevant way.
> (2) According to the block universe view, spatial and temporal change are not different in a metaphysically relevant way.
> (3) Therefore, our world is not a block universe.

Let's look at this argument in more detail. Why think that (2) is true? Chapter 3 offered the following sort of argument in favour of (2). On the block universe view, fundamentally there is just one kind of change: *spatio-temporal*

DOI: 10.4324/9781003105664-8

change, which is *variation across spacetime*. Spatial change then turns out to be variation in the *spatial* aspect of spatio-temporal change—or, as we might say, variation along one or more spatial dimension—while temporal change is variation in the *temporal* aspect of spatio-temporal change; that is, variation along the temporal dimension. There is, however, no deep difference in these two kinds of change, since they are just different ways of having spatio-temporal variation. Hence, (2) is true.

By contrast, for the presentist, spatial change and temporal change are quite different. Three spatial dimensions exist, and along these dimensions there can be spatial variation. There is, however, no temporal dimension as such. There is simply a three-dimensional object which is our world and which changes as time passes. So, temporal change is not variation along a temporal dimension at all. It is the coming into and out of existence of objects or the changing of a persisting object. So, according to presentism, spatial and temporal change are different in a metaphysically relevant way.

There is clearly something right about all of this.

I am happy to concede that, on the block universe view, fundamentally there is spatio-temporal change, of which spatial change and temporal change are two aspects. One could perhaps deny this, but I see no need to do so. Given this, I think there is some good sense in which these two kinds of change are similar.

But of course, two things can be similar in certain important respects and dissimilar in other important respects. Let's return to the argument for a moment and focus on (1). Why do we think (1) is true? I think that, insofar as any of us think it likely that (1) is true, it's because spatial and temporal change seem to us to be different. It's not, for instance, that we have some independent philosophical master argument for the truth of (1). (1) just looks to be right, given our experience of spatial and temporal change.

So, (1) is founded on the idea that it seems to us as though spatial change is different from temporal change. That, however, is not what (1) says. (1) says that there is some metaphysically relevant difference between the two. Now, I'm not really sure what a metaphysically relevant difference is (what sort of difference is metaphysically relevant, as opposed to being a metaphysically irrelevant difference?) so I am not sure if (1) is plausible. To be sure, we want to locate *some* difference between them, which explains and perhaps vindicates our intuitions that they are different. But it's not clear that the difference has to be metaphysical (depending on what you think that means). So, in what follows I am not going to try to argue that, on the block universe view, there is a metaphysically relevant difference between spatial and temporal change, since I don't know what it would take to do that and, at any rate, I am not sure that (1) is true. What I do think the block universe theorist needs to do, however, is to show that she can make sense of there being *some* important difference between the two kinds of change. For there is a nearby premise to (1) that is true; namely, that temporal and spatial change appear to us to be importantly different. We can then construct a slightly different argument to the one presented in Chapter 3, which is as follows:

The New Argument from Change

(1)* Spatial and temporal change are importantly different.
(2)* According to the block universe view, spatial and temporal change are not importantly different.
(3)* Therefore, our world is not a block universe.

My aim, in what follows is to show that the block universe theorist *can* accommodate spatial and temporal change being importantly different and, hence, to show that (2*) is false. Perhaps, in doing so, I will also show that (2) is false, but if not, then this will not unduly worry me, since I think we only have reason to accept (1*), not (1).

Let's start by asking ourselves in what sense spatial and temporal change are different. One very notable difference is that we can, as it were, experience spatial change all at once. We can experience it at a single moment of time. Consider a river that changes as it meanders through the countryside. In principle, you or I could see the entirety of that change at one moment. Of course, to do that, we'd need to get quite high up into the sky, and then perhaps we'd need a telescope. But we could. We cannot, even in principle, see all of temporal change at a time. In order to see temporal change, we have to be located at different times. That suggests one way in which spatial and temporal change are different from an experiential point of view. We can experience spatial change of some object at a single moment, while we cannot experience temporal change of an object at a single moment.

Of necessity, we experience temporal change unfolding through time. Given this, we would expect the *experience* of spatial and temporal change to be quite different in a block universe world. Since one important way in which spatial and temporal change can be different lies in them producing different experiences, it follows that, on the block view, there is one important difference between spatial and temporal change.

Moreover, recall that the reason we are supposed to conclude that temporal change is like spatial change (and hence that (2*) is true) is that they are both members of the same genus: spatio-temporal change. But does this give us reason to think that (2*) is true?

No. To be sure, it gives us reason to think that there are similarities between the two kinds of change. But it certainly does not give us reason to think that there are not also important dissimilarities. Dogs and (grey) wolves are members of the same genus: *Canis*. Moreover, dogs and wolves are similar in lots of respects. That, however, does not undermine the fact that there are important differences between them. There is all the difference in the world between having a dog lying on your couch and a large grey wolf. So, our reason to think that they are similar does not undermine our reason to think that they are also dissimilar. The same is true for spatial and temporal change. (Moreover, returning to (2) for a moment, we pretty clearly don't need to posit some deep *metaphysical* differences between dogs and grey wolves in order to explain why having a dog on your couch is very different from having a grey wolf on your couch. That is one good reason to think that, even if (2) were true, it wouldn't give us any reason to think that there are not important differences between spatial and temporal change (i.e., it wouldn't give us any reason to doubt the truth of (1*)).

The general point here is that we've been given no reason to think that spatial and temporal change are similar in a way that is in tension with the truth of (1*).

Now, we might have some reason to think that this was so if we believed that spatial and temporal change are basically exactly the same. We would believe that if we believed that the spatial dimensions are just like the temporal dimension, and so change along one is just like change along the other. Sometimes objectors to the block universe view make it sound as though this is what block universe theorists take to be true. It is, for instance, often said that the block universe view is a view on which the temporal dimension is *just like* the spatial dimension. It's a view on which, instead of supposing there to exist only three dimensions, we instead suppose there to exist four, with the fourth being the temporal dimension. Indeed, sometimes the view is even described as one on which we *spatialise time*.

There is some truth to these claims. It is true that the block universe view is one on which time is a dimension, just as space is a dimension (well, three of them). So, it is a view on which there are some important similarities between time and space. It is also a view on which it is most natural to think of spacetime as being more fundamental than either space or time.

But it's just false to think that it's a view on which the temporal dimension is just like the spatial dimensions. The equations of special and general relativity, for instance, clearly distinguish the three spatial dimensions from the fourth temporal one. One cannot simply treat the temporal dimension as though it is one of the spatial dimensions (and *vice versa*). Moreover, even if we move away from science itself and just consider metaphysical aspects of the block, it's clear that defenders of the view hold that the temporal dimension has quite different properties from any of the three spatial dimensions.

First, the temporal dimension is the dimension along which we find causation. Causes and effects are (typically at least) *temporally* separated. Earlier causes typically cause later effects. By contrast, we rarely (and perhaps never) find causation happening across space. So, if we want to causally intercede on the world, we do it by intervening at one time, in order to intervene at another time. We don't try to intervene at one location in space, in order to intervene at another location in space (at the same moment in time).

This marks an important difference between space and time on the block universe view. The temporal dimension is the only dimension along which causes propagate. This difference can, in turn, be expected to ground there being a significant difference between temporal change and spatial change. While both spatial and temporal change might be said to be variation along some dimension, spatial change is usually *mere variation*. That is, the variation along the spatial dimension is not the product of causation. By contrast, temporal change is often the product of causation.

Think about the kinds of ordinary changes we witness; the ways each of us is, tomorrow at least, in part a product of the choices we make and the causal influences upon us today. We change (*inter alia*) by making decisions, earlier in time, about what we will do and how we will be at later times. Indeed, these kinds of changes are important to us precisely because they are the sorts of things over which we have some control. These temporal changes, however, are quite different from spatial changes, in which it is very rarely (if ever) the case that how something is at one spatial location is causally connected to how it is at some other spatial location.

The point, then, is that it makes sense to deliberate about *how* to bring about temporal changes, while it makes no sense to deliberate about how to bring about spatial changes. Since deliberation (and causal connections more generally) are important to us, it can hardly be surprising that temporal change seems to us to be quite different from spatial change; for, in this respect, it is. The fact that causation only runs along the temporal dimension marks a real and important difference between temporal and spatial change—a difference that the block universe view can accommodate.

This difference, alone, it seems to me, is sufficient to show that (2*) is false.

There are, however, other differences to which we can appeal. Notice that we can (and do) make predictions about what will, or did, happen at future and past times, using information about how things are at the present time, in conjunction with the laws of nature. If the laws of nature are deterministic, then, in principle, someone who knows the laws and knows all of the particular matters of fact at a time can predict what did and will happen at any other time.

To be a bit more precise about this, let's imagine a block universe world. Let's imagine we are looking down on it from a God's-eye perspective. It's natural to imagine that there is one correct way to 'slice' the block into times. But the lessons we learned in Chapters 1 and 2 from thinking about special relativity show us that this is not so. There are lots of ways that we can slice up the block into 'times' that correspond to the events that will be observed to be simultaneous in various inertial frames.

So, there are various ways we can slice up the block so that each slice contains events that are space-like separated from one another and do not contain any events that are time-like separated from each other. Let's call each of these slices *space-like slices* (they are also sometimes known as *achronal slices*). Each of these slices looks a bit like a time, but they are called space-like slices because (very roughly) they are slices *through* space, rather than *through* time. Each way of slicing the block into space-like slices is one perfectly good way of dividing it up into times.

Notably, when we slice the block into space-like slices, we can take any slice and, with the laws of nature in hand, we can make predictions about what is happening at other space-like slices. To capture this idea, it is sometimes said that the laws of nature are *projectable along the temporal dimension*. That is to say, we can look at the ways things are on a space-like slice and we can project backwards or forwards in time, to see how things were (or probably were) or will be at other times in the block. This is pretty handy. Although you and I are probably not sitting in our kitchens using the laws of nature to work out what will happen tomorrow (or what did happen yesterday), we most certainly assume that our world is largely predictable along the temporal dimension. We assume that similar actions will result in similar effects. We assume that the kitchen that was here yesterday will be here tomorrow, barring hurricanes and bushfires. And so on. It would, in fact, be impossible to navigate our world if it wasn't predictable in this way.

Notice, though, that there are other ways we could slice up the block. We could, for instance, slice *along*, instead of *across*, the temporal dimension. We could call these slices *time-like slices*, because they contain events that are time-like separated. (So, time-like slices are slices along the temporal dimension and, consequently, are nothing at all like times). These slices contain events that light can travel between, and hence events that could be causally connected. So, time-like slices are slices of the block that contain lots of bits of space at different times, instead of containing lots of bits of space at the same time.

Importantly, if we take a time-like slice and use the laws of nature and try to predict what will happen at other time-like slices, we fail. Knowing everything about how the universe at a particular 'bit of' space, at *every* time (knowing how things at a time-like slice) is, alongside knowing the laws of nature, doesn't tell you everything about how things are at any other 'bit of' space at every time (how things are at some other time-like slice). This is not to say that we cannot learn something about how things are at one time-like slice by looking at how they are at another time-like slice. Sometimes, we can learn some things. Sometimes, knowing how things are at one bit of space does give us some information about how they are at a nearby bit of space. But our capacity to do this is limited. That's because, in general, the laws of nature don't allow us to work out how things are at one time-like slice from how they are at another time-like slice. We can capture this by saying that the laws of nature are not projectable along the spatial dimensions.

Again, this is something we are all pretty familiar with. I can predict what things will be like around here (in Bundanoon, Australia) tomorrow by knowing what they are like here, today. But I cannot use how things are here, in Bundanoon, Australia, to predict how things are 150kms away.

This marks another important difference between spatial change and temporal change. Temporal change, by unfolding along the temporal dimension, is the kind of change that we can predict, or at least, predict more often and with much more generality than spatial change. Of course, we don't have enough information to predict perfectly. Still, an important aspect of our very existence is that we are able to take information from one time and use it to figure out, to an approximation, how things will be at some other time. Being able to do so is what makes navigating our world possible. But this is typically not something we can do when it comes to spatial change. I typically cannot predict the ways in which spatial change will unfold by looking at how things are at one space and predicting how they will be at some other space.

This is another important difference between spatial and temporal change. That difference, too, is one that shows that (2*) is false. Hence, we should reject the conclusion to the amended argument. Even though (1*) is true, (2*) is not.

Although I said I would focus on the amended version of the argument, let's briefly return to the original argument. Are any of the differences to which I have pointed ones that would ground there being a relevant metaphysical difference between spatial and temporal change? I don't know. But here's the dilemma. If these differences are sufficient for there to be a relevant metaphysical difference between spatial and temporal change, then I've shown that (2) is false and the original argument fails. Suppose, though, that they are not sufficient for there to be a relevant metaphysical difference. Then (2) is true. But if these differences don't count as relevant metaphysical differences, then I think we have good reason to reject (1). For the only reason (1) seemed plausible was because there seem to be obvious and important differences between spatial and temporal change. (1) is an attempt to capture this. But if what is required, for the truth of (1), is something *more* than that there are important differences between spatial and temporal change, then, I submit, we have no reason to think that (1) is true. We only have reason to think that (1*) is true. And I've already shown that the amended argument, which makes use of (1*), fails because (2*) is false.

In sum, then, both the original argument and the amended argument fail. We have no reason to think that the block universe view fails to accommodate there being some relevant and important difference between spatial and temporal change.

In this section, I have argued that the block universe theorist can accommodate there being important differences between spatial and temporal change. Perhaps she cannot accommodate there being a metaphysical difference between the two (depending on what that would amount to). But there is no reason to suppose that she needs to point to a metaphysical difference. As long as she can explain why and in what regard the two are different, then that is sufficient to show that the argument from change fails.

2. Direction, Asymmetry, and Explanation

In Chapter 1, I argued that the block universe view better explains the sorts of asymmetries that we see around us. In Chapter 3, Nikk argued that this is false. In this section, I want to evaluate that response.

In Chapter 3 Nikk made the following concession: the fact that time robustly passes, or, as it's put in Chapter 3, the fact that reality is tensed, does not explain any of these asymmetries. On that, we agree. It's important to remember that many tensed theorists of time do not concede any such thing. Often, defenders of tensed theories of time think that it is the tensed nature of reality that explains how it is that time has a direction and, in turn, that it is this tensed nature that explains why we see the various asymmetries that we do. So, I'll take that concession as a win.

In Chapter 3, Nikk argued, however, that the block universe view is no better placed to explain these asymmetries than is the tensed theorist, and hence no better placed than the presentist. If that is right, then the argument I offered in Chapter 1 fails.

The argument offered in Chapter 3 is, roughly speaking, as follows. There are certain asymmetries that we want to explain. We can explain those asymmetries by appealing to physics. (I suggested in Chapter 1 that the explanation appeals to entropy, but for the purposes of this argument, it doesn't really matter). But, whatever the exact details of that explanation, Nikk says, it has *nothing at all* to do with metaphysics: that explanation is entirely orthogonal to whether our world is a presentist world or a block universe world. So, the presentist and the block universe theorist can appeal to that explanation equally. The presentist is not better off in this regard than the block universe theorist, but nor is she, as I argued, worse off.

Let's look at the argument offered in Chapter 3 in more detail. In principle, it's easy to see why one might think that the presentist and block universe theorist are equally well off when it comes to explaining the relevant asymmetries. To see this, suppose the explanation for time having a direction is that, at 10PM on Tuesday, the monster Swarb does a little *direction dance*. This is, of course, a terrible explanation. But go with me here. The block universe theorist will say that Swarb exists, out there is spacetime at 10PM on Tuesday, and that his doing his dance explains why time has a direction. The presentist thinks that 10PM Tuesday does not exist. But she thinks that there are truths about what did exist, and she thinks that it is now true that Swarb did exist on Tuesday at 10 and that he did a dance at that time. So, she can say that its having been the case that Swarb existed at 10PM on Tuesday and doing a direction dance is what explains why time has the direction it does.

Quite generally, any scientific explanation to which the block universe theorist can appeal it also one to which the presentist can appeal. Indeed, the only kind of explanation that would separate the two views, one might think, is one that explains time's having a direction by appealing to the existence, simpliciter, of past and future events; for the presentist denies there are any such events. But that is not the kind of explanation I offered (or indeed that anyone offers) for the relevant asymmetries.

Rather, I suggested that the block universe theorist should hold that the direction of time is fixed by the direction towards which entropy increases. In particular, I suggested (roughly) that she should say that we will call the direction towards which entropy increases, the future, and the direction towards which it decreases, the past. Then she can say that the direction of time always aligns with the direction of the asymmetries that we see *in* time, because the direction of time is fixed by those very asymmetries. So, the block universe theorist will first explain why there are the asymmetries there are by appealing to various facts about how things in time are distributions (such as facts about entropy). This, in turn, is meant to explain why there are the asymmetries there are and, in turn, why there seem to be the asymmetries there do. She will then say that there being these asymmetries is what makes it seem to us as though time has the direction it does. She will then go on to say that there being these asymmetries is what *determines* what direction time has. So, we have a neat explanation of why time seems to have the direction it does; namely, that the direction time seems to have been determined by the temporal asymmetries, and these in turn determine what direction time does in fact have! Hence, explaining why there are the asymmetries there are and explaining why time has the direction it does amounts to explaining one and the same thing. And that is why, once we explain why time seems to have a direction by explaining why the asymmetries are as they are, we don't then need to worry that time's true direction might be different from the direction that it *seems* to have.

The presentist, though, can say the same thing. Or so Nikk argued in Chapter 3. As Nikk noted, both the block universe theorist and the presentist have to be a little bit careful if they want to say that time's true direction cannot be different from the direction that time seems to have, and hence that time's having that direction explains why time seems to have that direction.

Suppose the block universe theorist posits *primitive* earlier-than and later-than relations, where these relations are primitive because they are not simply determined by the various temporal asymmetries. Then she will face a problem. *Those* relations will determine time's direction. If, however, those relations are not connected to the various temporal asymmetries, then it could be that they determine that the future is, in fact, the direction towards which entropy *decreases*, rather than the direction towards which it *increases*. If so, the true direction of time would be the reverse of the direction in which it *seems* to us as though time is pointed. Then, clearly, the block universe theorist would offer a very bad explanation of why it seems to us that time has a direction. For the direction she says it has would be completely contrary to the direction it seems to us to have.

I completely agree with Nikk here. This is not what the block universe theorist should say. She should instead say that, although, when we slice the block up into times, there is a fundamental fact of the matter regarding which times are between which others, there is no fundamental fact about which *direction* that order has. Rather, which direction along time is past, and which future, is determined by the various contents of time: the temporal asymmetries. This is what determines whether one time is earlier or later than some other time. And that is why the apparent direction of time can be explained by the true direction of time; for the true direction of time cannot 'come apart' from the apparent direction.

Given that sort of picture, the block universe theorist has a nice explanation of why time appears to have the direction it does and why the temporal asymmetries align with the direction of time.

Can the presentist offer the same account? In Chapter 3, Nikk argued that they can.

The view that Nikk presented is one on which the presentist also rejects the idea that the direction of time is independent of the various asymmetries. By doing so, the presentist can then maintain that the apparent direction of and the true direction of time will always align, and hence she can say that time having the direction it does is what explains why time seems to have the direction it does.

Now, of course, the presentist does not have to say this. She could think that, for all we know, the true temporal direction does not align with the temporal asymmetries, and hence does not align with the direction that time seems to us to have. If we did live in such a world, then all of the ways things *seem*, with regard to temporal direction (the ways generated by the temporal asymmetries) would be misleading. We'd be living in a *sceptical scenario* in which we are consistently and massively mislead about temporal direction. Nikk's proposal is a way to avoid the idea that we could live in such a world.

How does this work? Well, in order to say that time's true direction is a function of the temporal asymmetries, Nikk suggested that the presentist deny that time's direction is simply the 'direction' in which the world changes: the direction in which time passes. Most presentists hold that it is the direction of robust temporal passage that determines the true direction of time. To see what that view amounts to, imagine a presentist world from a God's-eye perspective. What does God see? The most natural answer is that God sees a very large three-dimensional object—an object with only spatial dimensions and no temporal dimension—and he sees that object changing.

So, for instance, suppose that God gets up one morning and looks down on a presentist world and sees that it is entirely purple, then, as he watches, it turns green, then blue, then orange. God watches the changing of the presentist world and, in doing so, he watches time itself flowing (or passing) in that world. Suppose Mrs God gets up and asks Mr God which events in the presentist world are earlier, and which later. She asks God, "Was the presentist world first purple, then green, then blue, then orange, or was the presentist world first orange, then blue, then green, then purple?" Call the purple slice of the presentist world S1, the green slice S2, the blue slice S3, and the orange slice S4. Then is it the case that S1 is earlier than S2, which is earlier than S3, which is earlier than S4, so that time flows from S1 to S4, or is the reverse true, so that time flows from S4 to S1?

There appears to be an obvious answer to this question: time flows from S1 to S4, and it does that because the presentist world changes from being purple to being green (and so on), rather than the other way around. The process of the world changing from one state to another determines that the state from which it changes is earlier than the state to which it changes. It is this direction of change that determines the direction of the flow of time. This, I take it, is what a standard version of presentism will say.

On this view, if the world changes from purple to green to blue to orange, its doing so constitutes the direction of time. This is precisely what Nikk denies. And here is why. Suppose that entropy decreases from S1 to S4 (or, put the other way around, it increases from S4 to S1). Then it will seem, to those in the presentist world, as though the direction from S4 to S1 is the direction towards the future, and the direction from S1 to S4 is the direction towards the past, even though, in fact, the reverse is true. So, the true direction of time will be different from the apparent direction of time, and the former certainly will not explain the latter. That is an unfortunate result and one that Nikk wants to avoid.

Nikk's proposal, offered in Chapter 3, was to reject the idea that there is some fact of the matter which direction time flows in which determines the direction of time independently of the temporal asymmetries.

Recall that the block universe theorist I have in mind holds that there is no fact of the matter, given by the nature of time itself, as to whether, say, x is earlier or later than y and z, even though there is a fact of the matter that y is *between* x and z. Similarly, the presentist needs to say that there is no fact of the mater, given by the nature of temporal flow, as to whether S1 is earlier than S4 or S4 is earlier than S1. There is only the fact that S2 is between S1 and S3 (and so on). Then, she will say that, if entropy increases from S4 to S1, then S4 is earlier than S1; whereas if, instead, entropy decreases from S4 to S1, then she will say that S1 is earlier than S4. So, what determines the direction of temporal flow is the direction in which entropy increases. This is the version of presentism that Nikk offered us in Chapter 3.

I think this version of presentism is indeed the analogue of my preferred version of the block universe. Moreover, this version of presentism does indeed close the gap between the apparent direction of time and the true direction of time that I exploited in my arguments in Chapter 1. It is a view on which the true temporal direction cannot come apart from the temporal asymmetries, since the latter determines the former.

But, while this version of the block universe theory is really quite intuitive, this version of presentism is weird beyond belief. Let's see why.

This version of the block universe theory is one on which, when God looks down on the block, she just sees one big, unchanging block. The block does not have any little arrows 'tattooed' into it, which say that the future is one direction and the past the other. The direction of time is not a fundamental aspect of the block. There is nothing odd about this. Think of a Rubik's cube. Which surface of the cube is *really* top, and which *really* bottom? Which surface of the cube is *really* left, and which *really* right? You should be stumped by this question: the cube can be oriented in any number of ways, and there is nothing about the cube that determines that one surface is *really the top*. Of course, those who spend a lot of time with the cube could, for pragmatic reasons, give one of the surfaces a name and declare that it will be the 'top' of the cube. If you were going to give someone instructions on how to solve the puzzle, you might need them to orient the cube in a particular way so that they can follow your instructions. Declaring that one surface is the top would be one way to coordinate the cubes into the same orientation. Indeed, 'top', in the context of cubes, might just come to mean 'the particular surface that, for practical purposes, we declare to be the top'. Then people could come to talk about the top of the cube, and they would say true things about its nature. There would be nothing puzzling about this.

So, suppose that, looking down at the block, God notices that the contents of the block are asymmetric: entropy increases in one direction, causes point in one direction, and so on. The block universe theorist will say that, given what we mean by the words 'future' and 'past', once God notices those asymmetries in time, he will be able to infer which direction is past, and which future. For God will realise that 'past' just *means* the direction towards which we remember and have records (roughly), while 'future' just means the direction towards which we deliberate and have no records (roughly). Since the asymmetric phenomena in time determine which direction is the one towards which we have records, this determines which direction is the one we will call future and which direction we will call past. There is, as it were, no deep metaphysical fact about past and future that God discovers. God simply knows how we use those words and, given this, knows which direction will count, for us, as past, and which future. There is nothing odd about the resulting picture of the world. There are no arrows in a Rubik's cube, and it's not that odd to think there are not special little inbuilt arrows in the block. Instead, on this view, there are facts about which direction is past, and which future (at least relative to a location in time), but these are determined by the temporal asymmetries at that location.

According the presentist analogue of this view, though, there is no independent fact of the matter as to which direction time flows in—independent, as it were, of the facts about temporal asymmetries (such as entropy). That, however, is weird.

The presentist thinks that new things come into and pass out of existence. On her view, the totality of what there is constantly changes. There is no nice, static block which simply fails to have inbuilt arrows. Instead, she has to say that, although the world is one in which things come into and pass out of existence, *there is no fact of the matter as to whether x comes into existence before y, or the converse,* independently of the facts about whether entropy (say) is increasing from x to y or from y to x. That is monumentally bizarre. The presentist should think that, when God looks down on our world, He either sees that world changing from purple to green or from green to purple, and that what he sees fixes the direction of time. The version of presentism offered in Chapter 3 denied this. On that view, there is no fact of the matter as to whether the world changes from purple to green or from green to purple, independent of facts about the relative entropy of the green and purple states of the world.

But surely there *is* a fact of the matter as to whether the world changes from purple to green or from green to purple; surely there is a fact of the matter as to whether first x comes into existence and then y, or first y comes into existence and then x. What would it be for that to fail to be true?

To see how additionally puzzling this view is, let's consider a world in which entropy increases away from each boundary of the world. Suppose the world contains eight slices, (eight complete ways the world is at some time) and that they are ordered as follows: S1, S2, S3, S4, S5, S6, S7, S8. That is to say, there is a fact of the matter that S2 is between S1 and S3, and a fact of the matter that S7 is between S8 and S6 (and so on). But there is no fundamental fact (we are to suppose) as to whether S1 is earlier than S2 (and so on) or whether, instead, S2 is earlier than S1 (and so on). That is, there is no fundamental fact as to whether S1 is the first moment and S8 the last, or whether S8 is the first moment and S1 is the last. Rather, *which* of these is the case is determined by whether entropy is increasing from S1 to S8 or from S8 to S1.

Suppose, though, that, in this world, entropy is increasing from S1 to S4 and entropy is decreasing from S5 to S8. It's worth noting, as I did in Chapter 1, that this world (though a toy world) is perfectly consistent with the laws of nature. Entropy will increase away from a low entropy state. If both S1 and S8 have very low entropy states, then entropy will increase away from both of them, towards S4 and S5.

What are we to say about temporal direction in this world? Well, the block universe theory has no difficulties here. The block universe theorist will simply say that the block has *two local directions of time*. At one end of the block (the S1 end), people will, quite rightly, say that S1 is the past and S8 is future. At the other end of the block (the S8 end), people will, quite rightly, say that S8 is the past and S2 is the future. Since there is nothing metaphysically heavyweight about temporal direction on this view, there is nothing odd about this. One man's north is another man's south. From the perspective of Hobart, Sydney is to the north. From the perspective of Byron Bay, Sydney is to the south. That's not unduly puzzling. The same is true of 'past' and 'future' for the block universe theorist. After all, for her, talk about 'past' and 'future' is really just talk about the local temporal asymmetries.

According to the presentist theory developed by Nikk, the direction that time flows in is determined by the direction of entropy increase. So, the presentist is going to have to say that time flows from S1 to S4, because entropy increases from S1 to S4. But she is also going to have to say that time flows from S8 to S5, since entropy increases from S8 to S5. So, she is going to have to say that time flows in *two* different directions: it flows from S1 to S4, or, as we might say, it flows away from S1 and towards S8. But it also flows from S8 to S5, or, as it we might say, it flows away from S8 and towards S1. So, it both flows away from S1 and, hence, towards S8, as well as flowing away from S8 and, hence, towards S1. But it's hard to see how time can both flow away from, as well as towards, both S1 and S8. Now, the presentist could say that time flows from S1 to S4, but then, when it gets to S5, it somehow *reverses* its direction of flow, which is why it's also true to say that time flows from S8 to S5. But what can that mean? How can time flow backwards? The presentist has no account of backwards temporal flow. After all, most presentists simply think that temporal flow is what we get when the present moment changes from being one way to being another. On that view, we can't make any sense of time flowing in reverse; of course, time always flows in the direction in which the world changes.

The problem, then, is that we cannot coherently describe the world in question. It cannot both be that the between-ness relations are as we say they are (that S2 is between S1 and S3, and that S7 is between S8 and S6, and S5 is between S4 and S6) and *also* that time's direction of flow is given by the entropic gradient. For then, we have to say that time flows in two different directions in the same world!

So, while it's true that the presentist can ape the explanation offered by the block universe theorist, the view she ends up defending is very peculiar. That is because, on the block universe view, all the slices exist simpliciter, in some order. All that remains to be determined by the asymmetries of the contents of time is whether time has a direction and, if so, what it is; or, indeed, whether time has multiple different local directions. Time does not flow, so there is no fact of the matter as to in which order those slices came into existence. Hence, it makes good sense to think that direction is nothing but a matter of there being certain asymmetries of the contents of time. Direction is, on this view, pretty cheap. But direction and flow are not cheap for the presentist. The presentist thinks that things come into and out of existence; that there is a robust sense in which time passes. If there is this robust notion of passage, however, then it is very hard to square this with the idea that direction is cheap. It requires us saying that there is no independent fact of the matter as to which things come into existence first, and which later, and no independent fact of the matter as to which direction change occurs in, independent of the facts about the asymmetric contents of time. But I fail to see how that can be. And, even if I did see how that could be, it would strike me as a deeply peculiar view.

So, I conclude, the block universe theory does much better at explaining why time seems to have the direction that it does.

> In this section, I considered the view that the presentist explains the various temporal asymmetries by holding that these asymmetries necessarily line up with the direction of temporal passage because they determine that direction. I responded to this idea by offering what we might think of as 'the argument from God'. In that argument, I tried to show just how peculiar such a view is; for it is a view on which there is no fact of the matter what order events occur in, from a God's eye perspective, given by the nature of the changing present itself. Until God knows something about the distribution of entropy at different times, God himself knows nothing about the direction of time. This is a very peculiar view, and not one that most presentists will find amenable. So, I conclude, eternalism better explains the temporal asymmetries than does presentism.

Chapter 6

Presentism Returns
Reply to Kristie Miller's Reply

Nikk Effingham

Contents

1. Introduction 165
2. Ontological Parsimony 166
3. Truthmaking 170
4. Ontological Parsimony Again: Qualitative Parsimony 172
5. Ontological Parsimony Again, Again: Quantitative Parsimony 174
6. Do Propositions Exist? 176
7. Permissivism 177
8. Conclusion 180

1. Introduction

Chapter 4 covers a lot of ground. In the space allotted to me, I cannot adequately respond to every point, so I confine myself to discussing just two of Kristie's objections. These objections are related; each challenges my argument that presentism is true because it is ontologically parsimonious.

The first objection focuses on what I mean by 'ontological parsimony'. Mathematicians have proven that, if you have an infinite number of things and another infinite number of things, then there are the same number of both. The resulting worry is that, if there were an infinite number of things regardless of whether presentism was true or not, then the presentist's theory could never be more parsimonious than the block theorist's. In my response below, I argue that there's a way of understanding parsimony such that, even when there are an infinite number of things according to two theories, one theory can nevertheless be more parsimonious than the other.

The second objection I discuss focuses on how I respond to worries about truthmaking. In Chapter 2 I argued that some truths have no further explanation and that this includes (certain) past truths. In Chapter 4 it is argued that the introduction of such unexplained truths threatens the supposed parsimony of my presentist theory. Below, I explain in detail why believing there are such truths is not an ontological matter, thus not relevant to weighing which theory is more parsimonious than another.

2. Ontological Parsimony

2.1 Qualitative Versus Quantitative Parsimony

I have argued that we should favour presentism because it is ontologically parsimonious compared to the block universe theory. In Chapter 4, Kristie disambiguated what I might mean by 'ontological parsimony'. Do I mean that presentism guarantees a theory with fewer entities? Or fewer *kinds* of entities? The first type of parsimony is called *quantitative parsimony*. The second type is called *qualitative parsimony*. Kristie argued in Chapter 4 that either option leads to problems.

It is quantitative parsimony that I had in mind when I advanced my argument for presentism. That is, I believe presentism guarantees fewer entities, not necessarily fewer kinds of entities. (Indeed, I am suspicious of qualitative parsimony in general, since I am not entirely sure what a 'kind' is meant to be. Set this worry aside for now—although, below, I will discuss issues related to this worry.)

2.2 Problems With Infinity

Kristie argued that it could not be quantitative parsimony that I had in mind. Her worry stems from how *infinite cardinalities* work.

The 'cardinality' of a set of things is a measure of how many things are members of that set. In cases where sets contain a finite number of things, this is straightforward. A set of five objects has a cardinality of five; a set of ten objects has a cardinality of ten; since five is smaller than ten, there are fewer objects in the first set than the second.

But when we consider collections of infinitely many things, it all starts to get quite weird. Consider two sets. One is the set of all natural numbers—i.e., 1, 2, 3, 4 . . . The second is the set of all odd numbers—i.e., 1, 3, 5, 7 . . . Intuitively, there are fewer things in the second set than in the first; after all, the first set includes all members of the second and then adds some more! But Georg Cantor, a famous mathematician, proved otherwise. He demonstrated that those two sets have the same cardinality.

The proof is simple (although, if you're not interested in it, feel free to take my word for it and skip the next paragraph). Two sets have the same cardinality if and only if we can place their members in *one-to-one correspondence*. Take, for example, the Three Stooges and the national capitals of South Africa. There are three of each. The Stooges have Moe, Larry, and Curley as members. The national capitals of South Africa are Pretoria, Cape Town, and Bloemfontein. We can take those two sets and pair their members off with one another—e.g.,:

Moe	⇔	Pretoria
Larry	⇔	Cape Town
Curley	⇔	Bloemfontein

(The exact pairings don't matter, so by all means instead pair Moe with Cape Town, Larry with Bloemfontein, and Curley with Pretoria, or what have you.) Each member of one set is paired with the member of the other and vice versa. This is what it is to stand in one-to-one correspondence; this is what it is for those sets to have the same cardinality; this is what it is for there to be as many Stooges as there are national capitals in South Africa. And when we turn to the set of all natural numbers and all odd numbers, we see that they also stand in a one-to-one correspondence:

1 ⇔ 1
2 ⇔ 3
3 ⇔ 5
4 ⇔ 7
5 ⇔ 9
... and so on.

We never run out of odd numbers to pair the natural numbers with! And, similarly, we never run out of natural numbers to pair the odd numbers with! Thus, they stand in one-to-one correspondence, and there are as many odd numbers as there are natural numbers. (Cantor goes on to prove that some infinite cardinalities *are* bigger than others; indeed, for any cardinality, there are infinitely many larger cardinalities. But these larger cardinalities are irrelevant to what I am talking about here. So, assume that whenever I say 'infinite' below, I always mean to refer to a cardinality of the same size.)

This mathematical insight proves problematic when it comes to my argument for presentism. If there were infinitely many things according to both presentism and the block universe theory, then the former cannot be more parsimonious than the latter, since they both commit to the same cardinality of entities—i.e., there is the same number of things according to both theories.

One response to this would be to argue that the presentist need only commit to finitely many things. This is almost certainly an untenable line to take. Given the argument of Chapter 4, I'd have to argue that I know—indeed, know *a priori* nonetheless—that the universe isn't infinitely big and does not contain an infinite number of material objects spread throughout the infinite vastness of space. Along similar lines, I'd have to claim that presentism was incompatible with matter being infinitely divisible (for if matter were infinitely divisible, then if anything material exists, its infinitely many parts would also exist). Finally, there might be an infinite number of abstract objects according to both presentism and the block universe theory; for instance, Chapter 4 appealed to the example of spacetime points, and we might also have in mind examples like numbers. If numbers exist, then there are an infinite number of them. In that case, whether either presentism or the block universe theory were true, there would be an infinite number of things.

All that said, I will assume that there *is* an infinite number of things. Whilst that assumption might be wrong, I'm conceding it to make my life harder, not easier—it is a *charitable* concession that I am making on behalf of the block theorist. The next sub-section argues that, even given this assumption, presentism is nevertheless more parsimonious than the block universe theory.

2.3 Parsimony in the Face of Infinity

In Chapter 4, it was argued that, if two theories are such that neither has fewer entities than the other, then one cannot be more parsimonious than the other. That is, the argument presented in that chapter assumes:

(1) If theory T is quantitatively ontologically parsimonious compared to T^* then T commits to fewer things existing than T^*.

(In Chapter 4 this is called 'NUMB'.) I deny (1). However, I endorse its converse:

(2) If T commits to fewer things existing than T^* then T is quantitatively ontologically parsimonious compared to T^*.

(2) is obviously true. If one theory commits to five things and another to ten things, the former is more parsimonious than the latter. But (2)'s being obviously true does not mean (1) is true, for there may be other ways for one theory to be quantitatively parsimonious compared to another theory.

Consider the following example. Imagine we conduct an experiment with a particle accelerator. Inside the accelerator, a reaction is initiated which brings into existence certain particles. Theory T_1 says that, post-reaction, the accelerator contains an infinite number of hoovon particles. Moreover, each particle causes some given quantum event to occur (so there are an infinite number of such quantum events occurring shortly after the experiment is conducted). Theory T_2 agrees that exactly the same hoovon particles exist, each initiating exactly the same quantum events. However, T_2 adds there are, *in addition*, infinitely many extra hoovon particles which do nothing, interact with nothing, and are invisible to any method of detection. Those hoovon particles bring about no quantum event. In the same way that adding an infinite number of odd numbers to the infinite number of even numbers gets you a set of things with the same cardinality as both the two other sets, theory T_1 and T_2 commit to the same cardinality of entities—i.e., an infinite number of them. Yet, intuitively, T_2 is less parsimonious than T_1; even though the cardinality of T_2's commitments is no different from T_1's, the former theory is intuitively less parsimonious than the latter. Quantitative parsimony should favour T_1, even though it has the same cardinality of entities in it as T_2. Thus, (1) appears to be false.

We can capture what's going on here by introducing *subsets*. T_1 commits to a subset of the entities committed to by T_2; that is, every entity committed to by T_1 is committed to by T_2 and, further, T_2 commits to some entities not committed to by T_1. (Compare: the odd numbers are a subset of the natural numbers, since every odd number is a natural number, but some natural numbers are not odd.) Where a theory's commitments are a subset of a competing theory's commitments, it is correct to say that the former is more quantitatively ontologically parsimonious than the latter—i.e.,:

(3) If theory T commits to a subset of the entities T^* commits to, then T is quantitatively ontologically parsimonious compared to T^*.

Given (3), presentism is more parsimonious than the block universe theory. Even if the universe is infinitely wide and contains infinitely many galaxies, the set of entities committed to by presentism is nevertheless a subset of the entities committed to by the block universe theory. After all, the presentist commits to the presently existing objects (of which there are an infinite number) and does not commit to the past and future objects, whilst the block universe theory commits to exactly the same presently existing objects *plus* the past and future objects (of which there are also an infinite number). The cardinality of the presentist's set of commitments is infinite, as is the block universe theorist's. Yet the presentist's set of commitments is a subset of what the block universe theorist has to commit to. Thus, given (3), the presentist theory is quantitatively ontologically parsimonious compared to the block universe theory. This solves the worry articulated in Chapter 4 about using quantitative parsimony to motivate presentism.

(An interesting question is whether (2) and (3) are the only ways to be quantitatively ontologically parsimonious. I suspect there are other ways, but we need not explore that question here.)

In Chapter 2, I argued that we should prefer presentism because it commits to fewer things. Kristie argued I must mean fewer *kinds* of things, rather than fewer things. This is because, given either presentism or the block universe theory, it's fair to presume that there will be an infinite number of things. Since one infinite collection of things is the same in number ('cardinality') as another infinite collection of things, I would be wrong to believe presentism commits to fewer things than the block universe theory. So, my only option must be to talk about fewer *kinds* of things.

But I disagree. One way for a theory to be parsimonious compared to another is to commit to fewer things. I agree that both presentism and the block universe theory may well commit to the same number of things (i.e., an infinite number) and so I agree that presentism won't be parsimonious compared to the block universe theory in *that* respect.

But there's another way for a theory to be more parsimonious than another theory: it can commit to a *subset* of entities that the other theory commits to. This is true of presentism when compared to the block universe theory. So, even though both theories commit to the same number of entities, presentism is still more parsimonious.

3. Truthmaking

Kristie also takes issue with what I say about truthmaking. I will focus on the argument from Chapter 4, whereby my theory's commitment to certain past truths being inexplicable causes a problem for the presentist's argument from ontological parsimony. In response, I argue that such past truths are no extra *ontological* commitment for the presentist.

3.1 Fundamental Truths

In Chapter 2 I introduced 'fundamental truths'. Recalling that '<φ>' is just the name for any proposition φ:

<φ> is a fundamental truth iff (i) <φ> is true;
(ii) there is no proposition that metaphysically explains why <φ> is true.

Fundamental truths, then, are in some sense 'inexplicable' in that they are not metaphysically explained by any other truth. Imagine some tiny, partless particle of sub-atomic physics. Call it q (after 'quark'). <q exists> is the sort of proposition that is fundamental in the sense I have just defined—i.e., no other *proposition* metaphysically explains why it's true.

However, as was made clear in Chapter 4, <q exists> nevertheless has *some* explanation for being true. That explanation is not another proposition being true, however. Rather, there's some sense in which we can say that <q exists> is explained by q. Since q isn't a proposition (it's a sub-atomic particle!), <q exists> is a fundamental truth, at least given how I have defined the term.

The problem Kristie presented in Chapter 4 isn't a problem with fundamental truths *per se*; rather it's just a problem for any fundamental truth that does not have any explanation whatsoever. We might see this in terms of truthmaking, whereby q is the truthmaker for <q exists>; Kristie's worry would be that, whilst there can be fundamental truths, there cannot be fundamental truths with no truthmaker. Now, Chapter 4 doesn't quite cash it out in truthmaking terms. It instead cashes it out as the claim that <q exists> 'marries up' to some chunk of reality (namely the chunk of reality containing q). Even if you don't accept the entirety of truthmaking theory, Chapter 4 argues that every true proposition ultimately has to be matched by a piece of reality.

My claim—which Kristie took issue with in Chapter 4—is that some fundamental truths *don't* marry up to reality in this manner. We can say I believe in *unmarried fundamental truths* (i.e., fundamental truths that don't pair up with some slice of the world in order to make them true). Kristie does not believe in such unmarried fundamental truths. (What I call 'unmarried fundamental truths' are what are called 'Fundamental Truths' in Chapter 4—note the capital 'F' and 'T'!)

I will, very briefly, discuss the claim that unmarried fundamental truths are weird and counterintuitive. My reply is simple: Who says? I do not think it's obvious that truths must always marry up with some piece of reality. For instance, consider:

<It is possible for Dwayne 'The Rock' Johnson to have won the 2020 USA presidential election>

That proposition does not seem to be married to any part of reality; for what candidates are there for that marriage? One candidate would be that the proposition is married to some piece of reality where Dwayne Johnson is winning the presidential election. But that's just crazy!

Another candidate is that the proposition is married simply to Johnson as he actually is, even though he's never won an election. One problem is this: what is it *about* Johnson that means the proposition is paired with him in this manner? Another, more serious, problem is that, if Johnson alone can be what the proposition is married to, then I get to change my mind and say that truths about the past *are* married to some piece of reality. If Johnson gets to be the partner in the above marriage, then, when we consider potential unmarried fundamental truths like:

<209 years ago, it used to be the case that atom a_1 was located at region r_1 and was F>

I will say that the proposition is married off to some portion of reality; namely, the region of space in question (i.e., r_1). In that case, the proposition *would* be married to some presently existing thing. If it works for the proposition about Johnson, why would it not work for the proposition about a_1 having once been at r_1?

In short, I don't think that all truths are married to bits of reality. Note, though, that I do think there's some interesting relation between reality and true propositions (fundamental or otherwise). It would be weird if the two could be thoroughly disconnected, after all. How strange it would be if, say, <God exists> were true even though, in reality, no God existed! But I have already explained how to avoid that worry back in Chapter 1. Whilst <209 years ago, it used to be the case that atom a_1 was located at region r_1 and was F> is true and fails to latch onto any part of the world, there nevertheless *used to be* something which it latched onto. Truths about how the world presently is latch onto things that presently exist, but truths about how the world used to be need only for reality to *have once been* a certain way. So, where Kristie called for some sort of connection between truth and reality, I agree that there is one! I just don't think that the correct connection is the sort of connections that bears out block theory being true.

4. Ontological Parsimony Again: Qualitative Parsimony

The discussion above was only brief because I want to press on to discuss the second argument Kristie gave in Chapter 4. That argument sets aside worries about whether fundamental truths must marry up to some portion of reality and advances a further argument which charitably accepts that there can be unmarried fundamental truths. The idea is that such truths threaten the original aim of obtaining a parsimonious ontology. Focussing on qualitative parsimony, rather than quantitative parsimony, Kristie argued that, in introducing unmarried fundamental truths, the presentist has introduced an additional *kind* of entity. Thus, the presentist's theory is worse off compared to the block universe theorist's, since it includes an additional ontological kind.

Even though it is quantitative, not qualitative, parsimony that plays the crucial role in motivating presentism, I cannot ignore this argument. This is because there is more to motivating presentism than merely saying that it is quantitatively parsimonious compared to block universe theory; you must further believe that the block universe theory does not itself have any benefits that outweigh its lack of quantitative parsimony. And Kristie's argument, if sound, would show that the block universe theory had just such a benefit. Whilst the block universe theory might be quantitatively less parsimonious than presentism, the block universe theory would be qualitatively more parsimonious. Were that true, when we compare the two theories, it would no longer be clear-cut that we should prefer presentism.

Nevertheless, I think the presentist's theory is still at least as qualitatively parsimonious as the block universe theory. So I will argue, unmarried fundamental truths are not a different ontological kind—when we come to consider qualitative parsimony, it is only ontological kinds that we are looking to reduce, not any old kind of thing. If that is correct, then presentism is still at least as parsimonious as the block universe theory.

Let me elaborate (and, hopefully, cast some light on what the difference is between a 'kind' and an 'ontological kind'). Firstly, notice that, when weighing metaphysical theories, if we're trying to guarantee qualitative parsimony, then it isn't parsimony regarding any old kind that is important. To see why, consider two comparisons.

> The first comparison: Theory T_3 says that not only do objects exist (i.e., sub-atomic particles, chairs, mountains, etc.) but properties also exist (i.e., the property of *Red* or *Blue* or *Being a Chair*). Theory T_4 says that only objects exist and that there are no properties—it is what is called a 'nominalist theory'. Clearly, qualitative parsimony favours T_4. The kinds of entities that those theories disagree over (i.e., properties) are *ontological kinds*.
>
> The second comparison: Theory T_5 and theory T_6 differ only over whether some people have trained to become professional footballers: T_5 says they did; T_6 says they did not. Being a professional footballer is a kind of thing you can be. But whilst, in the first comparison, I see the reasoning behind thinking T_4 is more parsimonious than T_3, here I do not. This is because 'professional footballer' is not an 'interesting kind'. I don't see any reason to believe T_6 is better, at least vis-à-vis qualitative ontological parsimony. What business would metaphysics have with adjudicating between such theories; that is, why think that parsimony of kinds is in any sense a virtue *in this case*?

I draw two lessons from this. First, if qualitative parsimony is meant to be a virtue, then some kinds must be 'special'—they must be the 'ontological kinds'. Second, when it comes to adjudicating qualitative parsimony, we should favour theories with the fewest ontological kinds, not the fewest kinds in general.

There are good questions about what it takes for a kind to be ontological. As I mentioned earlier, I worry whether this question can ever be settled and so worry about using qualitative parsimony to help decide between theories. But, given the dialectic, it's charitable for me to set aside that worry and assume that there's an answer as to which kinds are ontological and which are not. So, I'll assume that, whatever the answer is, kinds like 'mortgage broker' and 'footballer' won't be ontological kinds whilst kinds like 'object', 'property', and 'number' are ontological. (Perhaps you think *other* kinds are ontological—e.g., 'universal' and 'particular'. I don't think such alternative assumptions make any difference to what I say below.)

Once I am in the headspace of thinking I know what an ontological kind is, it seems to me that unmarried fundamental truths are *not* an ontological kind. I agree that propositions are an ontological kind, but their being unmarried/married or fundamental/non-fundamental is *not* a difference in ontological kind; it's just a different way that those propositions might be. (Compare: if numbers exist, then odd and even numbers are not different ontological kinds; rather, being odd versus being even are just two different ways that a number might be.)

I can flesh this out with an argument. Continuing to assume that I know what ontological kinds are, I find it irresistible to believe:

(4) Nothing is a member of more than one ontological kind.

For instance, were objects and properties the only ontological kinds, then (4) would be true (since no object would be a property and no property would be a material object). I assume that the same thinking applies no matter which kinds end up being ontological kinds (and that (4) is true no matter what).

(4), in tandem with the belief that propositions *are* an ontological kind, gets the conclusion that unmarried fundamental truths are *not* an ontological kind. A 'truth' is just a proposition that is true. It follows that every unmarried fundamental truth is a truth and, since every truth is a proposition, every unmarried fundamental truth is a proposition.

Next, assume (for *reductio*) that unmarried fundamental truths are an ontological kind. In that case, an unmarried fundamental truth would be a member of *two* ontological kinds; namely, 'unmarried fundamental truths' and 'propositions'. Given (4), that's impossible. Thus, by *reductio ad absurdum*, the assumption is false and unmarried fundamental truths are *not* an ontological kind.

So, it is not a problem for presentism that there are unmarried fundamental truths, at least not when it comes to qualitative ontological parsimony.

> The presentist theory I'm advancing has it that there are fundamental truths that don't 'marry up with' any portion of reality. If those truths are an extra kind of entity, then presentism would be qualitatively unparsimonious, compared to the block universe theory. However, I argue that, whilst such truths exist, we should *not* take them to be a new 'kind' of thing.

5. Ontological Parsimony Again, Again: Quantitative Parsimony

But, whilst I might avoid problems with qualitative parsimony, I fear that the presentist stumbles right into another gut punch: even though there's no problem with unmarried fundamental truths and qualitative parsimony, there *is* a problem with introducing such truths, given quantitative parsimony.

There would not be a problem if the block universe theorist and presentist both believed in the same propositions. In that case, whilst they might disagree about what those propositions *were like* (e.g., disagreeing over which ones were fundamental and which weren't, or which ones were true or false), they wouldn't disagree over *whether they existed*. So, there would be no ontological disagreement and, if there is no ontological disagreement regarding propositions, then there are no grounds for thinking the block universe theory can be more parsimonious when it comes to them.

But the block universe theorist may well disagree over what propositions there are. The block universe theory denies that reality has a 'tensed aspect'. That is, where the presentist believes there are *tensed propositions* like:

<209 years ago, it used to be the case that atom a_1 was located at region r_1 and was F>

the block universe theorist might deny that they even exist. The block universe theorist says reality is static; that it has no tensed aspect. We might reasonably draw from this that there are no tensed propositions. Think back to the metaphor of God from Chapter 2. If reality is ultimately tenseless, God does not know any tensed truths. We might think that He does not know any such truths because there are no such tensed propositions for him to know in the first place.

Some propositions, both theories will agree over; namely, tenseless propositions (e.g., <In 1812, Napoleon is invading Russia>) and non-temporal propositions that have no temporal element (e.g., <1 + 1 = 2> or <Red is a colour>). So, the presentist believes in tensed propositions, tenseless propositions, and non-temporal propositions. The block universe theorist only believes in tenseless propositions and non-temporal propositions. But that means the block universe theorist believes in a subset of the propositions that the presentist believes in. And it is this that causes the problem for the presentist! Given (3) from above, presentism is ontologically parsimonious only if it commits to a subset of the things the block universe theory commits to. When we considered only material objects, that was the case (see Figure 6.1). But once we consider propositions, this is no longer the case (see Figure 6.2). Whilst presentism commits to a subset *of the material objects* that the block universe theory commits to, it does not commit to either the same propositions, nor a subset of those

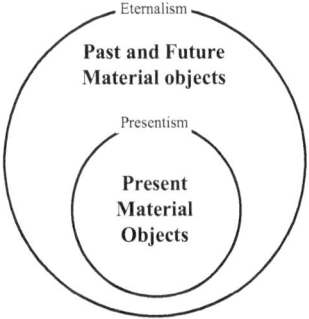

Figure 6.1 Ontological Commitments If We Consider Just Material Objects

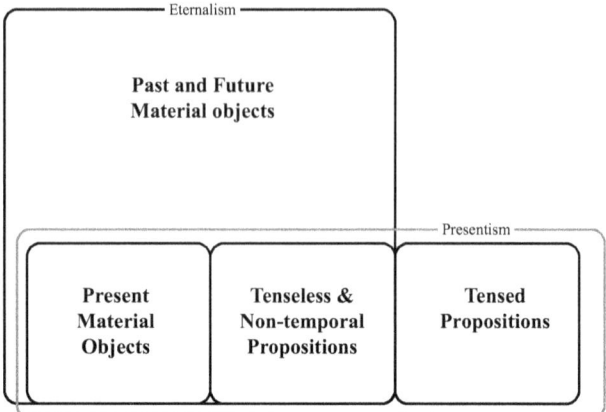

Figure 6.2 Ontological Commitments Including Propositions

propositions, that the block universe theory commits to (since it commits to the tensed propositions). Thus, the presentist's commitments are no longer a subset of the block universe theorist's. The argument from ontological parsimony to presentism is thereby scuppered.

This is a big problem. There are two solutions I will consider, both of which play down the ontological importance of propositions.

> My presentist theory talks about tensed propositions. The block universe theorist need not believe in tensed propositions, believing instead that the only propositions that exist are tenseless. This is a problem, because I said presentism was more parsimonious than the block universe theory, because it commits to a subset of the things that the block universe theory commits to. But now, it looks as if that's false! In committing to some things that the block universe theory does not commit to (i.e., the tensed propositions), presentism no longer commits to a subset of entities that the block universe theorist commits to.
>
> In the next section, I explain how the presentist can avoid this problem.

6. Do Propositions Exist?

The first solution plays down the importance of propositions by denying that propositions exist in the first place. Since they don't exist, the presentist *doesn't* commit to things that the block universe theorist does not.

I hear the complaint already: 'What madness is this? You're the one who keeps talking about propositions! Aren't some propositions being fundamental *crucial* to your presentist theory? And how can that be the case *if there aren't any propositions?'* In response, think back to Chapter 2. There, we talked about limps. For instance, I have had a limp in the past. But even though that's true, it's quite reasonable to deny that limps *exist*—I don't think that I should add limps to the list of entities that exist just because I once sprained my ankle.

Propositions might be like limps. Whilst I constantly *talk about* propositions, that doesn't mean that I want you to take such talk as being 'ontologically serious'. To talk about propositions is just a heuristic—a *façon de parler* with no commitment intended. And, just as limps don't exist but we can still demarcate them into categories (e.g., into being antalgic limps or being neuromuscular limps), propositions needn't exist for them to be true or false, fundamental or non-fundamental, married or unmarried etc.

Crucially, denying that propositions exist wouldn't be some claim idiosyncratic to the presentist. Lots of philosophers deny that propositions exist, since lots of philosophers are suspicious that *any* abstract objects exist. So, the presentist who took this road would be in good company. (Admittedly, those who believe that propositions *do* exist—what are called 'Platonists'—will still have a problem. But I would call it a win if this were the issue around which presentism's truth revolved.)

7. Permissivism

That is one way to deal with the problem. Now I shall consider another.

There are different ways of doing metaphysics. In the lingo of philosophy, questions about how we should do metaphysics are questions about *metametaphysics*. Some people's metametaphysical theories have it that we should argue about what does or does not exist. This is sometimes called a Quinean metametaphysics, after W. V. Quine. But not everyone is a Quinean. Some people believe that everything that you might think of exists. Numbers! Events! States of affairs! Fictional objects! They all exist! Call this view *permissivism* (because it is very permissive about what exists). As it stands, permissivism is not a metametaphysical theory, but just a metaphysical one. However, it's often associated with a certain way of doing metaphysics that repudiates the idea that the existence of things is the proper subject of metaphysical inquiry. Such a theory has it that, contrary to the Quinean, everything indisputably exists and we should not pause to question whether they do or don't. Rather, the correct metametaphysical theory is one whereby we try and figure out where things stand in the structure of *grounding relations*. To understand what that means, we must first understand what grounding relations are.

Some things are grounded in other things; that is, they depend for their existence on those other things in order for them to exist (they 'ontologically depend' on other things). A table is grounded in its parts—e.g., the table legs and the table-top. A galaxy is grounded in the stars and planets that compose it. The holes in a piece of Swiss cheese are grounded in the block of cheese itself—it's not as if you could have the holes without the cheese! The state of affairs of Amal Alamuddin and George Clooney being married is grounded in Alamuddin and Clooney. And so on. Given this metametaphysical theory, we should try to figure out which things ground which other things. Ultimately, we are interested in which things are at the 'bottom level'—i.e., which things ground all of reality whilst they, themselves, are ungrounded. For instance, were matter ultimately made up of tiny little particles that have no parts then, unlike tables and galaxies, those things would be ungrounded and would be of particular interest to the practising metaphysician. Define:

x is an ungrounded entity iff (i) x exists; and
(ii) there is no thing (or things) which ground x.

(In the literature, 'ungrounded entities' are often called 'fundamental entities'. Of course, I have already used the word 'fundamental' in a very different manner, so it would be confusing to have it do double service here. So, I shall stick with 'ungrounded', keeping 'fundamental' to apply only to truths that are not metaphysically explained by any other proposition being true.)

Grounding is central to the permissivist's understanding of ontological parsimony. Given permissivism, *every* theory must commit to *exactly the same* entities. So, no theory will commit to a subset of entities that any other theory commits to. But that just means the permissivist must revise how to understand ontological parsimony. Rather than seeking the fewest entities, the permissivist thinks a theory is parsimonious when it commits to the fewest *ungrounded* entities.

(If you look at the FUND and FUND* principles articulated in Chapter 4, you can already see this idea in action. Indeed, you might suspect that what's going on between myself and Kristie is that we have been talking past one another: I have meant 'fundamental' to mean 'inexplicable', whilst she has meant it to mean 'ungrounded'. It is far from unusual for such terminological differences to cause problems in philosophy, and that might well be the case here! The best resolution in such cases is to get ever clearer on exactly what one means by the problematic term(s), as I hope I have done in this chapter.)

With all this in place, we can now return back to the subject of propositions. Given permissivism, even the block universe theorist must believe that the proposition:

<209 years ago, it used to be the case that atom a_1 was located at region r_1 and was F>

exists. They will deny that it's true simpliciter, though; instead, they will say it is not true at all or that it is true, but only 'relative to' different times.

Given permissivism, we should see that it's not the existential status of propositions that is relevant to determining the comparative parsimony of theories. The question is, instead, whether those propositions are ungrounded or not.

Imagine the block universe theorist says that propositions are ungrounded. In that case, there's no way for the block universe theory to be more parsimonious than presentism. Either the presentist commits to those propositions being ungrounded or not. If they are ungrounded, then the presentist's theory is *as* parsimonious as the block universe theory when it comes to propositions. If they are grounded, the presentist theory is *more* parsimonious than the block universe theory when it comes to propositions.

Next, imagine, instead, that the block universe theorist says that propositions are grounded (e.g., they depend upon humans talking and thinking about them). In that case, the presentist can say likewise. And, if propositions are grounded, then we simply ignore them when it comes to adjudicating which theory is more ontologically parsimonious. So, again, when it comes to propositions, presentism would be as parsimonious as block universe theory.

In conclusion, either way, when we come to consider propositions, presentism is as parsimonious or more parsimonious than the block universe theory. (The only problem would be if the block universe theorist thought that the *tensed* propositions were grounded, whilst simultaneously demanding that the presentist think that tensed propositions were ungrounded. But why think that?)

There is an obvious objection, though. Given permissivism, past and future things *must* exist. So, Napoleon must exist. Dinosaurs exist. The outposts on Mars exist. So, it looks as if permissivism and presentism are just straight-out incompatible to begin with, and no presentist could try and be a permissivist.

But this isn't a problem either. When we changed our metametaphysical theory from being Quineans (and worrying about what exists versus what does not) to being permissivists (whereby we worried about which things were ungrounded), it was reasonable to reconceive what was involved in ontological parsimony. Similarly, the permissivist has to reconceive other debates in ontology.

Consider the question of theism (i.e., whether God exists), from the point of view of the permissivist. The permissivist says that, indisputably, God in some sense exists. But that doesn't mean you cannot be an atheist. It's just that, rather than being the question of whether God exists or not, the atheism vs. theism debate is instead reinterpreted as a debate about whether God is a fictional thing or not. Given permissivism, it's trivial that God exists, but it's debatable whether He's non-fictional (like you and I) or fictional (like Zeus and Odin).

For permissivists, the debate in temporal ontology should receive a similar treatment. It's trivial that Napoleon, dinosaurs, and outposts on Mars exist. What is being disputed is instead whether these things are more similar to a flesh-and-blood, presently existing thing like myself (as the block theorist would believe) or not (as the presentist would have you believe). For the permissivist-presentist, past and future things may exist, but in a sense much more similar to that in which Voldemort exists. For the permissivist,

Voldemort exists, but as a fictional thing; for the permissivist-presentist, past and future things exist but likewise fail to be concrete, material entities.

8. Conclusion

There are two types of ontological parsimony: qualitative and quantitative. It is quantitative parsimony that drives forward my argument for presentism. Whilst there are some nuances concerning how we understand parsimony when considering an infinite number of entities, above I detailed a way to do that.

There's then the question of whether unmarried fundamental truths make presentism less parsimonious than the block universe theory. I've argued that there's no reason to think this is the case if we have in mind qualitative parsimony.

Things are more complicated, however, when it comes to quantitative parsimony. My solution varied depending upon what metametaphysical scheme you were attracted to; that is, it varied depending upon what you think metaphysics is really all about in the first place. I laid out two metametaphysical schemes—one in the Quinean vein and one permissivist scheme—and argued that it's not unreasonable on either to think that propositions can be ignored when it comes to deciding which theory is more ontologically parsimonious.

There were other arguments in Chapter 4 that I would have loved to discuss—e.g., the claim that the block universe theorists have to revise their beliefs less in light of relativity than a presentist who relativises existence simpliciter to inertial frames. But space prohibits discussion of these matters. For now, my defence of presentism must come to a rest.

> I've offered two solutions to the parsimony problem concerning presentism's commitment to tensed propositions.
>
> One solution is to say that neither side—the block universe theorist nor the presentist—should believe in propositions at all. They both *talk about* them, but that doesn't mean *that they exist*. Since parsimony is measured only by which things exist, the presentist still commits to a subset of entities that the block universe theorist commits to (and so still has the more parsimonious theory!).
>
> The second solution is to say that both sides should be *permissive* about what exists, and so both sides must believe in the same propositions, no matter what. There is a snag in that permissivists think parsimony is about believing in the fewest *ungrounded* things. But whether the block universe theorist believes propositions are ungrounded or grounded, I say the presentist can say the same. Thus, when it comes to deciding which theory is more parsimonious, we can again ignore tensed propositions.

In this chapter, I have discussed some of the issues arising over how to understand parsimony when it comes to presentism. There are two types of parsimony: qualitative parsimony (i.e., having the fewest *kinds* of things) and quantitative (i.e., having the fewest things). I've argued that my original argument was that the presentist can secure a quantitatively ontologically parsimonious theory. This is even in light of worries about (i) both presentism and block universe theory committing to an infinite number of entities and (ii) worries about the presentist committing to there being tensed propositions.

Suggested Readings

Nikk Effingham

Presentism

An excellent go-to introduction is the Stanford Encyclopedia entry: Ingram, D. and Tallant, J. (2022). 'Presentism', *The Stanford Encyclopedia of Philosophy* (Spring 2022 Edition), ed. Edward N. Zalta, URL = <https://plato.stanford.edu/archives/spr2022/entries/presentism/>.

A classic presentation of the theory is Adams, R. (1981). 'Time and Thisness', *Midwest Studies in Philosophy* 11, 315–329. Some people also include Arthur Prior (1970). 'The Notion of the Present', *Studium Generale* 23, 245–248.

Contemporary defences include: Bourne, C. (2006). *A Future for Presentism*, Oxford: Oxford University Press; Ingram, D. (2019). *Thisness Presentism*, Oxford: Routledge; and Markosian, N. (2004). 'A Defence of Presentism', *Oxford Studies in Metaphysics* 1, 47–82. If you are interested in what non-philosophers think about time (and whether they find presentism intuitive), see Latham, Miller and Norton (2019). 'Is Our Naïve Theory of Time Dynamical?', *Synthese*. http://doi.org/10.1007/s11229-019-02340-4 (2021 198: 4251–4271)

Parsimony

Many of the arguments discussed in Chapter 2 have already been advanced elsewhere. Tallant, J. (2013). 'Quantitative Parsimony and the Metaphysics of Time: Motivating Presentism', *Philosophy and Phenomenological Research* 87(3), 688–705, provides an in-depth discussion of the argument from ontological parsimony for presentism. For a discussion of qualitative parsimony and what ontological kinds could be, see Effingham, N. (2015). 'Properties are Potatoes: An Essay on Ontological Parsimony', in *The Palgrave Handbook of Philosophical Methods*, ed. Chris Daly. I also discussed problems with infinity and parsimony—if you want to know more about infinity and its philosophy, see Moore, A. (2019). *The Infinite 3rd Edition*, London: Routledge. Finally, if you are interested in whether or not propositions exist, see Loux, M. and Crisp, T. (2017). *Metaphysics: A Contemporary*

Introduction 4th Edition, London: Routledge and Merricks, T. (2015). *Propositions*, Oxford: Oxford University Press.

Truthmaking

The relation between world and truth advanced in this book is very similar to 'nefarious presentism', discussed elsewhere. See: Tallant, J. (2009). 'Ontological Cheats Might Just Prosper', *Analysis* 69, 422–430; Tallant, J. (2010). 'Still Cheating, Still Prospering', *Analysis* 70, 502–506; and Tallant, J. and Ingram, D. (2015). 'Nefarious Presentism', *The Philosophical Quarterly* 65, 355–371. For more on truthmaking, see Merricks, T. (2007). *Truth and Ontology*, Oxford: Oxford University Press. For an example of someone defending eternalism using truthmaking theory, see Armstrong, D. (2004). *Truth and Truthmakers*, Cambridge: Cambridge University Press.

Metaphysical Explanation

For more on issues like metaphysical explanation, see Schaffer, J. (2009). 'On What Grounds What', in *Metametaphysics*, ed. Chalmers, Manley, and Wasserman, Oxford: Oxford University Press. For more on metaphysical completeness, see Sider, T. (2011). *Writing the Book of the World*, Oxford: Oxford University Press.

Metametaphysics and Permissivism

If you're interested in the two theories of metametaphysics, Quine, W. (1948). 'On What There Is' (reprinted in *From a Logical Point of View*, Cambridge, MA: Harvard University Press) is the classic source for the Quinean view and Schaffer, J. (2009). 'On What Grounds What', in *Metametaphysics*, ed. Chalmers, Manley, and Wasserman, Oxford: Oxford University Press. is the best thing to read on both permissivism and grounding.

Change

The historical precursor of the idea that the block universe theorist's 'change' is unsuitable can be traced back to McTaggart, J. (1927). *The Nature of Existence Volume II*, Cambridge: Cambridge University Press.

Open Future

A good introduction to the open future is Torre, S. (2011). 'The Open Future', *Philosophy Compass* 6, 360–373. A book-length discussion is Todd, P. (2021). *The Open Future: Why All Future Contingents Are False*, Oxford: Oxford University Press.

For more on the idea that there might not be any past truths, see Dawson, P. (2021). 'Hard Presentism', *Synthese* 198, 8433–8461.

Physics and Presentism

A short introduction to relativity and metaphysics is Hawley, K. (2009). 'Metaphysics and Relativity', in *The Routledge Companion to Metaphysics*, ed. Le Poidevin et al., London: Routledge. Important discussions by presentists include Bourne, C. (2006). *A Future for Presentism*, Oxford: Oxford University Press and Zimmerman, D. (2011). 'Presentism and the Space-time Manifold', in *The Oxford Handbook of Philosophy of Time*, ed. Callender, 163–244, Oxford: Oxford University Press.

The theory I defend is explicitly discussed by Godfrey-Smith, W. (1979). 'Special Relativity and the Present', *Philosophical Studies* 36(3), 233–244 and Hinchcliff, M. (1996). 'The Puzzle of Change', *Philosophical Perspectives* 10, 119–136.

An excellent discussion of the asymmetries of (and in) time is Price, H. (1996). *Time's Arrow & Archimedes' Point: New Directions for the Physics of Time*, New York: Oxford University Press.

Flatland

If you're interested in flatland, see Abbott, E. (1884). *Flatland: A Romance of Many Dimensions*, London: Seeley & Co.

Suggested Readings

Kristie Miller

For a detailed discussion of how appealing to entropy and statistical mechanics can explain various temporal asymmetries, see Albert, D. (2000). *Time and Chance*, Cambridge, MA: Harvard University Press.

For discussion of the relationship between temporal phenomenology and dynamical theories of time, see Baron, Samuel, Cusbert, John, Farr, Matt, Kon, Maria and Miller, Kristie (2015). 'Temporal Experience, Temporal Passage and the Cognitive Sciences', *Philosophy Compass* 10(8), 560–571, and Deng, N. (2013). 'Our Experience of Passage on the B-theory', *Erkenntnis* 78(4): 713726 as well as Hoerl, C. (2014). 'Do We (Seem to) Perceive Passage?', *Philosophical Explorations* 17, 188–202. More specific works that take up the question of what nature our temporal experiences have can be found in Le Poidevin, R. (2007). *The Images of Time: An Essay on Temporal Representation*, Oxford: Oxford University Press and in Miller, K., Holcombe, A. and Latham, A. J. (2018). 'Temporal Phenomenology: Phenomenological Illusion Versus Cognitive Error', *Synthese*, 1–21; Prosser, S. (2016). *Experiencing Time*, Oxford: Oxford University Press and in Paul, L. A. (2010). 'Temporal Experience', *Journal of Philosophy* 107(7), 333–359 and Prosser, S. (2016). *Experiencing Time*, Oxford: Oxford University Press.

A recent book-length defence of the block universe view can be found in Callender, C. (2017). *What Makes Time Special?* Another good introduction to the view is that of Mellor, D. H. (1998). *Real Time II*, London: Routledge.

For discussion of temporal asymmetries, particularly in the context of a block universe view, see Price, H. (1996). *Time's Arrow & Archimedes' Point: New Directions for the Physics of Time*, New York: Oxford University Press.

For more on the connection between dynamical theories of time and special relativity, see Putnam, H. (1967). 'Time and Physical Geometry', *The Journal of Philosophy* 64(8), 240–247, Zimmerman, D. (2011). 'Presentism and the Space-Time Manifold', *The Oxford Handbook of Philosophy of Time*, 163–244. New York: Oxford University Press, Savitt, S. (2000). 'There's No Time Like the Present (in Minkowski Spacetime)', *Philosophy of Science* 67, S563–S574, Saunders, S. (2002). 'How Relativity Contradicts Presentism', in *Time, Reality, and Experience*, ed. Craig Callender, 277–292, Cambridge: Cambridge University Press.

For discussion of the connection between presentism and truthmaking, see Baia, A. (2012). 'Presentism and the Grounding of Truth', *Philosophical Studies* 159(3), 341–356 and Caplan, B. and Sanson, D. (2011). 'Presentism and Truthmaking', *Philosophy Compass* 6(3), 196–208 and Tallant, J. and Ingram, D. (2015). 'Nefarious Presentism', *Philosophical Quarterly* 65(260), 355–371.

There are useful discussions of the nature of parsimony to be found in Baker, A. (2003). 'Quantitative Parsimony and Explanatory Power', *British Journal for the Philosophy of Science* 54(2), 245–259 and Cowling, S. (2013). 'Ideological Parsimony', *Synthese* 190(17), 3889–3908 and Nolan, D. (1997). 'Quantitative Parsimony', *British Journal for the Philosophy of Science* 48(3), 329–343 and Tallant, J. (2013). 'Quantitative Parsimony and the Metaphysics of Time Motivating Presentism', *Philosophy and Phenomenological Research* 87(3), 688–705.

Glossary

A-theory/B-theory: Often-used synonyms for 'tensed theory' (in the case of 'A-theory') and 'tenseless theory' (in the case of 'B-theory') and for 'dynamical view' (in the case of 'A-theory') and 'static view' (in the case of 'B-theory').

Block Universe Theory: Block universe theorists believe the combination of eternalism, permanentism, and the tenseless theory of time. The block universe theory is one of the two theories this book argues for.

Cardinality: A property of a set measuring how many elements are members of the set—e.g., a set with five members has a cardinality of 5, a set with seven members has a cardinality of 7, and a set with infinitely many members has an infinite cardinality.

Closed Future: The thesis that the future is not open. If the future is closed, then any proposition about the future is either true or it is false. For instance, if the future is closed, then <There are outposts on Mars in the year 2500 AD> is either true (in which case, there will be outposts on Mars) or it is false (in which case, come the year 2500, no such outposts will exist).

Compatibilism: The thesis that, even though determinism may be true, that does not mean that our actions are not free; that is, free will and determinism are 'compatible'.

Determinism: The laws are deterministic if and only if they fix exactly how the future will play out, given the way the world is now (or at any past time). So, a complete specification of the way the world is, at some time, plus the laws of nature, determine the way the world will be at each future time. Given deterministic laws, the future can only be one way, given the way it is at the present time. If the laws of nature allow the future to play out in multiple ways given the way the world is at the present time, we say that they are instead 'indeterministic'.

Eternalism: The thesis that whether something exists in the past, present, or future, it exists (in the same way that whether something exists near us or far away from us in space, it nevertheless exists). In this book, we assume eternalists believe the tenseless theory of time and permanentism, a combination called 'block universe theory'. (Eternalists who don't believe tenseless theory include 'moving spotlight theorists'.)

Fact: Used in one of two ways. (1) A fact is a state of affairs (see 'state of affairs', below). (2) A fact is a proposition that is true (see 'proposition', below).

Four-Dimensionalism: Used in one of two ways. (1) Used as a synonym for eternalism (in that the universe is a 'four-dimensional block'). Almost invariably, when used in this fashion, it picks out block universe theory. (2) The theory that objects have 'temporal parts', and thus objects are 'four dimensional', being stretched through time in the same way they are stretched through space.

Grounding: In metaphysics, some philosophers believe entities are 'grounded' in other entities. Standard examples include: I am grounded in my atoms; events are grounded in the things that participate in them; sets are grounded in their members. The things that ground an entity, in some sense, explain its existence.

Growing Block Theory: A third theory alongside eternalism and presentism. Growing block theorists believe that past and present things exist, but not future things.

Incompatibilism: The thesis that, if determinism is true, then no-one has free will—i.e., determinism and free will are 'incompatible'.

Indexical: A term that has a reference that varies depending upon the context in which it was uttered. 'Here' and 'I' are indexicals (for, if you say 'I', you refer to you, whilst if I use 'I', I refer to me). Arguably, 'now' is an indexical. Block universe theorists say that it is whilst presentists and other tensed theorists tend to disagree.

Moving Spotlight Theory: Usually used to refer to the combination of eternalism and the tensed theory of time. Given moving spotlight theory, everything permanently exists, but there's a metaphysically irreducible fact about which time is present. The present moment is like a 'spotlight' shining down on spacetime, moving along it as time passes.

Open Future: The future is open if and only if the propositions about the future are (in some sense) unsettled or undecided. For instance, if the future is open then <There are outposts on Mars in 2500 AD> is not true but might become true when we finally arrive at 2500 AD and it turns out we have built outposts on Mars.

Parsimony: When comparing two theories, one is more parsimonious than the other if and only if it has fewer things in it. There are different kinds of parsimony—e.g., qualitative ontological parsimony (whereby one theory has fewer kinds of entity than another) and quantitative ontological parsimony (whereby one theory has fewer entities than another).

Passage: Uncontroversially, time passes. 'Passage' (or 'temporal passage') refers to that phenomenon. Often, a distinction is made between 'anodyne'/'anaemic' passage and 'robust' passage. The idea driving the distinction is that even the block theorist can believe things are different from one time to another (and so time passes in some sense). But this type of temporal passage is less 'metaphysically robust' than the passing of time which the presentist (and other tensed theorists) believe in. So, the former is called 'anodyne' or 'anaemic', whilst tensed theorists are said to capture the 'robust' passage of time.

Permanentism: The thesis that there is no change in what exists simpliciter.

Presentism: The thesis that past and future things do not exist, whilst presently existing things do exist. It is an example of a tensed theory of time and a temporaryist theory. It is one of the two theories defended in this book.

Presentism, Nefarious and Upstanding: These are jocular terms for two different treatments presentists might give of truthmaking. Nefarious presentists say that there is no need to provide a truthmaker for propositions about the past; they are 'nefarious' insofar as they are trying to 'worm their way out of' having to provide the truthmaker. Upstanding presentists instead agree that truthmakers must be provided, suggesting that things like Lucretian properties can play the truthmaker role. The version of presentism presented by Nikk Effingham in this book is nefarious.

Propositions: We talk about the truth and falsity of sentences—e.g., 'Dinosaurs existed' is true. But two different sentences (such as sentences in two languages) can express the same idea, or have the same content. Propositions are what sentences express. In philosophy of language, propositions are usually taken to be what sentences mean (e.g., 'Dinosaurs existed', 'Es gab Dinosaurier', and 'םירואזוניד ויה םעפ' all have the same meaning—i.e., the proposition <Dinosaurs existed>). In this book, the authors adopted the standard approach of representing propositions using angled brackets, < and > (in a similar way to how quotation marks are put around sentences). In metaphysics, there are serious questions about whether propositions exist or not and, if they do, what their nature is

States of Affairs: States of affairs are a type of entity posited by some philosophers. According to these philosophers, in addition to objects like the Eiffel Tower, there also exist states of affairs concerning it—e.g., the state of affairs of its being made of metal or the state of affairs of its being located in Paris. Those who believe in truthmaking often believe that truthmakers are states of affairs.

Temporal Phenomenology: Often used just to mean our experience of time and temporal phenomena. Sometimes used more specifically to mean our experience of time passing or our experience as of robust passage. When it is used in this later sense, some people deny that we have such experiences.

Temporaryism: The view that there are changes in what exists simpliciter. The presentist introduced in this book would be a temporaryist. See also the entry for 'permanentism'.

Tense: Tense is a feature of language. Sentences are (usually) either past-, present-, or future-tensed. Philosophers disagree over the connection between tense in language and the nature of our world. In particular, they disagree about whether tensed sentences are only true if there are tensed facts (or if reality itself is dynamical) or whether tenseless features of reality can make true tensed sentences.

Truthmaking: Arguably, propositions/sentences are 'made true' by items in the world. For instance, the proposition <The Eiffel Tower exists> would be made true by the Eiffel Tower and <The Eiffel Tower is made of metal> is made true by the state of affairs of the Eiffel Tower being made of metal.

References

Abbott, E. (1884). *Flatland: A Romance of Many Dimensions*, London: Seeley & Co.
Albert, D. (2000). *Time and Chance*, Cambridge, MA: Harvard University Press.
Armstrong, D. (2004). *Truth and Truthmakers*, Cambridge: Cambridge University Press.
Austin, J. (1950). Truth, reprinted in Pitcher (ed.) *Truth*, Englewood Cliffs, NJ: Prentice-Hall.
Baron, S., Cusbert, J., Farr, M., Kon, M., and Miller, K. (2015). Temporal Experience, Temporal Passage and the Cognitive Sciences. *Philosophy Compass* 10(8): 560–571.
Bourne, C. (2006). *A Future for Presentism*, Oxford: Oxford University Press.
Callender, C. (2017). *What Makes Time Special?* Oxford: Oxford University Press.
Dawson, P. (2021). Hard Presentism. *Synthese* 198: 8433–8461.
Deng, N. (2013). Our Experience of Passage on the B-theory. *Erkenntnis* 78(4): 713726.
Effingham, N. (2015). Properties are Potatoes: An Essay on Ontological Parsimony. In Chris Daly (ed.) *The Palgrave Handbook of Philosophical Methods*, London: Palgrave McMillan.
Godfrey-Smith, W. (1979). Special Relativity and the Present. *Philosophical Studies* 36(3): 233–244.
Hawley, K. (2009). Metaphysics and Relativity. In Le Poidevin et al. (eds.) *The Routledge Companion to Metaphysics*, London: Routledge.
Hinchcliff, M. (1996). The Puzzle of Change. *Philosophical Perspectives* 10: 119–136.
Hoerl, C. (2014). Do We (Seem to) Perceive Passage? *Philosophical Explorations* 17: 188–202.
Latham, A. J., Miller, K., and Norton, J. (2019). Is Our Naïve Theory of Time Dynamical? *Synthese* 198: 4251–4271. http://doi.org/10.1007/s11229-019-02340-4
Latham, A. J. Norton, J., and Miller, K. (2020). An Empirical Investigation of Purported Passage Phenomenology. *The Journal of Philosophy* 117(7): 353–386. 10.5840/jphil2020117722
Le Poidevin, R. (2007). *The Images of Time: An Essay on Temporal Representation*, Oxford: Oxford University Press.
Lewis, D. (1986). *On the Plurality of Worlds*, Oxford: Blackwell.
Loux, M. and Crisp, T. (2017). *Metaphysics: A Contemporary Introduction*, 4th edition, London: Routledge.

Maudlin, T. (2002). Remarks on the Passing of Time. *Proceedings of the Aristotelian Society* 102: 259–274.
McTaggart, J. (1927). *The Nature of Existence Volume II*, Cambridge: Cambridge University Press.
Mellor, D. H. (1998). *Real time II*, London: Routledge.
Merricks, T. (1999). The Resurrection of the Body and Life Everlasting. In J. M. Murray (ed.) *Reason for the Hope Within*, Cambridge: William B. Eerdmans Publishing Company.
Merricks, T. (2007). *Truth and Ontology*, Oxford: Oxford University Press.
Merricks, T. (2015). *Propositions*, Oxford: Oxford University Press.
Miller, K., Holcombe, A., and Latham, A. J. (2018). Temporal Phenomenology: Phenomenological Illusion Versus Cognitive Error. *Synthese*: 1–21.
Moore, A. (2019). *The Infinite*, 3rd edition, London: Routledge.
Nolan, D. (1997). Quantitative Parsimony. *The British Journal for the Philosophy of Science* 48: 329–343.
Paul, L. A. (2010). Temporal Experience. *Journal of Philosophy* 107(7): 333–359.
Price, H. (1996). *Time's Arrow & Archimedes' Point: New Directions for the Physics of Time*, New York: Oxford University Press.
Prosser, S. (2016). *Experiencing Time*, Oxford: Oxford University Press.
Putnam, H. (1967). Time and Physical Geometry. *The Journal of Philosophy* 64(8): 240–247.
Quine, W. (1948). On What There Is. Reprinted in *From a Logical Point of View*, Cambridge, MA: Harvard University Press.
Schaffer, J. (2009). On What Grounds What. In D. Chalmers, D. Manley, and R. Wasserman (eds.) *Metametaphysics*, Oxford: Oxford University Press.
Sider, T. (2011). *Writing the Book of the World*, Oxford: Oxford University Press.
Tallant, J. (2009). Ontological Cheats Might Just Prosper. *Analysis* 69: 422–430.
Tallant, J. (2010). Still Cheating, Still Prospering. *Analysis* 70: 502–506.
Tallant, J. (2013). Quantitative Parsimony and the Metaphysics of Time: Motivating Presentism. *Philosophy and Phenomenological Research* 87: 688–705.
Tallant, J. and Ingram, D. (2015). Nefarious Presentism. *The Philosophical Quarterly* 65: 355–371.
Torre, S. (2011). The Open Future. *Philosophy Compass* 6: 360–373.

Index

absolute elsewhere 21–22, 141; *see also* special theory of relativity
Alamuddin, Amal 64–65, 178
argument from explanation 38–52
asymmetries *see* temporal asymmetries
A-theory 187; *see also* robust temporal passage
Augustine of Hippo x, xv

Being Explains Truth, principle 75, 76–80
Betty the Dinosaur 129–136
Big Bang x, 8, 12, 44, 52
block universe view, definition(s) 4, 11–12, 99, 185, 187
B-theory 187
Burj Khalifa 64–65, 100

cardinality 187; *see also* infinity
change: spatial change 102, 149; spatiotemporal 107, 149–156; and time xi, xiii, 25–26, 100–108, 149–156, 183
Clooney, George *see* Alamuddin, Amal
closed future 187; *see also* open future
completeness, metaphysical *see* metaphysical completeness
context shift and contextualism 102
continuity (of spacetime) 128
cost-benefit analysis 94; *see also* 59, 108, 121, 126–127

direction of time *see* time, direction of
dynamic time *see* Robust temporal passage

Einstein, Albert *see* special theory of relativity
entropy xiii, 45–52, 110–122, 156–163, 185
eternalism, definition(s) x–xi, 8, 54, 56, 95, 99, 187
Evil Demon 76–78, 110
existence: existence simpliciter 57; restricted quantification 6–7, 9; tensed *vs*. tenseless 6
explanation, metaphysical *see* metaphysical explanation

facts: different understandings of what a fact is 132, 188; 'fact of the matter' xii, 17–19, 23–24, 52–53, 119, 140, 158–163; facts about simultaneity principle 18–19; past-fact proposal 132–137, 139
fictional objects 179–180
Flatland 106–107, 184
four-dimensionalism 188
free will: and block theory xi, 33–38, 100; compatbilism 187; determinism 34, 187; incompatibilism 34, 188; and presentism 84, 100
FUND 127, 138–140; *see also* parsimony, quantitative *vs*. qualitative
FUND* 138–140, 178; *see also* fundamental, truths and fundamental truth; parsimony, quantitative *vs*. qualitative
fundamental xiv, 56, 79–86, 95, 111–122, 126–129, 133–140, 150, 152, 158–161, 170–174, 176, 178,

180; entities 178; facts, definition 79; truths and fundamental truth 134–135, 170–172; truths, married/unmarried 171
future, open *vs.* closed *see* open future

Gaunilo 70
genuine modal realism 69, 93
God's eye view 41, 106–108, 153, 158–161, 163
grounding relations *see* relations, grounding
growing block view 9, 56, 99, 188

indexicals 12–17, 188
inertial frame of reference 87; *see also* special theory of relativity
infinity 127–128, 166–168
intuition 54–55, 59–62, 71, 77, 103, 108, 121, 126
intuition pumps 60–62
Ittoqqortoormiit 61–62

Johnson, Dwayne 'The Rock' 67–70, 171

Kant, Immanuel 59
KIND 126, 128; *see also* parsimony, quantitative *vs.* qualitative

laws of nature 34–35, 44–46, 50, 110, 153–155, 161, 187
light cone 20–22
limps 71–72, 177
Lucretianism *see* truthmaking, Lucretianism

McTaggart, JME x, 183
metaphysical completeness 92–93
metaphysical explanation 73–76, 79–83, 94, 183; presentism and 75–83
metric 116–117
microstates (and macrostates), 46–47; *see also* entropy
moving spotlight theory 99, 188
Müller-Lyer illusion 29

nefarious presentism *see* presentism, nefarious

nomic possibility 44, 45–46, 48
NUMB 125, 127–128, 138, 168; *see also* parsimony, quantitative *vs.* qualitative

one-to-one correspondence *see* infinity
ontological argument 70
ontological commitment 125–127, 169, 175–176
ontology 126–127, 179; *see also* parsimony; temporal ontology
open future 83–86, 119–122, 183–184, 188
open past 119–122
operators 115–116

parsimony: argument for presentism xiii, 55–56, 62–64, 124–140, 182; definition 62–63, 186, 188; qualitative parsimony worries for presentism 172–174; quantitative parsimony worries for presentism 174–176; quantitative *vs.* qualitative 125–140, 166–170, 186
past-fact proposal *see* facts, past-fact proposal
permanentism and temporaryism 4, 5–17, 189
permissivism 177–180
phenomenology *see* temporal phenomenology
phlogiston 58
polysemy 104–105
possible worlds 65, 68, 73
presentism: argument from intuition 59–62; argument from the open future (*see* open future); definition(s) xi, 4, 9–10, 54, 56, 95, 189; nefarious 135–136, 183, 186, 189; suggested readings 182; trivial truth of 58–59; truthmaking (*see* truthmaking); upstanding 189
presentness principle 18
primitive relations *see* relations, primitive
propositions 189; existence of 176–180; modal propositions 67–68; as truth bearers 130

Quine, W.V. 177, 179–180, 183

relations: grounding 177–178, 180–181, 188; primitive 157–158
Riddle, Tom *see* fictional objects
robust temporal passage 3–4, 5n1, 10–14, 188–189

Shaw, George Bernard 118
special theory of relativity xi–xii, 17–25, 86–94, 140–145, 184, 185
state of affairs 41, 65–66, 71, 189; brute/ungrounded 69; constituents 66; tensed *vs.* tenseless 100–102
static time 11
supervenience 74–75

temporal asymmetries xii, 38–52, 109–119, 156–163, 185; asymmetry of influence 39, 42–43, 49–51, 109; deliberative asymmetry 40; epistemic asymmetry 39, 41–42, 109
temporal ontology 56–59, 99, 136–138, 179; *see also* eternalism; growing block view; presentism
temporal passage *see* robust temporal passage

temporal phenomenology xi, 27–33, 99–100, 185, 189
temporaryism *see* permanentism and temporaryism
tense 190
time: direction of 51–53, 156–163 (*see also* temporal asymmetries); and its analogy to space (*see* change, spatiotemporal; eternalism, definition(s))
time-reversal invariance 44–46
time travel 61–62, 101, 109
truth-bearers *see* propositions, as truth bearers
truth conditions 12–17
truthmaking xiv, 64–65, 190; Lucretianism 69–70, 131, 189; maximalism 66, 69, 71; nefarious presentism (*see* presentism, nefarious); and presentism 64–67, 129–140, 186; against truthmaking 71–72
truth supervenes on being *see* supervenience

ungrounded *see* relations, grounding

Voldemort *see* Riddle, Tom

For Product Safety Concerns and Information please contact our EU representative GPSR@taylorandfrancis.com
Taylor & Francis Verlag GmbH, Kaufingerstraße 24, 80331 München, Germany

www.ingramcontent.com/pod-product-compliance
Lightning Source LLC
Chambersburg PA
CBHW052021290426
44112CB00014B/2319